MEN
IN THE BIBLE

Examples to Live By

Don Charles

Dedication

I dedicate this book to the men in my life who have been role models for me. The[y] include my own father, my father-in-law, school teachers, pastors and a host of oth[er] men who have shared their lives and given their time to teach, guide and encourage me[.] With the writing of this book, I purpose to pass on to my peers, and those of generations to come, the challenge of being mature men of God as we look to Jesus the *"author and perfecter of our faith."*

Acknowledgments

In writing this, my first book, I am impressed at how much team effort goes into putting together such a Bible study. Without the publishers, editorial staff, friends who have prayed, and others who have shared their testimonies in the examples, I could not have accomplished the task. I am also deeply indebted to my wife, Sylvia, who took my unorganized material and put it into the form you now find it. Her diligent labor and counsel made my work much easier and we have proved to ourselves that a husband and wife can, indeed, work together as a team. Most of all, I praise God for giving me, through inspiration of the Holy Spirit, the messages He wants to convey to the readers of *Men in the Bible...Examples to Live By*.

Bible Version

Though other versions of the Bible were consulted in writing this material, the Bible version used in this book is, unless otherwise noted, the New International Version of the International Bible Society.

*"Proud People and Broken People" on page 119 is adapted from a message by Nancy Leigh DeMoss. Used by permission of Life Action Ministries, P.O. Box 31, Buchanan, MI 49107-0031

Men in the Bible...Examples to Live By
ISBN 1-56322-067-9

TABLE OF CONTENTS

FORWARD

There is a stirring of God among men today. Within and without the visible church, there are a number of renewal movements. As men are raising hands in prayer and praise, they are humbling themselves and seeking God's will for their lives. They are being drawn together, not only in large and impressive gatherings, but in small accountability groups where each man is challenged to be wholly submitted to God and to live a life of integrity…as husband, father, citizen, worker, and member of the Body of Jesus Christ.

This book is for men…to discover God's design for man by studying the men of the Bible. Focusing on a small portion of the more than 3,000 men named in Scripture, it begins with Adam, the first man. In chronological order, it not only introduces men as real-life characters with whom we can identify, but outlines a lesson appropriate to the concerns of men today. The final session looks at Jesus Christ…who was not only the Son of God, but the Word made flesh to dwell among us and Who is now interceding for us as our "Brother."

We live in a world of spiritual anemia and scriptural poverty where men are prisoners of addiction, compulsive behavior, and low self-esteem. So, we feel inadequate, guilty, hopeless. Thus, it is my prayer that a study of Bible men will help us be restored and conformed to the image of God's Son, and to be filled and anointed with God's Spirit so that we, like Jesus will *preach good news to the poor…proclaim freedom for the prisoners, and recovery of sight for the blind, to release the oppressed, to proclaim the year of the Lord's favor.* (Luke 4:18-19)

May the words of the old hymn, written in 1911 by William P. Merrill, encourage us not only to equip ourselves with the full counsel of God as found in Bible study, but also be our inspiration to pass God's truth and hope on to others.

Rise up, O men of God! Have done with lesser things;
Give heart and soul and mind and strength to serve the King of Kings.

Rise up, O men of God! His Kingdom tarries long;
Bring in the day of brotherhood and end the night of wrong.

Rise up, O men of God! The church for you doth wait,
Her strength unequal to her task; Rise up, and make her great!

Lift high the cross of Christ! Tread where his feet have trod,
As brothers of the Son of Man, Rise up, O men of God! Amen.

Lesson 1

ADAM

How am I Affected by the First Man's Sin?

For just as through the disobedience of the one man the many were made sinners, so also through the obedience of the one man the many will be made righteous.

Romans 5:19

SETTING THE STAGE

Sin! It's a universal problem experienced by **every** man, woman and child on earth, for, Romans 3:23 boldly states: ***all*** *have sinned and fall short of the glory of God.* Sin not only leads to death, it affects our relationship with others, even as it separates us from God.

There is no way man, in his own strength, can do away with sin. Some try, by proclaiming man innately good or by blaming environment and circumstances for his moral lapses. But only God, through His Word, has the true explanation for sin, its consequences, and what to do about it.

Thus before we become acquainted with a number of the men in the Bible and learn the lessons from their lives, we need to look at the matter of sin. For God has a plan. He doesn't just excuse our sin. Rather, He provides a way for our sin nature, and all the sins that result from it, to be dealt with — to be covered and taken away so not only can we be redeemed, but our relationships with others can be restored and, most of all, reconciliation with God Himself can take place!

As we begin our study with Adam, the first man, we will discover the root cause that led to his sinning and how it has been passed on to the rest of us. We will also learn how God has provided a way for our sins to be covered, so that we can be forgiven and enjoy restored fellowship with Him, now and in the life to come. Most importantly of all, we will discover what *we* are to do to enjoy this redemption and to receive salvation!

INTRODUCING ADAM

(Based on Genesis 1:26-28; 2:7-25; 3:1-25; 1 Corinthians 15:22, 45-47)

Adam was a created being, made from the dust of the earth. When God breathed into this first man, he became a living being, an integration of the divine and earthly. Earlier, in Genesis 1:26-27, God declared His intent to create man *in our image, in our likeness.* Being made in God's image meant that man would have some of His same attributes. God gave man free will and the power to rule. This latter capacity was important, because it was also God's plan that Adam have dominion over all the earth and its creatures. This would be a job with great benefits — living in a beautiful garden full of food, with a wife fashioned especially for him. And both Adam and his wife would have intimate fellowship with God. What more could one ask?

To see if Adam would be trustworthy, God placed a special tree in the midst of the garden, the tree of the knowledge of good and evil. God told Adam that this was the one tree from which they were not to eat, *"for when you eat of it you will surely die!"* (Genesis 2:17b)

God allowed Satan, in the form of a serpent, to tempt Eve who then gave some fruit to Adam to eat. When confronted by God for his disobedience, Adam blamed Eve, and Eve blamed Satan. The result was that Adam and Eve lost their innocence and were banished from the garden, as God pronounced consequences for their sin. God's glory was removed from them and He covered their nakedness with animal skins. By default, Satan became the *god of this world* (2 Corinthians 4:4 KJV). *Don't you know that when you offer yourselves to someone to obey him as slaves, you are slaves to the one whom you obey...?* (Romans 6:16)

Adam and Eve experienced separation from God, an evil ruler to contend with, and a cursed earth in which to work. (See also Genesis 3:17-19, 23-24)

In 1 Corinthians 15:45-47, Adam is referred to as "the first man Adam" and Jesus is called "the last Adam" or "second man." What was lost for man in Adam's "fall" would be regained for him by Jesus Christ.

LESSONS FROM ADAM

How Adam's Sin Was Passed On To Us

Therefore, just as sin entered the world through one man... (Romans 5:12a)

According to this and other scriptures, Adam's sin has passed on to us. The first man experienced a major change in his position and life as a whole. As God meted out punishment to Adam, Eve, and Satan (Genesis 3:14-19), it became evident that there was a different order of things; and this new order would be the experience of all Adam's seed (all mankind). No longer would man enjoy the peaceful setting of a garden where everything, including fellowship with God, was provided; now there would be pain and sweat and tears, and a struggle to exist. Also, Satan would be allowed to rule, since man obeyed him rather than God. (See Romans 6:16.)

Today we can see all of this being duplicated in our individual lives, as well as in society as a whole, for mankind, without the redeeming and life-changing Spirit of God, is doomed to its own self-destruction. Scripture confirms this in Romans 3:23: *For all have sinned and fall short of the glory of God.* All inherit Adam's sin nature.

Consider the following three sins. First write how Adam and Eve sinned; then write a way you have sinned in these areas:

Disbelief (disregarding God's Word and believing Satan instead) Genesis 2:16-17; 3:1-7

Adam and Eve _____

My sin _____

Disobedience (acting on personal desire and rejecting God's Word) Genesis 3:6

Adam and Eve _____

My sin _____

Lusting (not being content with what is given) Genesis 3:6; 1 John 2:17-18

Adam and Eve _____

My sin _____

How does the temptation of Adam and Eve compare with the temptation of Jesus as found in Matthew 4:1-11? _____

The Consequences of Sin

As a result of their disobedience, guilt entered into the soul and spirit of Adam and Eve, and they experienced a "fall" from God's grace, from the beautiful fellowship they had experienced with Him in the garden. They attempted to physically cover themselves with sticky fig leaves, and when God manifested His presence, all they could think to do was hide!

When God questioned him as to whether or not he had eaten from the forbidden tree, Adam responded by blaming someone else. Not wanting to take responsibility for sin has been the pattern of unredeemed man from that time to this. Sin still is man's major problem, and sin still has consequences.

God has declared, in Ezekiel 18:4b: *"The soul who sins is the one who will die."* And in 1 Corinthians 15:22a: *"For as in Adam all die."* So, the consequences of sin is death. In order to redeem man, God had to provide a way for sin to be covered. We'll look at that, and how man can appropriate this covering, later in this lesson. But, first, let's consider some of the consequences, recorded in Scripture, that man has had to pay for sin…sometimes even after forgiveness and reconciliation had taken place. Because sin often affects the lives of others, it's difficult to regain intimacy and trust from one who has been offended. Sometimes, too, the damage is so extensive it's impossible to return things to what they were.

Look at the following scriptures and write down how these men paid consequences of their sin, even though they may have been reconciled with God.

Adam (Genesis 3:17-19, 22-24) _____

Moses (Deuteronomy 34:4-8; Numbers 20:7-12) _____

Saul (1 Samuel 15:1-26) _____

David (2 Samuel 11:1-27; 12:7-14) _____

Ananias (Acts 5:1-6) _____

Herod (Acts 12:19b-23) _____

How God Covers Sin

From Genesis through Revelation, we can trace a "scarlet thread of redemption" — how God covers sin by blood. Hebrews 9:22b tells us *without the shedding of blood is no forgiveness.* It would take the offering of the innocent, on behalf of the guilty, to pay the debt incurred by sin.

Genesis 3:21: God covered Adam and Eve's sin with animal skins by replacing the fig leaves they had sown together. This implies that an animal had been killed…shed its blood…so that God could "cover" Adam. Adam would, indeed, have recognized this as a sacrifice, if it had been one of the very animals he had named and helped to care for!

Genesis 8:20 and 12:7: We find men of God building altars to make sacrifices to atone for sin and to free themselves from its curse.

Exodus 12:1-7, 22-23: We find the story of Moses preparing to lead the children of Israel out of Egypt into the Promised Land. The angel of death had been instructed to kill all the firstborn sons in the land one night. To protect the sons of the Israelites, God instructed them to paint the door posts of their homes with the blood of a sheep or goat so that the death angel would pass over them. This was another personal sacrifice; the animals had to be without blemish, ones that they had cared for.

Leviticus 1-7 & 16-17: These chapters contain commands concerning acceptable sacrifices and how to carry them out — so that people could have their sins covered and could be made a holy people before God. This very tedious and precise process became nearly impossible to keep, even though it was in effect during the wilderness wanderings, as well as when the Israelites settled in the Promised Land.

Joshua 2:17-18; 6:22-25: The spies told the harlot Rahab to let a scarlet rope down from her home on top of Jericho's wall so that she and her family could be spared when the walls came tumbling down as the Israelites took the city. She did, and her whole household was spared. The scarlet cord was another symbol of the blood.

1 Kings 8:62-64: At the dedication of the first temple, Solomon offered a large sacrifice of peace offerings which included 22,000 oxen and 120,000 sheep and goats. Much blood was shed that day! This was the beginning of temple sacrifices which lasted until Herod's temple was destroyed in A.D. 70.

Isaiah 53: We find God speaking through the prophet Isaiah concerning the one who would come to make the ultimate sacrifice for sin. Here Isaiah described the crucifixion of Jesus as a lamb being led to the slaughter, even though he didn't completely understand the coming of the Messiah and how Jesus would be God's Lamb, the One who would atone for sin.

Matthew 27:45-50: While Jesus was hanging on the cross, He cried out, *"My God, my God, why have you forsaken me?"* (v.46). With the burden of all man's sin upon His own body, He felt completely separated from His Father. *God made him who had no sin to be sin for us, so that in him we might become the righteousness of God* (2 Corinthians 5:21). According to 2 Peter 2:24, all of our sins were upon his body on the tree, so that we can die to sins and live for righteousness. He shed His sinless blood so that we can be saved from the second death — the flames of the lake of fire.

Various places in the Book of Revelation: We find mention of "the Lamb," which is Jesus, Who, according to John the Baptist in John 1:29, is *the Lamb of God who takes away* *the sin of the world.* In Revelation 5:9-13, we read of a beautiful song in heaven giving glory to Jesus, the Lamb who was slain, and, with His blood, purchased men for God. Revelation 7:14 tells us that the martyrs who die during the great tribulation on earth wash their robes in the blood of this Lamb. In Revelation 12:11, we find mention of those who overcome the "accuser of the brothers" by the blood of the Lamb. In Revelation 19:6-9, we find the Marriage Supper of the Lamb — the union of Jesus Christ and His Bride, the Glorious Church. With our sins covered, our ultimate destiny is to be this Bride, the "wife of the Lamb," as described in Revelation 21:9b-27.

God's Plan of Salvation

I am not ashamed of the gospel, because it is the power of God for the salvation of everyone who believes… Romans 1:16a

Those of us who live this side of the cross have been given specific directions in the Bible on how to receive God's forgiveness for our sins and how to receive eternal life. We call this being "saved," because we are saved from the second death and given eternal life with God. It is also known as being "born again," acknowledging the fact that our "first birth" is of the seed of man, while our "second birth" is of the incorruptible seed of God.

So, what are the steps that will lead to salvation, being born again?

We must recognize our sin.

Therefore, just as sin entered the world through one man, and death through sin, and in this way death came to all men, because all sinned. (Romans 5:12)

For all have sinned and fall short of the glory of God. (Romans 3:23)

Surely I was sinful at birth, sinful from the time my mother conceived me. (Psalm 51:5)

Once we have recognized our sin, we must repent.

In the past God overlooked such ignorance, but now he commands all people everywhere to repent. (Acts 17:30)

But unless you repent, you too will all perish. (Luke 13:3)

We must confess our sins — to God, and possibly to those we have wronged.

If we confess our sins, he is faithful and just and will forgive us our sins and purify us from all unrighteousness. (1 John 1:9)

Whoever acknowledges me before men, I will also acknowledge him before my Father in heaven. But whoever disowns me before men, I will disown him before my Father in heaven. (Matthew 10:32)

We must believe in the Lord Jesus Christ.

Believe in the Lord Jesus, and you will be saved…you and your household. (Acts 16:31)

If you confess with your mouth, "Jesus is Lord," and believe in your heart that God raised him from the dead, you will be saved. (Romans 10:9)

We should submit to water baptism.

We were therefore buried with him through baptism into death in order that, just as Christ was raised from the dead through the glory of the Father, we too may live a new life. (Romans 6:4)

Repent and be baptized, every one of you, in the name of Jesus Christ for the forgiveness of your sins. (Acts 2:38a)

If you've taken these steps and are assured of your salvation, your "new birth," write down when, where, and how this took place: _____

_____

What is the end of those who are not saved?

John 3:36 _____

Romans 6:23 _____

For God so loved the world that he gave his one and only Son, that whoever believes in him shall not perish but have eternal life. (John 3:16)

SUMMARY

It's fitting that the first lesson in this study begins with Adam, the "prototype" man…all of whom are sinners in need of God's grace. Because the first man "fell" in disobedience, he lost his close fellowship with God; so, God had to provide a way back. This He did by declaring shed blood as the covering for sin. All through the Old Testament, we see man trying to have his sin atoned for through a system of sacrifices. In time, God sent His own Son, Jesus, into the world to give His life as the ultimate sacrifice for sin. Since that time, all man needs to do is repent of his sin, confess it, and accept what Jesus has accomplished when He took all our sins upon His own body as He died upon the cross.

When man sincerely does this, God forgives and restores the relationship which He desired with man when He created Adam. He redeems us from Satan's control by the blood of an innocent victim. This provides for our salvation, victory over sin, and fellowship with Him, both now and for eternity. We are now "born again" with God's Spirit living in us.

Consider This

Are you assured of your salvation? If not, what can you do to be so?

_____

_____

If you have accepted Jesus' blood as a covering for your sin, what has been the result in your life? _____

_____

How do you continue to deal with sin?

_____

_____

What difference does this make in your attitude toward The Lord's Supper, Communion?

_____

_____

EXAMPLE

During a lengthy interim period between full-time pastors, I gave part-time pastoral leadership to a church we attended. During this time, I came to better know Doris, an elderly woman who often had to miss services due to poor health. When I called on her in her home, I visited with her husband, too, though he didn't want to talk about God or have anything to do with the church. It saddened me to think of how Doris always asked for prayer for Wilbur — at nearly every worship service or Bible study she attended. She so wanted him to be saved!

When she passed away, I was grieved that she had never seen her prayers answered for her husband of over fifty years. As I worked with Wilbur in preparing her funeral, I could see that he had loved her very much, but still didn't want to talk about God. He did, however, allow me the freedom to say what I thought would be appropriate at her service. So, after sharing what I knew about her life, I said I was glad to have the assurance that she would be with the Lord she so loved. I went on to tell about her faith and I gave a simple Gospel message, telling those present that they, too, could have the same assurance of eternal life as she did.

Imagine my surprise when, some weeks later, Wilbur called to say he wanted me to come see him, because he wanted to "get right" with God! He wanted to be where Doris is and have the peace she had! When he repented of his sin and accepted Jesus and the work of the cross into his heart, I was delighted. As he was baptized, I happily envisioned Doris rejoicing in heaven. Her prayers had been answered. I'm sure she never dreamed that it would take her *death* to bring *life* to her husband.

God is faithful, *not wanting anyone to perish, but everyone to come to repentance.* (2 Peter 3:9b) Even if it takes 86 years!

Lesson 2
NOAH AND KING SAUL

What Does God Expect of Me, as a Believer in Jesus Christ?

Don't you know that when you offer yourselves to someone to obey him as slaves, you are slaves to the one whom you obey…whether you are slaves to sin, which leads to death, or to obedience, which leads to righteousness?

Romans 6:16

SETTING THE STAGE

Obedience (or its counterpart, disobedience), one of the themes that runs throughout all of Scripture, is also one of the issues that permeates all facets of life and relationships. Beginning with our relationship as children to parents, we continue to deal with this issue into our adult years as we relate to employers and other authorities over us.

But the most important obedience we face is in our relationship with the God of heaven and earth, the Son as King of Kings and Lord of Lords, and the Holy Spirit who communicates the truth of the Godhead to us. As we seek to be conformed to the likeness of Jesus, we realize that, as a man, He also learned obedience. Not only are our lives affected by our obedience or disobedience to God, our position in eternal life is determined as well, for both obedience and disobedience have consequences — for blessing or for cursing, for eternal life or for eternal punishment.

We'll now look at two particular men in the Bible, Noah and King Saul. Noah was a man who did everything God told him to do and was rewarded by having his life saved. King Saul, on the other hand, lost not only his kingdom, but also his life as a result of disobedience to God.

INTRODUCING NOAH
(Based on Genesis 5:28-9:17)

Little is known about the first 500 years of Noah's life, before he was commissioned to build an ark. Noah was the son of Lamech a descendant of Seth, the tenth in line from Adam. Evidently his father was a religious man, because he gave Noah son a fitting name; it means "rest." (Isn't it significant that when we are "yoked to Jesus," as instructed in Matthew 11:29, we can have rest as we obey? See Hebrews 4:10-11.)

We do know that Noah lived during a time of terrible depravity and wickedness, a time much like our present world situation. Man was guilty of many sexual and moral misdeeds, to the extent that *every inclination of the thoughts of his (man's) heart was only evil all the time* (Genesis 6:5b). Verse 11 describes the earth as being *corrupt in God's sight and…full of violence;* and verse 12 tells us that *all the people on earth had corrupted their ways.* The Hebrew words translated "corrupt" and "corrupted" mean "to decay, mar, waste, ruin." Contrast this to God's declaration, at the end of creation, that "it was good."

In the midst of this age of moral darkness, Scripture declares, Noah was *a righteous man, blameless among the people of his time, and he walked with God* (Genesis 6:9). So, Noah found favor with God. When God determined to destroy all mankind by a flood, He instructed Noah to build an ark to exact specifications. This ark eventually carried the members of Noah's family, and representatives of the animal kingdom, to safety. Noah must have already learned to trust God through having walked with Him. This faith gave him the ability to obey God and build an ark when the earth had never before seen one drop of rain! Not only was Noah appointed to the difficult task of building such a boat amidst much ridicule from the people, but God also appointed him to preach to these people. (See 2 Peter 2:5.) Because Noah *did everything just as God commanded him* (Genesis 6:22), God rewarded him by delivering him and his family from death.

INTRODUCING KING SAUL

(Based on 1 Samuel 9-11, 13:1-15; 15)

Saul, son of Kish, was a "man of standing" who was *an impressive young man without equal among the Israelites…a head taller than any of the others* (1 Samuel 9:1-2). Because Israel had demanded a king, Samuel took steps to anoint Saul after a series of circumstances brought Saul on the stage of Israel's history. Saul, at first, seemed to doubt his ability to lead, saying that he was from the smallest clan of the smallest tribe of Israel. (Some have speculated that this lack of self-esteem may have been the seeds of Saul's later disobedience and turning to other gods while leading the nation of Israel into a crisis.)

The first few years of Saul's forty-year reign went fairly well. Military victories were won and his leadership was established. On two particular occasions, however, Saul didn't fully obey God's commands. And after being confronted by the Lord through Samuel, Saul found his kingdom taken from him. It was downhill the rest of his life. Toward the end, he sought information from a witch, something forbidden by God. In his last battle with the Philistines, after seeing his sons killed, Saul killed himself by falling upon his own sword.

LESSONS FROM NOAH AND KING SAUL

Obedience

God had given Noah a mission to preach to the wicked people of his day while also building an ark to very specific instructions. Noah obeyed God despite the ridicule and unbelief of those around him. No doubt he also experienced personal discouragement. Yet without God's written Word (or Christian fellowship or even knowing the hope of salvation through Jesus Christ) Noah stood firm and obeyed God. So what does God expect from us…those who have all these available, plus the infilling of the Holy Spirit to guide and comfort us? He still wants obedience to Him and His Word.

According to James 1:22-24, we are to be doers of the Word, not hearers only.

The parable Jesus told in Luke 12:41-48, also reminds us of how Jesus wants us, His servants, to be doing His will until He comes again. In fact, He spells out the consequences of disobedience to this when He says *that servant who knows his master's will and does not get ready or does not do what his master wants will be beaten with many blows* (v. 47*)*. He goes on to say in verse 48b: *From everyone who has been given much, much will be demanded; and from the one who has been entrusted with much, much more will be asked.*

From the beginning, God has required that His people obey Him: *If you fully obey the Lord your God and carefully follow all his commands I give you today, the Lord your God will set you high above all the nations on earth. All these blessings will come upon you and accompany you if you obey the Lord your God.* (Deuteronomy 28:1-2)

Name at least five blessings that verses 3-14 tell us will follow obedience:

1. _____

2. _____

3. _____

4. _____

5. _____

As a New Testament people, we are also called to obedience:
And this is love: that we walk in obedience to his commands. As you have heard from the beginning, his command is that you walk in love.

2 John 6

What insight do the following verses give on obedience?

1 Kings 3:14 _____

Matthew 7:21-27 _____

Matthew 12:50 _____

John 7:16-17 _____

John 14:23-24 _____

God has also given instructions on how to obey the various authorities in our lives:

The government	Romans 13:1-5, Titus 3:1-2
Our "masters"	Ephesians 6:5-8
Christ (as husbands)	1 Corinthians 11:3
Husbands (as wives)	Ephesians 5:22-24
Parents (as children)	Ephesians 6:1
Elders (as church members)	1 Peter 5:1-5

If you are one of the following authorities, what caution should you have toward those under your authority?

Fathers to children (Ephesians 6:4) _____

Masters to slaves (Ephesians 6:9) _____

Husbands to wives (Ephesians 5:25-29)_____

Elders to the flock (1 Peter 5:3) _____

The Cost of Obedience

Obedience has a price. It may require that we give up our own pleasures and wills. It may mean deferring gratification for something more valuable. It may be putting someone else's welfare and pleasure before our own. Look at the following examples of Bible characters and write down what it cost them to obey God:

Abraham (in Genesis 22:2) _____

Paul (in Acts 26:19-21) _____

What did the following do to obey God?

Joshua (See Joshua 11:15.) _____

Caleb and Joshua (See Numbers 13:1-2, 30; 32:11-12.) _____

King Asa (See 1 Kings 15:11-14.) _____

Elijah (See 1 Kings 17:2-6.) _____

King Hezekiah (See 2 Kings 18:5-7.)_____

Disobedience

Saul disobeyed God on at least two specific occasions. The first time, he became impatient because of Samuel's delay, and took things into his own hands. He offered burnt offerings, a responsibility of an authorized priest. Samuel reprimanded Saul (1 Samuel 13:13-14) by telling him that, due to his disobedience, his kingdom would not endure. On the second occasion, Saul and his army failed to totally destroy everything that belonged to their enemy, the Amalekites, as God had instructed. The Lord had said they were not to spare the people or even the animals. But Saul disobeyed. Not only did he spare the king, but he also saved the best of the sheep and cattle — everything that was good. Again, Samuel confronted Saul and told him that, because of this disobedience, the Lord had rejected him as king over Israel (1 Samuel 15:26). He said to King Saul (in 1 Samuel 15:22b-23) that *to obey is better than sacrifice, and to heed is better than the fat of rams. For rebellion is like the sin of divination, and arrogance like the evil of idolatry.* Tough words for one who thought he could do things his own way and that it wouldn't matter to God.

We don't have to learn disobedience. The sinful nature we inherited from Adam leads to disobedience — the tendency to make our will dominant over what God, or other authorities, wants us to do. With the help of God's Word, which *penetrates even to dividing soul and spirit...(and) judges the thoughts and attitudes of the heart* (Hebrews 4:12), let's look at some of the root causes of disobedience.

A lusting spirit: Man wants more of what the world offers than what God has provided.

People who want to get rich fall into temptation and a trap and into many foolish and harmful desires that plunge men into ruin and destruction. For the love of money is a root of all kinds of evil. Some people, eager for money, have wandered from the faith, and pierced themselves with many griefs. But you, man of God, flee from all this, and pursue righteousness, godliness, faith, love, endurance and gentleness…I charge you to keep this command without spot or blame until the appearing of our Lord Jesus Christ.

1 Timothy 6:9-14

Judas was a person who, for the lust of things and position, was willing to betray Jesus for thirty pieces of silver. (See Matthew 26:14-16.)

A bitter spirit: When a man becomes bitter, he justifies his actions even in the face of what he knows to be right and wrong according to God's Word.

Since they did not think it worthwhile to retain the knowledge of God, he gave them over to a depraved mind, to do what ought not to be done. They have become filled with every kind of wickedness, evil, greed and depravity…Although they know God's righteous decree that those who do such things deserve death, they not only continue to do these very things but also approve of those who practice them.

Romans 1:28-32

Esau, no doubt bitter because he had sold his birthright to Jacob, became a godless man unable to repent and, thus, did not receive a blessing. (See Hebrews 12:14-17.)

Lack of trust in God: Man is unable to trust authority, even God's. He blames God for things he does not understand.

Trust in the Lord with all your heart and lean not on your own understanding: in all your ways acknowledge him, and he will make your paths straight. Do not be wise in your own eyes; fear the Lord and shun evil.

Proverbs 3:5-7

Though Moses had seen miracles, he evidently still had a hard time fully trusting in God. As a result, he disobeyed God when he struck a rock twice instead of speaking to it in order to get water for the people and livestock. Hear what God said to him: *"Because you did not trust in me enough to honor me as holy in the sight of the Israelites, you will not bring this community into the land I give them."* (Numbers 20:12)

Lack of fear of God: When we fear people more than we fear God, we will disobey God. *Fear of man will prove to be a snare, but whoever trusts in the Lord is kept safe.*

Proverbs 29:25

Aaron is one man who feared the people more than he feared God. We see evidence of this when he capitulated to the wishes of the people to build a golden calf. (Exodus 32:1-3) His disobedience cost him entrance into the Promised Land. (Deuteronomy 32:48-51)

So what are some of the consequences of disobedience?

Death:

Therefore, just as sin entered the world through one man, and death through sin, and in this way death came to all men, because all sinned...

Romans 5:12

Defeat:

They forsook the Lord, the God of their fathers, who had brought them out of Egypt. They followed and worshipped various gods of the peoples around them...Whenever Israel went out to fight, the hand of the Lord was against them to defeat them, just as he had sworn to them.

Judges 2:12-15a

Captivity:

The king of Assyria departed Israel to Assyria and settled them in Halah, in Gozan on the Habor River and in towns of the Medes. This happened because they had not obeyed the Lord their God, but had violated his covenant...all that Moses the servant of the Lord commanded. They neither listened to the commands nor carried them out.

2 Kings 18:11-12

Punishment:

He will punish those who do not know God and do not obey the gospel of our Lord Jesus. They will be punished with everlasting destruction and shut out from the presence of the Lord and from the majesty of his power on the day he comes to be glorified in his holy people and to be marveled at among all those who have believed.

2 Thessalonians 1:8-10

Jesus, an Example of Complete Obedience

There is no one more obedient than Jesus. Even as a child, He "learned obedience" (Hebrews 5:8). Luke 2:51 tells us that he was obedient to his parents. It might appear that He was disrespectful when, as a 12-year-old, he remained at the temple talking with the teachers as the rest of the family returned to Nazareth. When reprimanded by his mother, He said that He had to be about his "Father's" business. He had a higher loyalty required of Him.

Obedience to His Heavenly Father would characterize the entire public ministry of Jesus. God's response was to say, *"This is my Son, whom I love; with him I am well pleased"* (Matthew 3:17). Jesus, with a heart undivided, desired to do God's will. In fact, according to John 4:34, His "food" was to do the will of the Father!

Jesus was completely dependent upon His father for everything He did and said. (See John 5:19; 8:28; 12:49-50; 14:10.) The culmination of Jesus' willingness to be completely obedient was in the Garden of Gethsemene where He felt the burden of spiritual darkness and evil and prayed to the Father that the cup of suffering be taken from Him. Yet, He ended the prayer saying, *"Not my will, but yours be done."* (Luke 22:42)

There is no doubt that Jesus had fully learned obedience, even when He experienced the pain that man's sin produced. But, because His trust was ultimately in the Father and knowing the joy that was set before Him, He was willing to suffer death upon the cross. (Hebrews 12:2) The result of His obedience is that we can be made righteous (Romans 5:19). Let us pray that we can participate in that same kind of obedience.

SUMMARY

God wants us to be submissive to those He has placed in authority over us, just as He desires our complete obedience to Him and His Word. There are many examples in Scripture of those who were blessed…like Noah… because they obeyed. There are also examples of those who disobeyed, like King Saul, and had to pay severe consequences. Jesus is the ultimate example of One who was in full obedience to His Father, even though He had to sacrifice His own life upon a cross. Obedience has a cost, but it is what God wants and expects of us. And, its reward is eternal joy!

Consider This

What problems do you have in obeying authorities in your life?

_____

_____

How do you know if you are obeying God?

_____

_____

What consequences have you had to pay for not obeying God?

_____

_____

What are some of the cautions you need to be aware of if you are in a position of authority over someone else? _____

_____

EXAMPLE

In a very hot July of 1924, the Olympic Games were being held in Paris, France. Harold Abrahams of England became the first Briton to win the 100 meters. Johnny Weissmuller, of the United States, took three gold metals in swimming. A Finn, Paavo Nurmi, won four gold metals in track events. And, Eric Liddell, of Scotland, won a gold metal running 400 meters.

Why is it that, of all these men, twenty-two year old Eric Liddell is the one who became a world-renowned hero and, decades after his death, the inspiration for an award-winning film? The answer is, of course, that this hero of "Chariots of Fire" refused to run on Sunday. He chose to drop out of a race to obey God rather than submit to the rules of men.

The decision had not been difficult for Liddell, even though the 100-meter race was his specialty. As far as he was concerned, the Sabbath was God's day and he simply would not run…not even in the Olympic games. On the following Friday, the day that he did run (the much longer 400 meter race), he received a note from the athletic masseur who attended Eric and the rest of the British team. The note read, "In the old book it says 'He that honors me I will honor'. Wishing you the best of success." This reference to I Samuel 2:30 spurred Eric on to win and glorify God that day.

Eric ran to win; he ran for enjoyment. But, he did not make sports his career. A year after standing in the limelight in the Olympic games, he returned to China where he had been born and raised by missionary parents. There he lived out his life in missionary service, spending his last days suffering from an inoperable brain tumor while interred in a Japanese prisoner of war camp. Eric had made the decision to obey God, regardless of the cost.

Lesson 3

ABRAHAM AND ISAAC

What Roles Does a Good Father Fulfill?

He will turn the hearts of the fathers to their children, and the hearts of the children to their fathers...

Malachi 4:6a

SETTING THE STAGE

Psalm 127:3 reminds us that *sons are a heritage from the Lord; children are a reward from him.* Many of us are blessed with children. It is God's will that fathers play a major role, as spiritual head of the home, in bringing these children into right relationships with others and with Him, our Heavenly Father. In fact Ephesians 6:4 admonishes us: *Fathers, do not exasperate your children; instead, bring them up in the training and instruction of the Lord.*

The roles of fathers have been changing the past few decades. The real victims of these changes are the children. Let's look at the roles God has ordained for fathers and see how to regain them in our homes. If we don't, Matthew 18:6 may be the result: *If anyone causes one of these little ones who believe in me to sin, it would be better for him to have a large millstone hung around his neck and to be drowned in the depths of the sea.* The One who welcomed children to come unto Him wants us to understand the importance of good fathering, as well as the consequences of causing little ones to sin because we have neglected to teach/train them.

In this lesson, we'll not only look at the Biblical roles fathers are to fulfill, we'll also see how God, the Heavenly Father, can be a father to the fatherless. We'll note how the lack of good fathering is affecting society. This, indeed, is sobering, when we realize that Malachi tells of a curse that will come on our land if the hearts of the fathers are not turned to their children and the hearts of the children to their fathers. (See Malachi 4:6.)

To accomplish our purpose, we'll look at the father/son relationship of Abraham and Isaac, especially significant because of Abraham being named, in Romans 4:16, the father of us all, a precursor of those who live by faith in God. We'll also consider other Biblical fathers and children whose examples can help us realize our roles as fathers pleasing to God and fulfilling the plan He has for families and for our land.

INTRODUCING ABRAHAM AND ISAAC

(Based on Genesis 15:1-6; 17, 21:1-7; 22:1-19; 24, 25:1-11)

Though Abraham was actually the father of several children — including Ishmael, born to Hagar, and at least six sons by Keturah, the woman he married after Sarah's death — in this lesson we're considering only his relationship with Isaac, the child born to him and Sarah as a result of God's promise and supernatural power.

We can assume that there was a special father/son relationship between Abraham and Isaac. God had given Isaac as part of the covenant He made with Abraham — that Abraham would be the father of a great nation. Though this is usually understood to be the nation of Israel, it also includes us. We can also accept Abraham as our father since we are believers in Jesus Christ and come (are adopted) into His family by faith. (See Romans 4:16-17.)

We can assume that Abraham and Sarah raised Isaac in the fear of the Lord, even circumcising Him as commanded by God (Genesis 21:4). But God still wanted to know what was in Abraham's heart, whether Abraham would put Him first above his son. So, when God told Abraham to take *"your only son, Isaac, whom you love"* (Genesis 22:2) to Mt. Moriah to offer him as a sacrifice, it must have been quite a shock. When Abraham obeyed God, even to placing his beloved son upon an altar, God spared Isaac by providing a substitute sacrifice. No doubt it was a grateful Abraham and Isaac who returned home having experienced, first hand, the mercy and provision of God.

Not much more is written about their relationship until after Sarah's death, when Abraham sent his servant to get a wife for Isaac, and the servant returned with Rebekah. Neither Abraham nor Isaac were perfect individuals. Abraham used his wife Sarah to save himself (Genesis 12:10-20; 20:1-18). Isaac did the same with his wife, Rebekah (Genesis 26:1-11). Yet, this father and son had hearts for each other unto the end. Though Abraham married and had other children after Sarah's death, and though both Ishmael and Isaac buried Abraham when he died at age 175, it was Isaac, the child of the covenant, to whom Abraham left everything he owned. Isaac, who can be considered a picture of Christ, was a submissive son… willing even to be a sacrifice. He shared in the promises of God's covenant and then passed the blessing on to his sons. (Hebrews 11:20)

LESSONS FROM ABRAHAM AND ISAAC

Roles of Fatherhood

Two of the very sad facts of our day are that not only are many children living without the benefit of fathers, but a growing number of adults believe that fathers are unnecessary in a child's life. Even more confusing is the idea that homosexual couples can fulfill the roles of mother/father for children. Yet states are grappling with this very issue right now. Thus, the God-ordained roles for fatherhood are being attacked from many angles.

Life itself does not happen without the seed of a father. Nor does a child become all he is meant to be unless his father fulfills his own various roles. Just as the sins of the fathers are passed on to succeeding generations (Exodus 20:5; 34:7; Numbers 14:18), the good influence of fathers is passed on as well (Exodus 20:6; Deuteronomy 7:9)).

To consider the various roles ordained by God, we'll look at some of the ways Abraham, as well as other Biblical fathers, fulfilled them.

The father as a source of identity

Proverbs 17:6 (KJV) declares *the glory of children are their fathers*. It's important, for a person's feeling of self-worth, to have a sense of roots…that we are part of something bigger than ourselves. Many of the difficulties of youth today stem from the fact that they don't know who they are. Many cannot identify with fathers since theirs is either absent from the home much of their lives, or gone altogether.

Scripture usually introduces characters by telling us whose son they were. Genesis 11:27 tells us that Abraham's father was Terah. 1 Samuel 17:12 introduces David as the son of Jesse. From Luke 5:10, we find that Zebedee was the father of James and John. Even Adam, who had no earthly father, is said to be *the Son of God,* in Luke 3:38. Though Jesus did not owe His life to earthly seed, some thought of him as the son of Joseph. (See Luke 3:23.) He was also identified as *Son of God, Son of Man, Son of David,* and *Son of Abraham,* depending upon what role He was fulfilling at the time.

Our identity as Christians is based upon the truth that we, as gentiles, are adopted (Romans 8:15) and have been named with God's name (Ephesians 3:14-15).

Can you identify with your own father, not only in name but also in who he is? If you can, what has this done for you? If you can't, why not?

The father as a covering authority

The delegation of authority for family life is found in 1 Corinthians 11:3: *I want you to realize that the head of every man is Christ, and the head of the woman is man, and the head of Christ is God.* Combine this with Colossians 3:20 — *Children, obey your parents in everything, for this pleases the Lord* — and we find that children are to submit to parents, the wife to her husband and the husband to Christ. While all are in proper order, God protects and blesses. Each is "covered." We find this was true in Abraham's family. Isaac submitted to his father (Genesis 22:7-10), Sarah submitted to Abraham (Genesis 26:1-11), and Abraham submitted to God (Genesis 22:2-3).

Do you see Jesus as your "head"? If so, what result does this have in your family?

The father as priest

As priest of his household, the father becomes the mediator between his family and God. He not only represents God to his family, he also brings the needs and concerns of his family to God. As priest, he passes on the truths and revelations of God to his family, so that they may become part of God's family and live the lives He intended. He not only teaches his children to pray, he intercedes for them

We can assume Abraham knew well the role of priest, because he built altars and interceded for the righteous people of Sodom, including his own nephew Lot and Lot's family. Job is also a father who fulfilled the role of priest of his family. As we read of the blameless and upright life Job led before God allowed Satan to test him, we find these words: *When a period of feasting had run its course, Job would send and have them (his children and their families) purified. Early in the morning he would sacrifice a burnt offering for each of them, thinking, 'Perhaps my children have sinned and cursed God in their hearts.' This was Job's regular custom.* (Job 1:5)

As spiritual head of the home, the father is to share his faith and insights from God's word. He is to pray for his children, even before they are born, as Manoah did in Judges 13:8: *"O Lord, I beg you, let the man of God you sent to us come again to teach us how to bring up the boy who is to be born."*

How are you fulfilling the role of priesthood in your family?

The father as protector

A father should not only have the desire to protect his children physically, he should also be concerned about their mental, emotional, and spiritual well being. He should be aware of what they are being taught, what they are reading and seeing, and who their friends are. He is to see that they are spiritually equipped for temptations and conflicts, as well.

Some fathers are now realizing the need to be more involved in protecting their children from wrong sexual relationships, as well. With television, the Internet, and the media all flaunting pornography and giving wrong ideas concerning sex, fathers must take more responsibility in teaching moral values, warning their children of deceptive dangers, and aggressively supervising their relationships with others.

In the Old Testament and in other cultures today, marriages were and still are often arranged. Abraham assumed the responsibility for finding a suitable wife for his son. Though well advanced in years, Abraham sent a servant to his native country to obtain the right wife for Isaac. Abraham reminded the servant of God's promise: *"To your offspring I will give this land"—he will send his angel before you so that you can get a wife for my son from there."* (Genesis 24:7b)

In what ways do you feel you can protect your children from dangers…physically, mentally, emotionally, spiritually?

The father as provider

Matthew 7:7-11, reminds us that a good father wants only good things for his children. Verse 11 tells us: *If you, then, though you are evil, know how to give good gifts to your children, how much more will your Father in heaven give good gifts to those who ask him!* God, as our Heavenly Father, wants to bless us with good gifts, even beyond what He says in Philippians 4:19, where He promises to meet all our needs.

Many fathers pride themselves in seeing that their family has a place to live, food to eat, adequate clothing and transportation. Abraham had the resources to provide well for his family, but also he acknowledged God's provision by giving Him a tithe of all he possessed. (Genesis 14:18-20)

How do you provide for your family?

The father as teacher/trainer

God wants fathers to pass on secular knowledge, even skills. But He wants a father to be the spiritual leader in the home, too. As God was calling out a people, He gave this instruction to Abraham: *Abraham will surely become a great and powerful nation, and all nations on earth will be blessed through him. For I have chosen him, so that he will direct his children and his household after him to keep the way of the Lord by doing what is right and just, so that the Lord will bring about for Abraham what he has promised him.* (Genesis 18:17-19)

When dealing with His people under the leadership of Moses, God said, *"These commandments that I give you today are to be upon your hearts. Impress them on your children. Talk about them when you sit at home and when you walk along the road, when you lie down and when you get up. Tie them as symbols on your hands and bind them on your foreheads. Write them on the doorframes of your houses and on your gates"* (Deuteronomy 6:6-9). God intended teaching/training children to be a full-time job.

The book of Proverbs (attributed to Solomon, the wisest man who ever lived) is full of teaching which is beneficial for fathers to pass on to children. Chapter 4 begins: *Listen, my sons, to a father's instruction; pay attention and gain understanding.... when I was a boy in my father's house, still tender, and an only child of my mother, he taught me and said, "Lay hold of my words with all your heart; keep my commands and you will live."* The father was recognized as the one who passed on wisdom and knowledge.

Joshua took the father's godly position in his home when he declared, *"But as for me and my household, we will serve the Lord."* (Joshua 24:15b)

In the Psalms, Solomon's father, David, also had words for fathers.

Psalm 78:1-4 commands: *O my people, hear my teaching; listen to the words of my mouth. I will open my mouth in parables, I will utter hidden things, things from of old...what we have heard and known, what our fathers have told us. We will not hide them from their children; we will tell the next generation the praiseworthy deeds of the Lord, his power, and the wonders he has done.*

The New Testament continues to urge fathers to teach their children. Paul singles fathers out in Ephesians 6:4: *Fathers...bring them* (your children) *up in the training and instruction of the Lord.*

In 1 Timothy 3:2-5, Paul lists the qualifications of overseers in the church. One of these is that *he must manage his own family well and see that his children obey him with proper respect.*

How are you passing on knowledge…especially spiritual truths…to your children?

The father as disciplinarian

Much of the discipline of children today is left up to the mother, babysitter, or teacher; but it's the father, the head of the home, whom God holds responsible. God, as our Heavenly Father, sets the example by disciplining us. In fact, Hebrews 12:7 admonishes: *Endure hardship as discipline. God is treating you as sons.* The next verses go on to say that if we are not disciplined, we are illegitimate children, not true sons. God disciplines us for our good, so we can share in His holiness.

What do the following scriptures say about God as a disciplinarian?

Deuteronomy 8:5 _____

Psalm 94:12-14 _____

Proverbs 3:11-12_____

Revelation 3:19_____

Some well-known men in the Bible didn't discipline their sons well. They all suffered the consequences. Consider what 1 Samuel 2:12, 25, 31-36 say about Eli, and what 1 Samuel 8:1-5 says about Samuel. David wasn't a good father. Because of his sin, his first baby by Bathsheba died, his son Solomon didn't end up being a good king; his son Amnon raped his half-sister, and his son Absalom tried to usurp David's throne. Yet, David is called a man after God's own heart, because he repented of his sins. God forgave David, though David and his family had to live out the consequences of those sins.

The father as mentor/role-model

One of the primary functions of fatherhood is that of being a role model, a mentor who teaches his children by living the example he wants to pass on. In 1 John 2:6, we Christians are admonished to do just this: *Whoever claims to live in him must walk as Jesus did.* Fathers can teach, discipline, and provide, but if they aren't living by God's principles, their message will not get through. Life's lessons are as much "caught" as they are "taught." If he wants to truly obey God and have the respect of his children, a good father will live the kind of life he wants his children to have. He will also do as 1 Thessalonians 2:11 instructs: *For you know that we dealt with each of you as a father deals with his own children encouraging, comforting, and urging you to live lives worthy of God, who calls you into His kingdom and glory.*

A child will learn many character qualities as he observes them lived out…good or bad…in his father. He also determines how to relate to the opposite sex as he watches the way his father treats his mother, sisters, and other women.

Listed below are some of the character traits (and accompanying scriptures) which we teach our children by example. Check the ones you think you are demonstrating satisfactorily.

Consider those not checked and think of how you can improve in these areas.

___ servant leadership (Matthew 20:26-27	___ humility (Philippians 2:3)
___ purity (1 Timothy 4:12; 1 Thess. 4:3-8)	___ honesty (Ephesians 4:25)
___ self-discipline (1 Timothy 4:7-8; 1 Peter 1:13)	___ integrity (Proverbs 10:9)
___ perseverance (Galatians 6:9; James 1:12)	___ love (Genesis 37:4: 1 John 2:9-13)
___ compassion (James 2:14-17)	___ patience (James 5:7-11)
___ forgiveness (Matthew 6:14; Ephesians 4:32)	___ thankfulness (1 Thessalonians 5:18)
___ handling anger (James 1:19-20; Ephesians 4:26)	___ not greedy (Ephesians 5:5)

God's "Plan B"

In Psalm 68:5, God declares that He is *a father to the fatherless.* In 2 Corinthians 6:18, He has promised to *be a father to you, and you will be my sons and daughters.* For the person who hasn't had the benefit of the life-giving nurture of an earthly father, God can and will provide what is lacking. He can protect them, provide for them, and give them love and encouragement. All it takes is trust and the faith to accept His provision. He can give strength and wisdom to single parents, to stepfathers, to grandparents, or to others in the life of a fatherless child. God can provide surrogate earthly fathers as well. Paul became a spiritual father to Timothy, as recorded in 1 Timothy 1:2, 1 Corinthians 4:17, and Philippians 2:19-20. He was also a spiritual father to Titus. (See Titus 1:4.)

Though God wants to be a father to the fatherless, it is often hard for those who need this relationship the most to accept it, for if we have had a poor experience and/or image of what our earthly father is like, we will often be unable to trust God as a father. For most people, this may not come about until past hurts have been dealt with, forgiveness has been given, and healing accepted. Only then are they truly able to accept God in this role.

One of the most sobering books of our time, *Fatherless America* by David Blankenhorn, says that in 1995, forty percent of American children went to bed in homes where their fathers did not live. The author estimated that by the year 2,000 this number would rise to at least 50 percent! Another book on present-day fathering, *Raising a Modern-Day Knight,* uses Jeffrey Dahmer, the man convicted in Milwaukee in 1992 for murdering and dismembering seventeen people, as an example of what can happen to a life without a father's influence. Lionel Dahmer, Jeffrey's father, wrote his own book, *A Father's Story,* attempting to piece together the tragic events of his son's life. And, Lionel concluded that, because he had been too busy to participate in his son's life, Jeff had begun to withdeaw into himself and drift… eventually to become a loner, a serial killer. Lionel accepted the blame, as he searched his soul and found that only fathers can halt the drift of sons.

As Christian fathers, we are called not only to have great responsibility in our homes, but also to introduce our Heavenly Father to the great number of fatherless children around us.

SUMMARY

Abraham and Isaac illustrate the relationship God desires for fathers and children. God wants to be first in the father's life, and He wants fathers to assume responsibility by fulfilling various roles, such as source of identity, covering authority, priest, protector, provider, teacher, trainer, disciplinarian, and mentor/role-model. Fatherlessness is increasing today due to divorce, drugs, violence, pornography, abuse, and abandonment. But God can be, and wants to be, a father to the fatherless. His desire is for all children — including fathers — to recognize Him as their Heavenly Father!

Consider This

Which of the father roles do you believe you fulfill in your home?

_____

_____

Which of the father roles do you need to improve?

_____

_____

What fatherless child can you relate to...perhaps even help bring into a relationship with His Heavenly Father?

_____

_____

What is your fatherly role after your children have grown and left the nest?

_____

_____

EXAMPLE

In some Christian circles today, fathers have a ceremony for their sons, much like the Bar-Mitzvah for young Jewish men.

One such event that I attended was very meaningful. My friend, Ken, invited several men who were acquainted with his son, Jacob, to his home for an evening while his wife and other children were away. Though we each knew Jacob in different ways...as relatives, teachers, family friends, etc...we all recognized his transition from childhood into adolescence, and all the spiritual implications this will involve as he makes decisions during his teenage years. Each guest shared scriptures which had been meaningful in his own life, as well as the importance of seeking God in everything. We laid hands on Jacob and prayed for him in very specific ways, even as we encouraged him to submit to the advice of his father, his pastor, and us, as Christian men. We closed the time together by welcoming him to manhood, reassuring him that, though life would not always be easy, we all were standing with him in his maturing process. Ken has since reported that this evening of sharing made quite an impact upon Jacob and he is grateful for the fruit he is seeing in his son's life.

Since attending Jacob's "calling out," I have heard of other such ceremonies. Some ceremonies have been more of a family affair, perhaps with a nice dinner out. Some fathers and sons have gone on a special outing and made a covenant with each other. Some fathers and sons have combined with other fathers and sons for a more elaborate celebration. Some do it at time of puberty, others at High School graduation. Some give special tokens, such as rings or a family crest. However creative the occasion, it is a very meaningful experience for both fathers and sons...and for others who participate in such a ceremony to recognize a special time in a young man's life.

Lesson 4

JACOB AND ESAU

How Can I Handle Anger?

In your anger do not sin. Do not let the sun go down while you are angry, and do not give the devil a foothold.

Ephesians 4:26-27

SETTING THE STAGE

How can I control my temper? Is all anger bad? What does it mean to be angry and yet not sin? Why is it important to deal with anger before the day is over? We all ask these questions as we struggle to live the new life in Christ while realizing we still have a sinful nature, an "old man" that doesn't want to die. We should be able to understand Paul, and the battle he experienced in doing the very things he didn't want to do, as he learned to live by the Spirit instead of yielding to the flesh. (Romans 6-7)

Jacob and Esau were twins who, along with their parents, became victims of their own deception and anger. These acts of their sinful nature led to the disintegration of their family life.

In this lesson we will particularly look at anger, and what it does to us as well as to those around us. Most importantly, we will consider what God says about anger, and how He wants us to handle it.

INTRODUCING JACOB AND ESAU

(Based on Genesis 25:21-36:8,except chapters 26 and 34; and Hebrews 11:21; 12:16-17)

Jacob and Esau were the sons of Isaac and Rebekah. Esau, the firstborn, was an outdoorsman and was his father's favorite, while Jacob stayed closer to home and grew up a "mama's boy." As a young man, Jacob took advantage of Esau's hunger to get him to sell his birthright for some bread and stew. He later schemed with his mother to rob Esau of the paternal blessing — a blessing which would have been given to the oldest son. When Isaac realized he had been deceived into giving the blessing to Jacob, he *trembled violently* (Genesis 27:33). Verse 41 tells us that Esau held a grudge against Jacob and told himself, *"The days of mourning for my father are near; then I will kill my brother Jacob."* When Rebekah heard what Esau was planning, she became afraid and sent Jacob to Paddan Aram, her ancestral homeland. So Jacob fled, while Esau remained behind and married Canaanite women, much to the displeasure of his parents. Deception and anger had destroyed a family.

While living in Paddan Aram, Jacob married Leah and Rachel. Years later, he took his wives, children, and herds back to his homeland. But he feared an encounter with Esau. When he received word Esau was approaching him with 400 men who would be overwhelmingly superior if Esau planned to carry out his earlier threat, Jacob sent gifts on ahead to appease him. He then divided his entourage into two groups, in case one group was killed. Though Jacob wanted to spend a night alone before joining them, God had other plans. A "man" appeared to Jacob and the two wrestled all night. The man touched Jacob's hip, even as Jacob cried out for a blessing. God commended Jacob for his prevailing attitude and gave him a new name, Israel, meaning "He struggles with God." Jacob suffered a permanent limp, God's way of reminding him of the weakness of his own natural strength. (Hosea 12:2-6 gives Jacob as a model for us to follow whenever we are facing difficulty resulting from our sinful nature.) By morning, Jacob was a changed man. As he approached Esau, he bowed down to the ground seven times. Then Esau ran to meet Jacob and they embraced and wept in each other's arms. After this brief meeting, they went their separate ways. Eventually, Jacob entered the Promised Land as "Israel" and was reunited with his father. He and Esau must have seen one another again; Genesis 35:29 tells us that they both buried Isaac. Jacob's family settled in the Promised Land and became part of the lineage of Jesus Christ. Esau, according to Hebrews 12:16-17, was remorseful over losing the birthright, but never experienced true repentance (change of heart). His descendants were the Edomites who continued to hold a grudge against Jacob (Israel) because of the loss of their birthright. Their story and how God said He would deal with them is found in the book of Obadiah.

LESSONS FROM JACOB AND ESAU
Dealing with Our Sinful Nature

Before we look specifically at anger, we need to consider how we deal with our flesh, for in Galatians 5:20, we find that *fits of rage* are acts of our sinful nature. When we receive the gift of salvation, we become new creatures in Christ — the old is gone, the new has come (2 Corinthians 5:17). From that time on, we experience struggles between our new life, as Christians, and our old flesh, our sinful nature that still wants to rise within us. Paul describes this struggle in Romans 7:21-25: *So I find this law at work: When I want to do good, evil is right there with me. For in my inner being I delight in the Lord's law; but I see another law at work in the members of my body, waging war against that law of my mind and making me a prisoner of the law of sin at work within my members. What a wretched man I am! Who will rescue me from this body of death? Thanks be to God…through Jesus Christ our Lord!* Through Christ we have provision for dealing with our sinful nature, for reckoning the old man dead:

- We have the benefit of the blood of Jesus, which cleanses us from sin.
- We have God's Spirit within us to mature fruit, such as self-control.
- We have God's Word to claim His promises of victory over sin.
- We can pray, even coming boldly before God, because Jesus is now our high priest and intercessor.

Jacob and Esau represent the struggle of two kinds of persons. The scheming, deceiving Jacob ultimately desired to be rightly related to a covenant-making God and to be blessed by Him. One night, when Jacob was alone, a "man" wrestled with him, supernaturally touching him until his physical strength was weakened and his carnal nature was subdued. In the process, Jacob was given the name "Israel," which means "Prince of God" or "he strives with God." Jacob was a different man from that time on. Esau, however, is a picture of a godless or profane man who didn't have the desire to please God or enjoy His blessing. According to Hebrews 12:17, Esau never fully repented, and even passed his anger on to future generations.

The struggle within us always demands a choice. Will we yield to the Spirit, or will we submit to the flesh? Will we let anger control us, or will we look to God to help us handle it His way?

The Many Faces of Anger

Though we have just seen that anger can be of our sinful nature, a simple definition of anger is difficult. In his book *Overcoming Hurts and Anger*, Dwight Carlson defines anger as "an automatic reaction to any real or imagined insult, frustration, or injustice, producing emotional agitation, which the person may or may not be aware of, but which will seek expression in some sort of aggressive, defensive, or destructive manner to oneself or others." On the other hand, Drs. Les Carter and Frank Minrith in their book, *The Anger Workbook*, define anger as "an intent to preserve (1) personal worth, (2) essential needs, and (3) basic convictions." A dictionary simply defines anger as a strong feeling of displeasure.

We can also say that:

Anger is a legitimate emotion, a neutral one that can be righteous or of evil intent.

Anger is a bio-chemical reaction, as well as an emotional one. Our bodies have an automatic "flight or fight" mechanism which prepares it for action. Adrenaline starts pumping, blood pressure increases, eyes dilate, our hands become sweaty; all are involuntary responses to anger.

Anger can be pictured as a volcano. Its outward eruptions are the result of inward build-up of pressure. These eruptions are unpredictable and usually hurt those closest to them. Even after the eruptions have ceased, damage may be felt for a long time.

Anger operates in two directions: We can be the perpetrator or the victim. We can offend, or be offended. Both can hurt.

Anger is a demand. It thrives on unmet needs. So it says: "I want an apology." "I want appreciation." "I want to be heard." "I have unfulfilled expectations."

Anger is control, a way to use power over someone.

Just as we can see various aspects of anger by looking at Jacob, Esau, Isaac and Rebekah, we can observe the different ways anger is manifested in our own lives, as well as the lives of those around us.

It appears that Isaac might have repressed his anger, while Rebekah camouflaged hers. Jacob fled the situation, and Esau's anger erupted into rage. So it is today. Different people evidence anger in different ways.

Check the ways you manifest anger:

_____ Become silent	_____ Become critical or judgmental
_____ Blame others	_____ Lash out verbally
_____ Disguise my true feelings	_____ Become physically abusive
_____ Erupt like a volcano	_____ Other _____

In recent years we have become painfully aware of how anger leads to domestic violence and spousal, elder, or child abuse. It affects the poor of the inner city and small hamlets of our land, as well as prominent members of society who live in luxurious city suburbs. It is found in non-Christian, as well as Christian homes, even in the homes of pastors.

The Bible doesn't say that Jacob's anger erupted into domestic violence. It does tell us of two instances when he became angry with family. Genesis 29:19-27 tells us he was angry when he found that his father-in-law, Laban, had tricked him into marrying Leah after he had worked seven years for Rachel. Then, in Genesis 30:1-5, we find him angry with his wife, Rachel, because she was blaming him for not giving her a child.

Anger is also displayed in the lives of other Bible characters. We'll look at a few of these and determine what made them angry, and how they responded.

Numbers 32:13: God became angry. What did He do? _____

He made them wander in the desert for 40 years until all had gone (died)

1 Samuel 18:6-8: What made King Saul angry? *They credited David with*

tens of thousands, but me with only thousands

What happened as a result? (See v. 9-11.) *evil spirit from God to Saul*

_____

2 Kings 5:9-12: Why did Namaan become angry? *he told him to go wash himself*

7 times in the Jordan and did not cure his leprosy

Who confronted him about this? What was the result? (See v. 13-14.) _____

 # Naaman's servant confronted him - he did - he was cleansed

Esther 3:5-6: Why did Haman become enraged at Mordecai? _____

Mordecai would not kneel down or pay him honor

Matthew 21:12-13: Why did Jesus become angry? What did He do? *he saw buying*

+ selling in the temple - he overturned the tables of the
money changers + the benches of those selling doves

Luke 4:16-29: Why were the people in the synagogue furious? _____

page 15 + 3

What did they want to do? _____

_____

Since Ephesians 4:26 alludes to the fact that not all anger is sin, some anger might be called righteous anger. Certainly the wrath of God and the anger of Jesus do not come from their sinful nature. Put a check by those incidents above where you think it is a case of righteous anger.

In your opinion, what justifies anger or makes it righteous? _____

_____

32

Handling Anger God's Way

Many books and counselors proclaim a variety of methods to handle anger. Some of these may be very beneficial from a psychological point of view. In this lesson, however, we'll look primarily at Scripture to see what God says about anger and how we are to handle it.

From the beginning of time, God knew that man would have to deal with anger, so He has much to say about it in His Word. In the Old Testament, we find this admonition in Leviticus 19:18: *Do not seek revenge or bear a grudge against one of your people, but love your neighbor as yourself. I am the Lord.* And, in the New Testament, we have this instruction in Ephesians 4:31-32: *Get rid of all bitterness, rage and anger, brawling and slander, along with every form of malice. Be kind and compassionate to one another, forgiving each other, just as in Christ God forgave you.*

God has much more to say about this aspect of our sinful nature. Here are a few verses:
- *Refrain from anger and turn from wrath, do not fret...it leads only to evil. (* Psalm 37:8)
- *Do not make friends with a hot-tempered man, do not associate with one easily angered, or you may learn his ways and get yourself ensnared.* (Proverbs 22:24-25)
- *An angry man stirs up dissension, and a hot-tempered one commits many sins.* (Proverbs 29:22)
- *In your anger do not sin; when you are on your beds, search your hearts and be silent.* (Psalm 4:4)
- *My dear brothers, take note of this: Everyone should be quick to listen, slow to speak and slow to become angry, for man's anger does not bring about the righteous life that God desires.* (James 1:19-20)
- *But now you must rid yourselves of all such things as these: anger, rage, malice, slander, and filthy language from your lips.* (Colossians 3:8)

What can we do to handle our anger God's way?

Recognize that you are a sinner and that God hates sin. (Romans 3:23; Psalm 11:5; Psalm 51:4)
When does anger become a sin against God?

_____

_____

Accept responsibility for your anger. (Ezekiel 18:20)
Do you have a choice of whether or not to become angry?

_____

_____

Discover the root cause of your anger and deal with it. (Romans 8:5-8; Galatians 5:16-21)
What do pride, fear, hurt, frustration, etc. have to do with anger?

_____

_____

Make your anger a matter of prayer. (Acts 15:8-9; 1 John 3:20; 1 Corinthians 2:10b-11)
How can God help you handle your anger?

_____

_____

Be sensitive to the leading of the Holy Spirit. (Ephesians 4:17-24)
How do you determine which is "of the Spirit" and which is "of the flesh?"

_____

_____

Watch your thoughts. (Philippians 4:8; 2 Corinthians 10:3-5)
How does thinking affect your actions?

_____

_____

Communicate your grievances to the one who has offended you. (Matthew 18:15)
Have you ever averted an angry confrontation by first going to the one who has offended you and talking it out? If so, what was the result?

_____

_____

Get counsel from others. (James 5:16; Proverbs 24:6)
To whom do you go to get counsel on how to handle a situation when you are so angry you can't think straight?

_____

_____

Repent and forgive. (Matthew 6:12; Mark 11:25; Luke 17:4; 2 Corinthians 2:10-11)
What does forgiveness do for you…for the other person? How does unforgiveness give the devil a foothold?

_____

_____

Make amends. (Matthew 5:22-24)
Can you remember a time when an enemy became a friend because you took the initiative to make amends for your anger?

_____

_____

Bless the one who made you angry. (1 Peter 3:9)
How does blessing the one you have forgiven help you forget the offense?

_____

_____

SUMMARY

In the story of Jacob and Esau, we saw how acts of the sinful nature (deception and anger) separated them as brothers. We also saw how anger, especially, destroyed their whole family. Through Esau's unrepentance, his descendants carried a grudge against the people of Israel — a grudge which has had a long-term effect. God supernaturally dealt with Jacob's "old man" and Jacob emerged with a new name and new relationship with God and with others. As we learn to handle our anger God's way, and let Him deal with us, we'll experience the fruit of self-control, be slower to anger, and be unwilling to give the devil a foothold. Unrighteous anger, anger that results from pride, fear, etc., is part of our old nature, the carnal man that continues to give us a struggle as we live as new creatures in Christ. Because we are new creatures, however, we have many provisions of God with which to handle our anger and live at peace with others.

EXAMPLE

As star pitcher for the San Francisco Giants, Dave Dravecky often let his anger get out of control, particularly before he became a Christian. After winning several games on the road, he would return home feeling quite invincible. And when he entered the door and didn't find everything in perfect order, he lashed out at his wife and two small children for even the most minor things — like leaving towels on the bathroom floor. Once, after a day of unending blame and rage, his wife, Jan, told him that she'd had enough, that she couldn't live up to his expectations any longer. This made him so angry that he threw towels, clothes, and even furniture, all the while glorying in the power he felt he had.

In 1991, Dravecky suffered a blow which eventually led to the end of his promising baseball career. His left pitching arm and shoulder were amputated due to cancer. Bottling his feelings inside and refusing to recognize them not only kept him from understanding his true worth as a man, but also eventually led to uncontrolled anger and deep depression. Frustration with new difficulties (such as putting on his pants with only one arm) would cause him explode in anger, and everyone around him would suffer the effects of his rage. Finally, with the help of a Christian counselor he was able to see the other feelings — hurt, frustration, pride, etc. — that produced his anger. And he saw that he needed to learn to recognize and deal with these feelings. Then, when he learned to recognize frustration, he would let go of his pride and ask for help. He got his pants on, his family didn't have to suffer his rage, and he felt better.

Dravecky admits that he'll probably continue to wrestle with anger the rest of his life, but he knows that he's improving and is able, now, to share what he has learned with others. Life is more enjoyable for those around him, and he is better able to live out his God-given worth as a man, and he hasn't thrown any furniture in a long time!

Lesson 5

JOSEPH AND JOB

How Do I Respond to Trials, Afflictions, and Persecution?

In this you greatly rejoice, though now for a little while you many have had to suffer grief in all kinds of trials. These have come so that your faith...of greater worth than gold, which perishes even though refined by fire...may be proved genuine and may result in praise, glory and honor when Jesus Christ is revealed.

1 Peter 1:6-7

SETTING THE STAGE

It's relatively easy to understand trials and suffering on the part of a person who lives a life of immorality, rebellion, and violence. Proverbs 13:15b (KJV) tells us that *the way of transgressors is hard.* It's more difficult to explain why good people suffer, especially those who are trying to follow Christ and His teachings. We probably never will understand the reason. Isaiah 55:8-9 reminds us that God's thoughts are not our thoughts, nor are our ways His ways. He has higher purposes for our lives, and this may include our having to endure trials, afflictions, and persecution. etc.

Scripture does give us clues as to why there is some suffering. It also tells us how to respond to the difficult, hurtful things that come our way.

In this lesson we will highlight two men in the Bible, though we'll look at a number of men to see how they responded when suffering came into their lives. Through Joseph, we'll consider the trials and afflictions we endure because of what other people have done to us. In Job, we'll look at the ways we may suffer because of what God has sovereignly let come through circumstances or by allowing Satan to "do his thing." In learning from these examples, we should, in the end, be most grateful for the One who *suffered for you, leaving you an example, that you should follow in his steps.* (1 Peter 2:21)

INTRODUCING JOSEPH

(Based on Genesis 30, 35, 37, 39-50)

Joseph was the eleventh son of Jacob, and the first for Rachel. Since Jacob had another wife and some handmaids who also gave him children, Joseph was born into a household which included envy, anger, competition, and bargaining for favor. When Joseph was still very young, his mother, Rachel, died during the birth of his brother, Benjamin, as Jacob's whole household was returning to his homeland.

Missing his favorite wife, Jacob favored her oldest child. This didn't please Joseph's half-brothers, particularly because he had told them of dreams in which he saw them bowing down to him. A day finally came when they had opportunity to get rid of Joseph by selling him into slavery. They deceived their father by making it look like an animal had killed him.

Taken to Egypt, Joseph was given responsibility in Potiphar's house. However, Potiphar's wife tried to seduce him and then accused him of sexual misconduct. As a result, he was thrown into prison where he eventually earned the trust of the warden and was given opportunity to interpret some dreams. Because of his explanation of one of the Pharoah's dreams concerning a coming of seven years of famine, Joseph was given a position of rulership so that he could collect and distribute food.

When the famine spread to the north, Joseph's father and brothers heard about the food distribution in Egypt, and went there to get some. Imagine Joseph's surprise when he saw his brothers! At first, he didn't let them know who he was. After requiring them to return home and bring back his younger brother, he revealed himself to them. They were at first terrified, and then overjoyed. All ended well. Joseph was reunited with all his family, including his father. He forgave his brothers for what they had done to him as a young boy. And he reminded them of God's goodness.

Sold into slavery; thrown out of Potiphar's house; betrayed by fellow prisoners; Joseph experienced suffering because of many people. But God had a purpose for it all.

INTRODUCING JOB
(Based on the book of Job, particularly chapters 1-2, 13:15, 16, 19, 42)

Job's name is significant, for it is the Hebrew word *Iyowb,* which means "hated (persecuted) one ever returning to God" or "he that weeps." Job was a descendant of Aram, son of Shem. He was possibly a contemporary of Abraham. He was 240 years old when he died. Some have speculated that his trial of suffering took place within one year's time. Ezekiel 14:14, & 20 imply that Job was in high standing with God, because Ezekiel includes Job with Noah and Daniel as intercessors. Great though they were, they weren't be able to change God's mind in regards to sending judgment. In James 5:11 Job is lifted up as a model of perseverance.

In the book of Job, we also find that Job was a man declared by God to be righteous. He had faith in a personal, living, eternal God who would redeem him as He would appear in the flesh on earth some future day. Job prayed for both his children and friends, and his prayers were answered. Most of all, his trust and hope in God remained intact despite all God had sovereignly allowed him to suffer.

LESSONS FROM JOSEPH AND JOB
The School of Suffering

To understand some of the reasons God seems to allow suffering resulting from trials, afflictions and persecution, we will consider the following:
- Suffering as a result of sin, both our own and that inflicted upon us by others
- Suffering as perpetrated by Satan
- Suffering as allowed by God for His purposes

Suffering as a result of sin, both our own and that inflicted upon us by others
Later Jesus found him (the paralyzed man He had healed) *at the temple and said to him, "See, you are well again. Stop sinning or something worse may happen to you."* John 5:14

If one has had his sins forgiven, and goes on to sin without asking forgiveness, he often must pay the consequences for sin…and it can be worse than before as God deals with him.

Cain killed his brother, Abel, because he was angry that Abel's offering, not his own, had been accepted by God. God meted out punishment for Cain's sin — Cain became a fugitive, wandering from place to place on the earth. Cain's reply was, *"My punishment is more than I can bear"* (Genesis 4:13).

The prodigal son in Luke 15:11-32 is another who suffered the consequences of his own sin. As he lived with pigs (which in itself was an atrocity for a Jew), he found that rebellious living results not only in diminished finances, but poverty of soul and spirit.

What consequences (suffering) have you had to endure because of your own sin?

_____

_____

Who is going to harm you if you are eager to do good? But even if you should suffer for what is right, you are blessed. (1 Peter 3:13-14a)

In 2 Samuel 16:5-14, we have a story of a deposed David leaving Jerusalem. He was being pelted with stones as he was cursed by Shimei, a man from Saul's family. David didn't fight back, and he told others to leave Shimei alone. But David was inflicted with pain because of another person's sin.

What have you suffered because of someone else's sin?

_____

_____

Suffering as perpetrated by Satan

Do not be afraid of what you are about to suffer. I tell you, the devil will put some of you in prison to test you, and you will suffer persecution for ten days. Be faithful, even to the point of death, and I will give you the crown of life. (Revelation 2:10)

Satan, as an instrument of God, can never move out of God's sovereign will. God will allow him to function, at times, as a means of dealing with our sins and unbelief. Isaiah 54:16b-17 says, *"And it is I who have created the destroyer to work havoc; no weapon forged against you will prevail….This is the heritage of the servants of the Lord…."* One of the interpretations of this verse is that God has created the destroyer (Satan) to deal with sin. But we, His servants, can prevail. (See also John 8:44; 10:10.)

The story of Job is a familiar example of one who suffered because God allowed Satan to do what he wanted…with limitation. In Job 1:6-12, we find God giving this permission to Satan even while considering Job a very righteous man. God's "hedge" around him was removed and Job experienced the loss of his children, his possessions, his health and even his wife's respect.

A New Testament example of suffering caused by Satan is found in 1 Corinthians 5:1-5. Paul turned a man over to Satan so that his sin of fornication could be dealt with and his spirit saved. It isn't clear what kind of trial or difficulty this man suffered, but if he's the same man referred to in 2 Corinthians 7:8-13, whatever it was it brought him sorrow, which led him to repent.

Today, one of the ways Satan inflicts suffering on us is by getting us involved in the occult. This may come through things such as playing certain games, living by horoscopes, going along with New Age beliefs, or becoming involved with eastern religions. Adherents to cults (such as Heaven's Gate) are deceived by Satan and often have to suffer consequences.

Have you ever suffered because God allowed Satan to supernaturally deal with you? How?

_____

_____

Suffering as allowed by God for His purposes

God seems to have several reasons for allowing us, His children, to experience various types of suffering as a result of trials, afflictions, and persecution. Let's look at some of them:

1. God allows suffering so that His works are displayed...so people can see Him as the awesome God He is:

    This happened so that the work of God might be displayed in his life. (John 9:3b)

    Sometimes, this is seen through what we term miracles, such as in John 9:1-34, when the blind man was healed. The attempt by men to explain why this man suffered blindness all his life was all wrong. He wasn't blind because of his or his parents' sin (v.3). After this man's miraculous healing, Jesus said that he had been blind only so that the work of God could be displayed in his life. This is how God received glory for Himself.

    The prophet Hosea is another person who suffered because of what God was trying to show through his life. Hosea's relationship with his wayward wife was a picture of God's relationship with unfaithful Israel. The entire book of Hosea is very moving as it shows Hosea's suffering, even as he saw wanton, disheveled Gomer at a slave market and paid the price for her redemption. He loved her enough to suffer, himself, in order to restore her to the relationship he so desired with her.

    Have you ever suffered, and then received a miraculous demonstration of God's power in your life? If so, how did God receive the glory from your suffering?

    _____

    _____

2. God allows suffering as part of His discipline for us:

    Endure hardship as discipline; God is treating you as sons. (Hebrews 12:7a)

    Hebrews 12:4-11 reminds us that God's purpose in His discipline is to produce a harvest of righteousness and peace for those who have been trained by the discipline. Such discipline is not pleasant; it's painful.

Jonah had a difficult time obeying God. In fact, he ran the opposite direction, and ended up in the belly of a big fish. Even after he got out of this predicament and did what God had originally asked him to do, he had to be disciplined again. This time he sat in the blazing sun under a withering vine with the scorching wind blowing in his face. God had to teach him a lesson; and Jonah suffered in the process.

That Peter endured suffering through discipline is evident from reading his letters. Second Peter is filled with statements concerning suffering. Peter, who had failed His master a number of times, was *sifted like wheat* (Luke 22:31) and was restored to become a leader in the early church.

How have you experienced God's discipline in your life?

_____

_____

3. God allows suffering to prepare us for a larger task:

    You (my brothers) intended to harm me, but God intended it for my good to accomplish what is now being done, the saving of many lives. (Genesis 50:20)

    As noted earlier, God allowed Joseph to suffer much in order to prepare him for leadership and to get him into a position that would benefit others.

    David went through many trials between being anointed king and assuming that role after Saul's death. (See 1 Samuel 18:5-11; 19:1-16: 23:7-29.)

    Have you endured suffering because God was grooming you for a new and/or larger task/ministry? _____

    _____

4. God allows suffering for our own spiritual growth:

    We also rejoice in our sufferings, because we know that suffering produces perseverance, perseverance, character, and character, hope. And hope does not disappoint us, because God has poured out his love into our hearts by the Holy Spirit, whom he has given us. (Romans 5:3-5)

    Like baby birds struggling out of their shells, or butterflies from cocoons, sometimes we must suffer in order pass from one stage to another. As has been said, "No pain, no gain"

    Zechariah 13:9a says there will be a remnant who will go through a great time of tribulation: *This third I will bring into the fire; I will refine them like silver and test them like gold.*

    Precious metals are refined (reduced to a pure state and cleansed of foreign or objectionable elements) over a very hot fire. As the ore melts, that which is impure floats to the top where it is then skimmed off. When the refiner can see his own image on the surface of the liquid metal, he knows the refining process is complete.

    God put Paul through the fire to refine him, to make him in the great apostle that he became. As Saul of Tarsus, Paul had previously persecuted Christians, but God had chosen him to be His instrument to carry the Gospel to the Gentiles. After being confronted on the road to Damascus, Paul was converted. When Ananias came to him three days later, Paul was baptized and filled with the Holy Spirit. In the process, God told Ananias: *"I will show him (Paul) how much he must suffer for my name"* (Acts 9:16). God did eventually display his power through Paul, and Paul suffered much because of this. (See 2 Corinthians 11:23-33 for some of the details.)

Can you think of some way you have grown spiritually because of having to endure trials and/or suffer persecution?

_____

_____

The Suffering of Jesus

Christ suffered for you, leaving you an example, that you should follow in his steps. He committed no sin, and no deceit was found in his mouth. When they hurled their insults at him, he did not retaliate; when he suffered, he made no threats. (1 Peter 2:21b-23a)

Crucifixion was the worst possible death. Jesus suffered excruciating physical pain. The realization that many had not received His message and that even His own disciples would desert Him must have caused Jesus much mental anguish. He suffered so from his separation from God that He cried out from the cross: *"My God, my God, why have you forsaken me?"* (Matthew 27:46b)

Why did God allow Jesus to pay the ultimate price of suffering? Let's look at a few scriptures:

But we see Jesus, who was made a little lower than the angels, now crowned with glory and honor because he suffered death, so that by the grace of God he might taste death for everyone. (Hebrews 2:9)

Although he was a son, he learned obedience from what he suffered, and, once made perfect, he became the source of eternal salvation for all who obey him.... (Hebrews 5:8)

Let us fix our eyes on Jesus, the author and perfecter of our faith, who for the joy set before him endured the cross, scorning its shame, and sat down at the right hand of the throne of God. (Hebrews 12:2)

Persecution for Christ's Sake

In fact, everyone who wants to live a godly life in Christ Jesus will be persecuted. (2 Timothy 3:12)

Read the verses on the following page, then draw a line to the words that describe what each selection tells us we may have to endure for Christ's sake:

Luke 9:23	leave our family
Luke 12:49-53	be insulted by others
Mark 10:29-30	see division in our family
Matthew 5:10-11	deny ourselves
John 15:18-20	be hated by the world

What are we to do when we are persecuted for righteousness sake?

Matthew 5:11-12; Acts 5:41 _____

2 Thessalonians 1:1-4 _____

James 1:2-3 _____

What is our reward upon graduation from of the school of suffering? 2 Timothy 2:12 (KJV) says *if we suffer, we shall reign with him.*

SUMMARY

Suffering as a result of trials, affliction, and persecution is inevitable, even for Christians who have many promises of God's goodness and blessings. Joseph and Job are two among many men in the Bible who are examples for us regarding how to face and/or endure difficulties that come our way…whether from others, or the devil or God. Most important of all, we must realize how much Jesus suffered for our salvation. In the midst of our suffering, God's character is not marred. He is still a God of integrity, goodness and grace. Because He desires, most of all, our relationship, He will allow suffering to come into our lives so that we will be drawn closer to Him.

As we follow Jesus with sold-out commitment, we will suffer persecution, for the world is against God and His ways. This is especially true these days, as the return of Jesus draws near.

Consider This

How do you handle trials and afflictions that come your way?

_____

_____

Has looking at the examples in this lesson given you a different attitude toward suffering?

_____

_____

What does meditating on the suffering of Jesus do for you?

_____

_____

Have you ever experienced persecution because you are a Christian? If so, how did you respond?

_____

_____

EXAMPLE

While in the process of choosing from among many stories for the best illustration of this lesson, I received a letter from the wife of a long-time friend, Jim Marsh. The letter was to tell us of Jim's final suffering and of the victory he had in it.

As Wycliffe Bible Translators, Jim and Marjorie Marsh gave all their adult years to living among the Aboriginal peoples of Australia, learning their language and putting it into written form so that they could give them the Bible to read.

Jim was often plagued with asthma attacks and eye problems, yet he and Marj raised two daughters while living among the Martu Wangka people along Jigalong Creek. Not only did this mean living in the most meager of conditions, far from both their families, it also meant extreme frustration, at times, attempting to gain the confidence of the people and then to decipher their spoken language. Over a lifetime, little by little, they made progress. With the help of other translators, they finally put together a dictionary, a translation of much of the New Testament and an abridgment of Genesis. I especially remember the joy they experienced when, after fifteen years, they had the privilege of seeing Jigalong people gathered under a white gum tree praising the Lord!

Jim's final suffering came in the form of colon cancer, diagnosed a little over a year before he died. Between surgeries, chemotherapy, and other hospital visits, Jim made at least two trips back to Jigalong to work more on translation. When the cancer finally spread to his lungs, he and Marj spent hours in his hospital room reciting scripture over and over.

During his lifetime, the trials, afflictions, and persecution of Jim Marsh were many. And his final suffering came through a difficult battle with cancer. Yet Jim was willing to endure it all so that the Aboriginal people could have God's Word and a personal relationship with Him. How fitting it was that Marj took his ashes to Jigalong to be buried among the people he loved so much.

In her letter, Marj enclosed a poem Jim wrote entitled "He's Coming for Me"…a declaration of his faith in God and His Word. His poem confirmed what we knew all along…that Jim, with God's help, had victory despite suffering much his whole life through. To God be the glory!

Lesson 6
MOSES, JOSHUA AND NEHEMIAH

What Are the Traits of a Good Leader?

Be strong and very courageous. Be careful to obey all the law my servant Moses gave you; do not turn from it to the right or to the left, that you may be successful wherever you go.

Joshua 1:7

SETTING THE STAGE

Following the last meal that Jesus had with His disciples before going to the cross, He told them that they would fall away from Him that very night. Then he quoted from Zechariah (13:7b) *"I will strike the shepherd, and the sheep of the flock will be scattered."* Though the disciples didn't fully understand what He was saying, He was warning them that He would be crucified and His people would scatter. People without a leader are like sheep without a shepherd. According to Matthew 9:36, they become harassed and helpless.

Throughout the Bible, there were leaders. Some were without specific titles, such as Abraham, Noah, and Jacob. We know others by the major responsibilities they were given: Moses, Joshua, Ezra and Nehemiah. Interspersed were kings, prophets, and judges…most of whom tried to bring the people together for the common good and under the ultimate rule of God.

As we'll discover in our study of the Old Testament prophets, God speaks through human instruments and expresses His authority and ultimate rule through human leaders. He is the authority behind all leaders. He puts them in their positions, and He removes them, as well.

The purpose of this lesson will be to consider three men…Moses, Joshua, and Nehemiah…to discover what traits allow for good leadership. This should help us appreciate the role of leaders in our lives, as well as give guidance to those of us who are, or may become, leaders.

INTRODUCING MOSES
(Based on Exodus, especially chapters 2-4, 18; Numbers 12-14, 16; Hebrews 11:24-30)

The first eighty years of Moses' life were not what we would call successful. He was born while the Hebrews were slaves in Egypt, during a period when the Pharaoh had decreed that all boy babies be thrown into the river. Through divine intervention, Moses was spared and was raised in Pharaoh's own household by his daughter. There, he was thoroughly trained in the ways of the Egyptians, being groomed for royal leadership. However, since Jochebed (Moses' mother) was his nurse, she was able to teach him the heritage and beliefs of the Israelites as well. One day, Moses went out to observe the Israelites at hard labor, and killed an Egyptian who was beating a Hebrew. He became a fugitive and fled to Midian. There, he lived with Jethro's family, and eventually married Jethro's daughter Zipporah.

God used this time of solitude to teach Moses some important things about himself. One day, while Moses was tending Jethro's flock, God spoke to him from a burning bush. He asked Moses to return to Egypt and to lead His people from there into a land flowing with milk and honey. After Moses asked God how he could lead when he couldn't even speak well, God provided his brother Aaron to be his spokesman…an arrangement that later caused some grief.

The saga of Moses, and his leadership of the Israelites, is reflected in the first five books of the Old Testament, which he authored. These books of the law became a very important basis for the whole Jewish religious system. There are a number of parallels between Moses and Jesus, as well as the fact that Jesus was called a *prophet like Moses* (Acts 7:37). One of the most important descriptions we see of Moses is that of the Lord speaking to him face to face, as a man speaks with his friend (Exodus 33:11). Undoubtedly this is one of the most important traits any God-chosen leader could have.

INTRODUCING JOSHUA

(Based on Exodus 17:8-15; 24:12-18; 33:11; Numbers 11:26-30; 13:16; 14:26-45; 27:18-23; 32:6-13, 28; Deuteronomy 1:37-40; 3:21-29; 31:1-8, 14, 23, 24; Book of Joshua)

Joshua was a loyal assistant to Moses. Moses had been Joshua's mentor during the forty years of wilderness wandering. Although Moses was a "hard act to follow," Joshua stepped into a position of leadership with the best qualifications anyone could have. Deuteronomy 34:9 says *Joshua son of Nun was filled with the spirit of wisdom because Moses had laid his hands on him. So the Israelites listened to him and did what the Lord had commanded Moses.* And God assured Joshua: *"No one will be able to stand up against you all the days of your life. As I was with Moses, so I will be with you; I will never leave you nor forsake you."* (Joshua 1:5)

Joshua had already exhibited courage by bringing back a good report after spying out the promised land with Caleb. Joshua and Caleb were the only two spies who believed God; and it was reckoned to them as faith. Everyone else died in the wilderness; only Joshua and Caleb were permitted to enter the promised land, although they had to wait forty years.

INTRODUCING NEHEMIAH

(Based on book of Nehemiah)

Nehemiah was born to Hachaliah while the Jews were in captivity in Babylon. He was taught well concerning his people and the Jewish faith. This made him love and long for Jerusalem, the place where God had put His name. So when his brother returned from visiting Jerusalem and reported the devastation and low morale among the remnant of Jews there, Nehemiah wept and prayed with great sorrow. As cupbearer to the king, he tried to hide his sorrow, because if anyone approached the king with a sad face, he was executed. God protected Nehemiah, for when King Artaxerxes did happen to notice his sorrow, Nehemiah shared his concern for Jerusalem. The King not only gave him a leave of absence, but also authorized him to go there and rebuild Jerusalem's walls. With vision and perseverance, Nehemiah was able to carry out his task without being stopped by ridicule, fear, and false accusations. He demonstrated his dependence upon God as he encouraged the people to complete the work of rebuilding the broken down walls of his beloved city.

LESSONS FROM MOSES, JOSHUA, AND NEHEMIAH
Who Selects Leaders?

When we see kings ascend the throne because of family lineage, dictators come to rule because of power struggles, and presidents take office because of election by the people, we tend to think that men select leaders. Man does have a part, for God does answer the cry of people for leaders. We are even told to pray for them so *we may live peaceful and quiet lives in all godliness and holiness* (1 Timothy 2:2b). But the truth is, God is the authority behind all leadership. Psalm 75:6-7 tells us *no one from the east or west or from the desert can exalt a man. But it is God who judges; He brings one down, he exalts another.* And Proverbs 21:1 tells us *the King's heart is in the hand of the Lord, he directs it like a watercourse wherever he pleases.*

When Jesus was on trial before Pilate, He didn't say anything. When an exasperated Pilate asked, *"Don't you realize I have power to free you or to crucify you?"* Jesus answered *"You would have no power over me if it were not given to you from above"* (John 19:10b-11a).

In Romans 9:17 (and Exodus 9:16), what did Paul tell us about God's purpose for Pharaoh?
He raised him up for this purpose, that God might display my purpose in you & that my name might be proclaimed in all the earth.

According to Genesis 45:8, what did Joseph tell his brothers after they found him a ruler in Egypt? *So that God sent me here, he made me father to Pharaoh, lord of his entire household & ruler of all Egypt.*

According to 2 Samuel 7:8 and Isaiah 55:4, who put David in his position as king over Israel? *God*

According to Daniel 2:21, who sets up kings and deposes them?
God

According to Romans 13:1-7, who establishes all authorities?
God

When the antichrist comes to rule, he will also be in his position by God's authority, even though he will represent all rebellion and deception, for in Isaiah 54:16b God says, *"It is I who have created the destroyer to work havoc."* So God allows even rulers submitted to Satan to be used for His purposes.

Preparation for Leadership

Some people prepare for leadership through formal training, such as attending college, Bible School, and seminars. Others are mentored by an already-proven leader. And, some are educated by learning from work and life-experience. God has His own methods of training men for leadership. Let us look at a few:

Moses   was removed from worldly training and put in desert solitude. (Exodus 2:15-3:10)

Joshua   was assistant to Moses while Moses was leading God's people through the wilderness. (Exodus 24:12; Numbers 27:12-23)

David	was given the task of caring for real sheep. (Psalm 78:70-72; 1 Samuel 16:19)
Nehemiah	served a pagan king as a cupbearer. (Nehemiah 1:11; 2:1)
Jesus	was given specific directions from His Father. (John 5:19; Hebrews 5:7-10)
The Disciples	were put into a three-year course of in-service training with the Master. (Mark 10:46; Luke 9:18-21; John 3:22)
Paul	was sent to Arabia, Syria and Cilicia for revelation. (Galatians 1:15-24)
Timothy	was mentored by Paul. (2 Timothy 1:8-14)

Because we don't always realize how God is working, we may not think He's preparing us for anything. Many times, it's only as a leader looks back with the perspective of time and the eyes of the Holy Spirit, that he can see how God prepared him in a very unique, but excellent way. *"For my thoughts are not your thoughts, neither are your ways my ways,"* says God in Isaiah 55:8.

What God Expects of Leaders

God is very zealous of those who lead, teach, pastor in His name. James 3:1 says of teachers: *You know that we who teach will be judged more strictly.* Satan also knows the importance of leadership positions. If he can cause leaders to fall, he can cause many to turn from God.

God didn't mince words concerning shepherds who are overseers of His flock. In Jeremiah 23:1-4, He warns that shepherds who do not care for the flock properly, or who allow it to scatter, will be punished and replaced by other shepherds. In Ezekiel 34:1-10, God gives shepherds warnings as He tells them He will hold them accountable for His flock and punish them if they don't take care of it properly. This standard is reiterated in Philippians 2:3-4: *Do nothing out of selfish ambition or vain conceit, but in humility consider others better than yourselves. Each of you should look not only to your own interests, but also to the interests of others.*

Traits of Good Leadership

A leader must be able to share a vision and mobilize others.

It takes good and effective communication skills and an understanding of people to inspire and challenge. It also requires the ability to keep followers from becoming discouraged. Joshua knew he must have commitment from the people, so he said to them, *"Choose for yourselves this day whom you will serve...But as for me and my household, we will serve the Lord."* (Joshua 24:15)

And, Nehemiah, after surveying the city, issued a challenge to the people (Nehemiah 2:17-18). He had to deal with discouragement because there were those who opposed the rebuilding of the wall. So he divided the workers into two groups and had them alternate — half of the men working while the other half stood guard (Nehemiah 4:12-23).

Nehemiah also showed he knew how to resolve conflict as he dealt with injustices between workers. (Nehemiah 5)

Are you able to share a vision with others in a way that will enable them to commit to it? Give an example. _____

_____

A leader must be able to delegate responsibilities.

A leader can implement a vision, but its permanency and effectiveness are greatly reduced, and the cost to the leader is high if he tries to do everything by himself. This was true for Moses, whose responsibility it was to lead two million or more people from Egypt to the land God promised them. Even though Moses had Aaron and Joshua to assistant him, he still carried most of the load. His father-in-law, Jethro, saw the need for organization, and helped him delegate responsibilities to others. (Exodus 18:13-26) Other scriptural examples of delegation leadership include:

Seventy Elders

   The Lord put His Spirit on seventy elders of Israel when dealing with unbelief in His people. They were to help Moses carry the burden when the people complained about the food. (Numbers 11:4-34)

Nehemiah

   He assigned responsibility of the rebuilding of Jerusalem's walls to different leaders. (Nehemiah 3)

Elijah

   When he thought he was the only one who had not bowed to Baal, God told him that there were 7,000 others,. (1 Kings 19:10, 18)

A leader must also recognize (acknowledge) other leaders whom God sends to do specific tasks. Jesus said, in Matthew 23:39, *"For I tell you, you will not see me again until you say, 'Blessed is he who comes in the name of the Lord.'"*

Can you delegate responsibility, or do you tend to do everything yourself? Give a specific example. _____

_____

A leader must know how to deal with rebellion.

People are rebellious and unsubmissive and leaders may be hindered from doing their jobs. Moses experienced this from the grumbles of the people (Exodus 16:2-15), from Korah, Dathan, and Abiram (in Numbers 16), and even from his own brother and sister (in Numbers 12:1-5)! As Moses looked to God, the Lord provided food for the people, caused an earthquake which swallowed the three Levites and their followers, and afflicted Miriam with leprosy!

God takes care of the leaders whom He has anointed and who look to Him. (Psalm 105:15)

How do you handle unsubmissiveness by those under you...even as leader in your home?

_____

_____

A leader must be a person of integrity.

A leader is susceptible to special dangers because of his position. These dangers fall into three main categories: pride, sexual temptation, and greed. Pride can cause a leader to stumble when the leader realizes how God is using him, especially if people are looking to him and not to God. Sexual temptations may follow closely on the heels of pride. Because the leader feels he needs special attention, he may look to women for intimacy. If he's a workaholic with a family, his wife and family may feel rejected because he is never there for them, which only drives him away even further from the closeness they could and should provide. Sometimes men in leadership positions believe they aren't being compensated fairly for their long hours. When they feel entitled to more money, this becomes a trap for getting it, even in illegal or unethical ways. A leader who compromises his integrity is actually listening to lies of Satan. Proverbs 29:12 tells what will happen: *If a ruler listens to lies, all his officials become wicked.*

Have you ever experienced the "fall" of someone in leadership? How was integrity involved?

_____

_____

A leader must persevere.

According to Proverbs 24:10, *if you falter in times of trouble, how small is your strength.* A leader must be ready for all kinds of difficulties, for leaders are always facing challenges, whether from his subordinates or others. Discouragement is probably one of the greatest enemies of a leader. Coupled with fear, it can lay low the most enthusiastic and capable leader.

Nehemiah faced real discouragement. When Sanballat and his friends attempted to keep Nehemiah and his people from rebuilding the walls of Jerusalem, Nehemiah faced their accusations by praying to God (Nehemiah 4:4-5), making a clear statement to the enemy of God's favor toward them (Nehemiah 2:20), and encouraging those working on the project (Nehemiah 4:13-14). To counter rebellion, a leader cannot succumb to fear. He must put his trust in the Lord, no matter how discouraged he becomes or how long his task takes.

What do you do when you become discouraged, whether in leadership at home, in your workplace or elsewhere?

_____

_____

A leader must look to God.

Since God is the One who puts men into leadership positions, good leaders look to God for direction. Even a Pharisee named Gamaliel recognized God's part in protecting and guiding leaders. In Acts 5:38-39 he said, *"Leave these men alone! Let them go! For if their purpose or activity is of human origin, it will fail. But if it is from God, you will not be able to stop these men; you will only find yourselves fighting against God."* A paraphrase of Psalm 127:1 would be: "Unless God is part of the plans of leaders, all they do is in vain." Moses was assured of God's help through communication with Him. (Exodus 33:12-23)

Do you have more confidence in a leader if you know that leader prays? Why?

_____

_____

A leader must accept final responsibility.

No matter how involved other people become, the leader must know that ultimately he is the one who is accountable. For this reason, a leader must be willing to make the hard decisions. Although Aaron and Joshua helped Moses, it was up to Moses to make the final decisions. He was the one whom God held responsible. God does deal with the people under a leader, but He also exalts or deposes those in leadership. (Psalm 75:6-7)

What takes place when a leader won't take responsibility for whatever happens?

_____

_____

Learning from the Master

Jesus was the leader of leaders. In fact, He was called "Master." Several Greek words refer to this aspect of Jesus' position. *Didaskalos,* meaning "teacher," is used to address Christ in Matthew 8:19. *Dospotes* meaning "one who has absolute ownership and uncontrolled power," is used of Christ in 2 Timothy 2:21. And *epistate*s, denoting "chief, commander, overseer," is used of Christ in Luke 5:5.

What leadership traits can we learn from Christ?

He was not self-appointed. (John 6:38)

He spoke with authority. (Mark 1:27)

He portrayed servant-leadership. (John 13:12-17)

He prayed for His followers. (John 17)

He was confident of His calling. (John 3:12-23; Luke 2:49)

He was resolute in carrying out His mission. (Luke 9:51)

He shared his vision and mission with others. (Matthew 10:1)

SUMMARY

God uses human leaders to accomplish His divine purposes. Some of these will be good and some bad, but each is ultimately raised up by God and deposed by Him. To be good, leaders one must have certain skills and character traits to accomplish their tasks. These skills and traits include having a vision, being able to communicate that vision to others, working well with people, and looking to God for direction and guidance. People are blessed when good leaders are in authority.

Consider This

What leaders to do you respect...in our land, in your city, in your church?

_____

_____

What is the most important quality you think is necessary for a leader?

_____

_____

Are you a leader or follower? How do you know?

_____

_____

Can a leader develop good leadership traits, or is he born with them?

_____

_____

EXAMPLE

God has His own way of raising up leaders, and it isn't always the way we would do it. I know that from experience!

After receiving a music degree in college and graduating from seminary, I served several churches in different states, in various capacities — music ministry, Christian education, associate pastor, and pastor. After twenty-five years, I left one position to take another…which fell through before I could begin. Since we had always lived in houses provided by the churches we served, we suddenly found ourselves homeless, as well as without work — a new and frightening experience for me, as breadwinner with a wife and three growing daughters.

We decided to move near my wife's aging parents to help with their care, and I found a secular job. I became acquainted with some of the pastors in the community and began meeting with them for weekly prayer.

After an especially wet winter, which kept the farm laborers from work, the local Salvation Army found itself on overload. The pastors began praying about an interchurch, community-wide outreach, not only to these workers, but to the many transients who came to the churches for help, as well as for local citizens who found themselves in need of emergency aid. Within months, a governing board accountable to the participating churches was formed. As contributions of food and money started coming in, we opened a "Center" manned by volunteers. Little had I dreamed I would be giving twelve years of my life to such a ministry! My part-time volunteer leadership eventually grew to the position of full-time paid Director.

The world would have hired someone with a degree in social work or counseling to help the 10,000+ clients we served each year; or, a person with a degree in business administration to oversee the 100 volunteers and procure food to help feed the growing multitude. Instead, God chose a used-to-be pastor working in a hardware store who, himself, had experienced the trauma of sudden life changes. He chose a violinist who, from experience in playing in ensembles and orchestras, knew the value of working together with all kinds of instruments in harmony. He chose one who had never experienced chemical dependency or domestic violence, but only knew the Word of God.

As the name chosen for this ministry suggests, Loaves and Fishes experienced daily miracles of provision…and, for me, the miracle of God's sustaining wisdom, guidance, and endurance. As I came into "retirement," the Lord raised up a new director and it became my privilege to gather together musicians from the various local churches to perform an annual concert to benefit the ongoing ministry of Loaves and Fishes. To Him be the glory!

Lesson 7
AARON AND DEMETRIUS

Whom…or What…Do I Truly Worship?

You shall have no other gods before me.

Exodus 20:3

Therefore, my dear friends, flee from idolatry.

1 Corinthians 10:14

SETTING THE STAGE

Is idolatry really a problem facing today's Christian man? Is it possible that we worship idols without even realizing it? J. R. Miller writes "anything which we keep in our hearts in the place which God ought to have is an idol, whether it be an image of wood or stone or gold, or whether it be money, or desire for fame, or love of pleasure, or some secret sin which we will not give up. If God does not really occupy the highest place in our hearts, controlling all, something else does. And that something else is an idol." So, if we truly search our hearts, the answer to the above questions will be: "Yes! Idolatry is a problem facing today's Christian man." It's possible that we worship idols without even realizing it.

To help us consider ways we may be caught in the trap of idolatry and to see how idols may be affecting our walk with the Lord, we'll look at two men in scripture: Aaron, of Old Testament times, was party to the building of a golden calf for people to worship while Moses was up on the mountain receiving the Ten Commandments from God. And Demetrius, silversmith of New Testament times, made it possible for people to worship their gods through images that he crafted.

We'll also look at some modern-day idols and see why the Holy Spirit, through John (1 John 5:21), warns us to keep ourselves from idols.

INTRODUCING AARON

(Based on Exodus 4-8, 16, 19, 28-29, 32)

Aaron was an older brother of Moses, the lawgiver and deliverer of God's people. Aaron, Moses, and Miriam, their sister, were the ones God chose to bring His people from Egypt to the Promised Land. With Aaron acting as Moses' spokesman (because of Moses' speech problem), the three formed a leadership team. God worked His miracles through them as they represented God before the Pharoah and the Israelites. Aaron and his sons were named priests and, thus, were equipped to represent the people to God through sacrifices and worship.

While Moses was a long time on Mt. Sinai receiving the Ten Commandments and details of tabernacle worship, Aaron gave in to the pressure of the people to provide a god who would lead them. He helped them build a golden calf from the jewelry they had brought with them from Egypt. Aaron built an altar in front of this calf (which the people proclaimed as a god) and announced a festival to the Lord. In response, the people ate and drank and indulged in revelry before their idol. God was angry, but Moses interceded and God withheld His wrath. When Moses came down the mountain and saw the golden calf and dancing people, he threw down the tablets containing the commandments and took the calf, burned it in the fire, ground it to powder, and made the Israelites drink the water in which he had scattered the powder. Aaron tried to make excuses both for himself and for the people, but the Lord punished them for their sin by striking them with a plague. According to Numbers 20:22-29, Aaron died on Mount Hor. God had forbidden him to enter the Promised Land because of both his and Moses' rebellion at the Lord's command at the waters of Meribah. (Numbers 20:24)

INTRODUCING DEMETRIUS

(Based on Acts 19:1-41)

Demetrius was involved in the very prominent worship of idols in the prosperous city of Ephesus. Extraordinary miracles took place through Paul in Ephesus. People were delivered of demons and received the Holy Spirit. Many came to belief in Jesus, confessed their evil deeds, and publicly burned their scrolls and other objects of sorcery.

While this brought much rejoicing to the delivered people, it also threatened the idol industry. Demetrius, a silversmith, sounded the alarm to his fellow business and craftsmen by saying, *"Men, you know we receive a good income from this business. And you see and hear how this fellow Paul has convinced and led astray large numbers of people here in Ephesus and in practically the whole province of Asia. He says that man-made gods are no gods at all. There is danger not only that our trade will lose its good name, but also that the temple of the great goddess Artemis* (Diana) *will be discredited, and the goddess herself, who is worshipped throughout the province of Asia and the world, will be robbed of her divine majesty"* (Acts 19:25b-27). Not only was the false worship of the whole city threatened, but Demetrius' livelihood was also in jeopardy. He had much to lose if people turned from worshipping idols to worshipping the true God that Paul preached.

LESSONS FROM AARON AND DEMETRIUS

Biblical Examples of Idolatry

Idolatry didn't start with Aaron and the golden calf. Nor will it end with us. A quick survey of the Bible, beginning in Genesis, will give us a few examples of idolatry and how it will end with the worship of the Antichrist and the False Prophet just before Jesus comes again.

Genesis 31:19-35

As Jacob was fleeing from Padanaram to return to his homeland, his wife, Rachel, hid some idols that she had stolen from her father, Laban. This is the first mention of idols in scripture, though it is evident that idolatry was prevalent in Abraham's past and other beginnings of civilization when substitution for one true God was desired.

Exodus 20:1-6; 32:1-35

God gave Moses the ten commandments in which He demands that He is the only God to be worshipped. When Aaron helped the people built a golden calf to worship, God dealt with them severely.

Numbers 33:4

Along with smiting the firstborn, God executed judgment upon the gods of the Egyptians.

Joshua 24:15, 20-24

As the Israelites were entering the promised land, they chose to put away their strange gods and serve only the Lord God of Israel.

Judges

We find various incidents of the worship of Baal, a title used for a number of deities which were worshipped to ensure good crops and general welfare during the time of the Judges of Israel. Judges 6:25-32 records an incident when God told Gideon to throw down the altar to Baal and build one to God.

1 & 2 Kings

As kings began to rule Israel, idol worship continued to be a problem, even with the various kings themselves. During the golden reign of Solomon, idol worship actually increased because it was introduced by many of his foreign wives. By the time of Ahab and Jezebel, worship of God was nearly supplanted by worship of Baal. This climaxed during the contest between the Baal worshippers and those who worshipped God when a demonstration was held on Mt. Carmel to prove which God was the greatest. Of course, God won in a dramatic way! According to 2 Kings 17:7-23, idol worship by the people of the northern kingdom of Israel was one of the reasons God allowed them to be taken into captivity by Assyria. Likewise, 2 Kings 23 tells us that even though King Josiah tried to put down the idolatrous priests and places of worship, God was angry (v. 26-27) and allowed the southern kingdom of Judah to be banished into exile by Babylon. (2 Kings 25:21)

The Prophets

All during the time of the prophets…before, during, and after the exile… various prophets called the people to worship the one true God. An example is found in Jeremiah 16:10-21 where God told Jeremiah that when the people asked him why God had brought punishment upon them, Jeremiah was to say, *"It is because your fathers forsook me…and followed other gods and served and worshipped them."* During Israel's captivity, the people finally got the message and eradicated all obvious forms of idolatry.

New Testament Times

Idol worship continued to be prevalent in the Greek and Roman societies during the time of Christ, as attested to by the magnificent temples built during that time. Jesus did not address the problem directly, since His major thrust was to the *lost sheep of Israel* (Matthew 15:24). When He was being tempted to worship the devil (Matthew 4:10), He did quote and refer to Deuteronomy 6:13-14, concerning worshipping the only God. It's significant that Peter's declaration that Jesus was *the Christ, the Son of the Living God* took place in the region of Caesarea Philippi, where there were a number of shrines dedicated to various gods and idols (Matthew 16:13-16). As the church spread into the Roman and Greek world, there were clashes between true Christianity and the societies that were given to idol worship. Christians were persecuted because they weren't willing to accept the pantheon of idols. The uproar in Ephesus involving Demetrius was an example of this. Idol worship, and the meat that was used in this worship and later sold in markets, was a problem confronting the early church. Paul discussed this in Romans 14:13-21.

Revelation

Here we find that, according to Revelation 9:20, in the last days idolatry will continue to be a major issue causing man to miss the mercy and grace of God. The final and most abhorrent of all idol worship will be the worship of the image of the Beast, the antichrist, the one who will claim to be God. (Revelation 13:11-17)

What God Says about Idolatry

Idolatry…putting something, someone, or an activity before God…is a problem that has plagued man throughout history. It's not surprising that the very first of the ten commandments given by God to Moses is: *You shall have no other gods before me* (Exodus 20:3). Or, that the second commandment (Exodus 20:4-5) continues to spell this out: *You shall not make for yourself an idol in the form of anything in heaven above or on the earth beneath or in the waters below. You shall not bow down to them or worship them, for I, the Lord your God, am a jealous God.*....Jesus confirms this in Mark 12:29b-30, when He gives the greatest of all commandments: *"Here, O Israel, the Lord our God, the Lord is one. Love the Lord your God with all your heart and with all your soul and with all your mind and with all your strength."*

In Leviticus 19, as God told Moses to speak to the entire assembly of Israel, He gave them various commands. He told them He wanted them to *be holy because I, the Lord your God, am holy* (v.2). What command is given in verse 4?

_____

_____

According to Deuteronomy 11:16-17, what will God's punishment be for those who worship other gods?

_____

_____

What does Isaiah 44:9-11 tell us about those who make idols?

_____

_____

In Ezekiel 36:24-26, what did God say He would do for His people when He brought them back into their own land?

_____

_____

According to Romans 1: 25, what helps begin the downward spiral of reprobate man?

_____

_____

In 1 Corinthians 10:6-10, how did Paul describe the idolaters who built the golden calf?

_____

_____

What warning did he give us? (In those verses and continuing to verse 14?)

_____

_____

According to 1 Corinthians 10:20, to whom are the sacrifices of pagans offered?

_____

_____

What does Scripture say about worshipping idols and partaking of the Lord's Supper? (1 Corinthians 10:21-22)

_____

_____

How did Paul counsel concerning eating meat which had been sacrificed to idols? (See 1 Corinthians 10:23-33)

_____

_____

According to Galatians 5:19, idolatry is one of the

_____

_____

What does Colossians 3:5 say is another form of idolatry?

_____

_____

Idolatry Today

Western culture — especially in America — has a pantheon of gods to worship. The cult that has risen around Elvis Presley is a case in point. The almost fanatical veneration for Princess Diana is another example of how the world is prone to idolatry. (Is it coincidental that the modern Diana has the same name as the Greek goddess who ruled over Ephesus? See Acts 19:24 KJV.) A number of other potential idols can serve as substitutes for the love and worship we should give to God. The following are some examples:

Computers	Internet	Knowledge
Jobs	Political candidates	Music
Food	Sports	Cars
People	Family	Pets
Hobbies	Wife	Children
Cult leaders	New Age ideas	Occult enticements
Possessions	Money	Self
Television	Houses	Church/Ministry

Circle any of these which tempt you to give more thought or time to them than to God.

Let's look in more detail at how some of these have an effect on men.

Sports

What man, young or old, doesn't enjoy some aspect of the sports scene…either as a participant or spectator? Much in various sports is good. Sports — athletics — can build character, provide a worthy outlet for physical energy, and give diversion from work. However, sports can also take the time, energy, and attention that should be given to God, especially when they take first place in our lives. As an article entitled "Golden Calf in the Superdome" says, "it (sports) is a religion for our time. Its theology is one of enduring hope. It honors the strong with prosperity and celebrity. And there are miracles in sufficient number to keep the congregants contented and ever expectant for more."

Have sports become an idol to you? If so, what can you do to change that?

_____

_____

Cars

Many men take pleasure in maintaining their cars and keeping them looking good. Others, as a hobby, spend hours restoring cars, sometimes to participate in shows and parades so that people can see what they have done. When does the latter become idolatry?

_____

_____

Possessions

The gold and silver often connected with idolatry in Bible times, has its counterpart today in our possessions — stocks, houses, tools, electronic equipment, etc. We often have so much pride in these, we spend too much time expanding their usefulness in our lives. Some people suggest that our shopping malls are modern counterparts to ancient temples!

What does Deuteronomy 8:10-20 say about desiring and getting more than we need?

_____

_____

What does Hebrews 13:5 say about money and contentment?

_____

_____

What does Matthew 6:19-34 have to say concerning our attitude toward our possessions?

_____

_____

Wives, Children, and Parents

We can almost unconsciously put family members on pedestals. We may not think of this as idolatry, but it is if we look to them to satisfy us. We can put expectations on them to fulfill our emotional and physical needs, instead of looking to God as our source. No one can meet our need for acceptance and affirming love as can Jesus. So, our love and devotion to Him should not be eclipsed by our love for any person.

What do Matthew 10:37 and Luke 14:26 say about this?

_____

_____

How to Deal With Idolatry

Scripture gives specific directions in dealing with idolatry:
   We are not to listen to those who would entice us to worship other gods. (Deuteronomy 13:6-11)
   We are to flee idolatry. (1 Corinthians 10:14)
   We are not to associate with idolaters. (1 Corinthians 5:11)
   We are to keep ourselves from idols. (1 John 5:21)
   We should turn from idolatry to God. (1 Thessalonians 1:9; Acts 14:15)
   The best way to deal with idols is to not have any room for them. Be filled with the Holy Spirit and love God with all your heart, soul, and strength, so God can receive all your attention and meet all your needs. Pray that God lead you not into temptation…that you have the strength to flee idolatry when you are tempted due to your desires of the flesh.

SUMMARY

Throughout Scripture, we have seen how man has been lured to worship beings other than the one true God. Both Aaron and Demetrius illustrate how we can become party to those who serve idols. In Biblical times, idols and idolatry were more identifiable. We read of graven images, ashteroth groves, and temples to gods and goddesses. Today, idolatry is more subtle. Our gods include sports, cars, material possessions, and people, among other things. Our best defense against becoming involved in idolatry of any kind is to be so filled with the Holy Spirit, so in love with Jesus, and so committed to God that we won't be tempted to worship anyone else but Him

Consider This

1. Can you identify any idols in your life? If so, how can you put them secondary to God's place in your heart?

   _____

   _____

2. Are there any issues, today, that can compare to eating meat sacrificed to idols? (as described in Romans 14:13-23; 1 Corinthians 10:14-22)

   _____

   _____

3. How do cults, New-Age teachings, etc. get people involved in idolatry?

   _____

   _____

4. Is it possible that even our ministries for God and the church can become a substitute for the worship of God Himself? Explain.

   _____

   _____

EXAMPLE

Youth With a Mission (often called YWAM), is a ministry God has used to train and send thousands of young people into all parts of the world with the gospel of Jesus Christ. This is done in a variety of ways…from establishing medical clinics on the city dump in Manila, Philippines, to helping farmers in Central America, to witnessing to people living in houseboats in Hong Kong harbor. However, it was at the beginning of one of their more unique forms of ministry that God dealt with Loren Cunningham, founder of YWAM, concerning idolatry.

Cunningham had had a vision of what would become "mercy" ships…ships fitted with medical centers, which would be able to go to the very places where the needy of the nations lived. These ships could also carry construction supplies and be used as training centers for those desiring to carry the gospel into all the world. As his dream began to take shape through various supernatural provisions, Loren and the staff of YWAM began to be all-consumed with finances, recruitment, ministries that would be on board, and myriads of other details needed to get such a ship afloat.

Then, on his way to Osaka, Japan for a conference, Loren had a vision which changed the course of his ministry. While laying on a pallet in Seoul Korea, he was trying to focus upon the Lord and get direction for what he would say at this special meeting of YWAM leaders. Quite vividly, he saw himself standing before the group exuberantly announcing that all the money for the ship was now in. The crowd cheered wildly, waving their arms and shouting. Then he saw a figure standing in the shadows to his left, unnoticed by anyone, including himself. He looked at the face of the man and saw he was grieving. Cunningham realized that this "man" was none other than Jesus. In cheering the ship, they had ignored the very One for whom they were readying it for ministry. He buried his face in his pallet and cried out to God for mercy. After a long time of weeping, he felt the peace of God's forgiveness, and determined to give a more somber message at the conference. He wanted to make sure everyone's attention was off the hunk of metal and given to God, who, rightfully, should receive all the glory for what **He** had done!

When Cunningham did give his speech, the group fell to its knees, using the six days to confess their sins and seek purification from the pride in what **they** had accomplished. They put the ship into God's hands, determined not to look to it as an idol, but to give the glory to the true and living God.

Lesson 8
SAMSON

What Does God Say About My Sexual Life?

The body is not meant for sexual immorality, but for the Lord, and the Lord for the body.

1 Corinthians 6:13b

SETTING THE STAGE

God has much to say about your sexual life. After all, He created sex. Furthermore, after He had created male and female, He *saw all that he had made, and it was very good* (Genesis 1:31). In the animal realm, the mating of the male and female was to be a means of reproducing each after its own kind. In humans, sexual intercourse would accomplish the same purpose, but this relationship was to be much more. It was to be an expression of intimacy that would fulfill Adam's need for a companion. It was to be the ultimate bonding of two people, different in their gender; the way to become one flesh. It was to bring fulfillment, joy, and satisfaction, and yes, aesthetic pleasure.

Because of the beautiful experience sex was designed to be, we'll consider the positive side as we look at the parameters and protection outlined in Scripture. However, due to all the perversions we face today, we'll also consider what God says about homosexuality, pornography, adultery, pre-marital sex, incest, etc. We'll consider the fact that as the Church, the ultimate Bride of Jesus Christ, God wants us to be a holy people and thus, desires sexual purity for us.

We'll look at Samson, one whom some have claimed was a he-man with a she-weakness. Though he was sent by God to be a man of strength and faith, Samson's weakness for women nearly destroyed his ministry and took his life. No man alive is immune from sexual temptations. As Christian men with all the desires He gave to us, we must know what God says about sex — especially, how He can help us live according to His plan for man.

INTRODUCING SAMSON

(Based on Judges 13:1-16:31)

Samson's birth and mission were foretold by God even before he was conceived. An angel delivered the prophecy first to Manoah's wife, of the clan of Danites. Though she had been barren for some time, an angel told her that she would have a son and that he was to be a Nazarite — which required him to abstain totally from fermented drink, and not cut his hair. The Lord would use Samson to deliver the Israelites from the hands of the Philistines.

At Manoah's request, the angel was later sent to instruct them on how to raise this son.

Samson grew into manhood blessed of the Lord, a man of physical prowess and spiritual strength. If he had been born today, he would have made the cover of a sport's magazine…and even some Christian periodicals! Scripture tells us *the spirit of the Lord came upon him in power* on a number of occasions (Judges 14:6, 19; 15:14).

The first indication we see of Samson's womanizing (which apparently became addictive) was when he saw a young Philistine girl in Timnah and demanded of his father and mother:

"Now get her for me as my wife" (Judges 14:2b). His parents weren't happy that he wanted to marry outside their faith, but Judges 14:4 tells us that God was going to use this relationship to confront the Philistines who were, at that time, ruling over Israel. After several unusual episodes that took place during the wedding celebration, Samson went to his parents' home without his wife. Samson's wife was given to a friend who had attended him at the wedding; eventually she was burned to death by the Philistines. An angry Samson took his revenge on them and they were defeated.

Scripture also tells us of a one-night stand Samson had with a prostitute in Gaza. This put him into the hands of the Philistines, but he used his great strength to escape.

Then, Samson fell in love with Delilah, another Philistine woman. Loyal to the Philistines, who had offered to pay her if she could discover the secret of Samson's strength, she tried to trick Samson into telling her where he got his strength. Worn down by three days of her constant nagging, he finally disclosed the source of strength as being in his long hair. So she had it cut, and Samson grew so weak that the Philistines were able to capture him. Then they blinded him by putting his eyes out, and put him in prison — where his hair grew back. When the rulers of the Philistines assembled to offer a great sacrifice to their god Dagon, to celebrate the capture of Samson, they had a servant bring Samson out of prison to perform for them. While Samson and the servant were standing among the pillars, Samson asked the servant to position him where his hands could feel the pillars that supported the temple because he wanted to lean against them. Then, with all the rulers filling the temple, and thousands of other Philistines standing on the temple roof, Samson began to pray. He asked God to strengthen him one more time so that he could take revenge on the Philistines for gouging out his eyes. Bracing himself against the pillars, he also asked God to let him die with the Philistines. *Then he pushed with all his might, and down came the temple on the rulers and all the people in it. Thus he killed many more when he died than while he lived* (Judges 16:30b). Samson, because of his faith in God and despite his sexual weakness, won out over his enemy…an event which gave him a place (see verses 32-34) in the Hebrews 11 "Hall of Faith."

LESSONS FROM SAMSON
God's Standard of Sexual Purity

From the time God called out a people of His own, He required a holy people. In Leviticus 11:44 God says: *"I am the Lord your God; consecrate yourselves and be holy, because I am holy."* Then in the New Testament, in 1 Peter 1:16, He gave the same command to the Church: *But just as he who called you is holy, so be holy in all you do.* When Jesus returns, He will be coming for a glorious Church. Ephesians 5:25-27 tells how *Christ loved the church and gave himself up for her to make her holy, cleansing her by the washing with water through the word, and to present her to himself as a radiant church, without stain or wrinkle or any other blemish, but holy and blameless.* There is no doubt God wants a holy people for the Bride of His Son, Jesus Christ.

We also know that, by His grace and His blood, He has provided the only way for us to become righteous: *If we confess our sins, he is faithful and just and will forgive us our sins and purify us from all unrighteousnes.* (1 John 1:9). On the other hand, Isaiah 64:6 reminds us: *All of us have become like one who is unclean, and all our righteous acts are like filthy rags....* Only through Jesus Christ can we be made clean and have the purity to make us holy.

The New Testament term that most often deals with sexual immorality is "fornication," which is translated in the NIV as "sexual immorality." It comes from the Greek word *porneia* which means "unlawful lust." This is an umbrella term that covers any sexual activity outside of God's law — pre-marital sex, adultery, incest, homosexuality, etc. Though the Old Testament also has much to say about sexual immorality, let's look at some of the scriptures in the New Testament, which were given to the Church.

Hebrews 12:16a:

See that no one is sexually immoral...

1 Thessalonians 4:3-7:

It is God's will that you should be sanctified; that you should avoid sexual immorality, that each of you should learn to control his own body in a way that is holy and honorable.... For God did not call us to be impure, but to live a holy life.

Ephesians 5:3:

But among you there must not be even a hint of sexual immorality, or of any kind of impurity, or of greed, because these are improper for God's holy people.

Galatians 5:19-21:

The acts of the sinful nature are obvious: sexual immorality, impurity and debauchery (lack of restraint)...those who live like this will not inherit the kingdom of God.

So, what are the consequences of sexual immorality? Read the following scriptures and then write the consequence:

Ephesians 5:5 *No inheritance in the kingdom*

Hebrews 13:4 *God will judge*

Hebrews 12:14 *will not see God*

Jude 7 *eternal fire*

Revelation 21:8 *second death - fiery lake*

We, who are being formed into the image of God's Son (Romans 8:29) must make a choice: Will we obey God, submit to His Word, and follow Jesus Christ as Lord, or will we choose the way of this depraved world and indulge in various kinds of sexual immorality?

The Depravity of Man

The first chapter of Romans describes the downward spiral of man. It begins, in verse 21, with man not giving God thanks or glory, even though God has made His eternal power and divine nature clear. It ends with man not only knowing he deserves death, but also encouraging others to do evil.

We have only to look around us to see the utter depravity of man…the television programs, Internet, videos, movies, billboards, newsstands, streets of our cities, and adult book stores. What is even sadder, though not always so obvious, is the amount of sexual immorality going on in the lives of Christians.

Temptation and Lust

It's interesting to note that man's "original" sin was responding to temptation with lust. (See Genesis 3:1-7.) As Jesus was beginning His ministry, He, too, was tempted. But, He responded differently (Matthew 4:1-11). Though neither of these instances were sexual lust, they do indicate that temptation is always with us and that we have a choice in how we will respond. In the case of Adam and Eve, sin led to shame and guilt and God had to provide a means of covering with a blood sacrifice (Genesis 3:10-11, 21). In the case of Jesus, who did not sin, God allowed Him to become the ultimate blood sacrifice for man's sin. Now, through belief in Jesus and His atoning work on the cross, we can have victory over both temptation and lust. Let's consider what Scripture says about temptation and lust, and the relationship between the two.

Temptation — a testing designed to strengthen, or corrupt

James 1:13 says that God does not tempt anyone. So, who does? Satan does (Matthew 4:1). However, James 1:14 puts the burden on man: *Each one is tempted when, **by his own evil desire**, he is dragged away and enticed.*

From the following scriptures, what would you conclude was the reason for succumbing to temptation?

Hear, O earth: I am bringing disaster on this people, the fruit of their schemes, because they have not listened to my words and have rejected my law. (Jeremiah 6:19. See also 2 Kings 17:14-18; Hosea 4:6; 2 Peter 2:1-2, 13-19.)

_____

God knows that when you eat of it your eyes will be opened, and you will be like God, knowing good and evil. (Genesis 3:5. See also Isaiah 14:14; 2 Thessalonians 2:3-4)

_____

Therefore God gave them over in the sinful desires of their hearts to sexual impurity for the degrading of their bodies with one another. They exchanged the truth of God for a lie, and worshipped and served created things rather than the Creator…who is forever praised. (Romans 1:24-25)

_____

I denied myself nothing my eyes desired; I refused my heart no pleasure. My heart took delight in all my work, and this was the reward for all my labor. (Ecclesiastes 2:10. See also Psalm 10:3-4; Ephesians 2:3.)

_____

Lust — an intense longing

Though we can lust in other ways, man succumbs most easily to sexual lust, sexual desire to an intense or unrestrained degree.

Look up the following scriptures and write the different sources of lust:

1 John 3:8a _Devil_

2 Peter 1:4 _world_

James 1:14-15 _our own evil desire_

Matthew 15:19 _heart_

Ephesians 2:2f _ways of the world_

Temptation and lust, for men, usually come through sight. It's what we *see* that turns us on. And, we think that if we can have what we have *seen*, we'll be satisfied. This was Solomon's downfall. In Ecclesiastes 2:10 he wrote that he had denied himself nothing that his *eyes* desired. David got into big trouble when he *saw*, from his own rooftop, a woman bathing next-door (2 Samuel 11:2). And Samson's failure began with his *seeing* a young Philistine woman (Judges 14:1). Jesus, however, did not succumb to temptation when the devil *showed* him all the kingdoms He could have if only He would bow down and worship him (Matthew 4:8). Satan knows the temptation that comes from what a man sees…and he knows the consequences that come from falling into such temptation.

What should a man do:

When watching television and/or videos? _____

When using the Internet? _____

When buying reading material at a newsstand? _____

A Matter of the Heart

Though it's our eyes that get us into trouble, the source of the sin comes from our heart, *for from within, out of men's hearts, come evil thoughts, sexual immorality, theft, murder, adultery, greed, malice, deceit, lewdness, envy, slander, arrogance and folly. All these evils come from inside and made a man 'unclean'* (Mark 7:21-23).

They are darkened in their understanding and separated from the life of God because of the ignorance that is in them due to the hardening of their hearts. Having lost all sensitivity, they have given themselves over to sensuality so as to indulge in every kind of impurity, with a continual lust for more. (Ephesians 4:18-19)

So, how do we change our hearts? Read the following scriptures and write what each one suggests.

Proverbs 4:23 _guard your heart_

Ezekiel 11:19 _a new spirit_

Psalm 51:10 _____

1 Peter 3:15 _____

Sexual Sins

God has made sex beautiful and for His purpose, saying to honor marriage and keep the marriage bed pure (Hebrews 13:4). He has also condemned sex outside of the husband-wife relationship that He designed. So, what are some of these sins/perversions and what does scripture say about them?

Pre-Marital Sex

If a man happens to meet a virgin who is not pledged to be married and rapes her and they are discovered, he shall pay the girl's father fifty shekels of silver. He must marry the girl, for he has violated her. He can never divorce her as long as he lives. (Deuteronomy 22:28)

Now to the unmarried and the widows I say: It is good for them to stay unmarried as I am. But if they cannot control themselves, they should marry, for it is better to marry than to burn with passion. (1 Corinthians 7:8-9)

Adultery

You shall not commit adultery. (Exodus 20:14; Deuteronomy 5:18)

If a man commits adultery with another man's wife...both the adulterer and the adulteress must be put to death. (Leviticus 20:10)

Do not be deceived: Neither the sexually immoral nor idolaters nor adulterers nor male prostitutes nor homosexual ...will inherit the kingdom of God. (1 Corinthians 6:9b-10)

Divorce and Remarriage

So guard yourself in your spirit, and do not break faith with the wife of your youth. "I hate divorce" says the Lord God of Israel... (Malachi 2:15b-16a)

Jesus answered: *"Anyone who divorces his wife and marries another woman commits adultery against her. And if she divorces her husband and marries another man, she commits adultery."* (Mark 10:11-12)

Homosexuality

Do not lie with a man as one lies with a woman; that is detestable. (Leviticus 18:22)

In the same way the men also abandoned natural relations with women and were inflamed with lust for one another. Men committed indecent acts with other men, and received in themselves the due penalty for their perversion. (Romans 1:27)

Do not be deceived: Neither the sexually immoral nor idolaters nor adulterers nor male prostitutes nor homosexual offenders...will inherit the kingdom of God. (1 Corinthians 6:9b-10)

Incest

No one is to approach any close relative to have sexual relations. I am the Lord. (Leviticus 18:6. For more detail, see Leviticus 18:8-18.)

Pornography

But I tell you that anyone who looks* at a woman lustfully has already committed adultery with her in her heart. If your right eye causes you to sin, gouge it out and throw it away. It is *better for you to lose one part of your body than for your whole body to be thrown into hell.* (Matthew 5:27-29. See also Ephesians 4:19; 2 Corinthians 12:21.)

*Pornography uses the eye gate to get a strangle-hold on man's sinful desires.

The Addictive Cycle

If you don't deal with temptation daily, and align yourself with God's Word, you can easily fall into the trap of an addictive cycle:

Preoccupation — thinking about doing something that will take away pain and boredom

Ritualization — beginning to think of what it would take to satisfy the urge

Acting Out — going through with what has been imagined

Shame and Guilt — resulting in shame and guilt.

Preoccupation — as one becomes preoccupied with the shame and guilt, the cycle begins again

God is great. His Word will not return to Him empty, but will accomplish what He desires and will achieve the purpose for which He sent it (Isaiah 55:11). If, however, you are deep in an addictive cycle, you may need more help. There are many Christian ministries available to those with various kinds of addictions. Seek them out through your pastor, family or friends.

Standing Against Sexual Impurity

Since, for men, sexual impurity is a constant battle…no matter how old one is…there are some scriptural standards by which we must constantly align ourselves. As you read the following, put a check by those you feel you are doing regularly now. Consider the ones you leave blank, and determine, if you can, how and when you will do these in order to maintain sexual purity and become the holy man God wants.

_____ Recognize your sexual sin for what it is—SIN. (Romans 7:7-25; 1 John 1:8)

_____ Sincerely repent of your sin. (Ezekiel 14:6; Acts 17:30)

_____ Confess your sin to God for cleansing. (1 John 1:9)

_____ Confess your faults to another person who can pray for you to be healed. (James 5:16)

_____ Seek help and encouragement from someone to whom you can be accountable. (Hebrews 10:24-25)

_____ Think on these things: Whatever is true, lovely, admirable, and whatever you have learned of God's Word. (Philippians 4:8-9; Psalm 119:11)

_____ Realize that thoughts are preludes to acts. (James 1:14-15)

_____ Make a covenant not to look with lust at any woman or replica thereof. (Job 31:1; Colossians 3:5-6)

_____ Don't make provision for the flesh (Don't pick up porn material, watch certain TV shows, surf the Internet, etc.) (Romans 13:14; Galatians 5:24)

_____ Study God's Word, so that it becomes part of you. (2 Timothy 2:15; Hebrews 4:12-13)

_____ Ask God, and rely on Him, for help. (Romans 8:6, 27; Hebrews 4:16; 1 Corinthians 10:13)

_____ Keep your eyes upon Jesus and allow Him to develop holiness in you. (John 15:1-7; Romans 13:14; Hebrews 3:1; 12:2-4)

_____ Walk by the Spirit. (Galatians 5:16-18)

_____ Don't associate with men who may entice you to do the wrong things. (2 Peter 2:17-19)

_____ Consider the consequences of sexual immorality. (1 Corinthians 6:9-10; 1 Thessalonians 4:3-7)

_____ Take radical action to change your behavior. (Matthew 5:27-30)

SUMMARY

In looking at the life of Samson, we have seen a man who was tempted in the area of sex. Though his life was ordained by God, and his ministry was empowered by the Spirit, his weakness for women eventually cost him his life.

God wants a holy people...which includes men who are sexually pure. Society, our own flesh, and the devil bombard us daily with temptation to sin, particularly through lust. Only through obedience to God's Word and the empowering of His Spirit, as well as possible help from those who are led of Him, can we recognize our sin and deal with it. We, as men, must especially realize how much our "looking" gets us into trouble. We must also take seriously God's admonition that those who are sexually immoral will not inherit His kingdom

Consider This

What causes you to be tempted sexually?

_____

_____

Have you discovered ways to keep from succumbing to everyday temptations? If so, what are some of them?

_____

_____

Who helps you most to deal with your temptation? Pastor? Friends? Wife? Other?

_____

_____

Has fear of God and the consequences outlined in His Word helped you deal with sexual sin? If so, how?

_____

_____

EXAMPLE

Author Bill Perkins shares how he has been sexually tempted even though he is Christian who has been happily married for over twenty-five years.

Late one evening, as he was turning on his sprinkler system, he noticed lights on in a house next door. He glanced at the house and, quite unexpectedly, through the fence slats saw a beautiful young woman standing at the window talking on the telephone…completely naked. The sight set the adrenaline rushing through his body.

On another occasion, he found himself alone in a Phoenix, Arizona motel room. It was too hot to do anything outside, so he started channel surfing on the television. When he came across a partially nude female dancer, he again realized how vulnerable he was — how what he *sees* can entice that evil desire!

In helping Christian men deal with these temptations, Perkins gives four steps to freedom:

1. Know who you are in Christ…that He has the power to set you free from sin.
2. Believe that you live with Christ…that He dwells in you by His Spirit.
3. Give yourself to God…thank Him that you are not alone in your struggle.
4. Don't give lust a foothold…be diligent in what you can do.

For Perkins, the latter means doing specific things. Men need male buddies with whom they can be accountable. They need to focus on meeting their wives' sexual needs, not just their own.

For Perkins, it has meant journaling, taking his daily spiritual temperature. It has also meant signing up with an Internet provider that blocks out all pornographic web sites. It has meant no longer allowing himself to even turn on the television when he's alone in a motel room. He knows that, in our sex-laden society, even good men can be tempted.

Lesson 9

BOAZ

What Are My Responsibilities As a Husband?

Husbands, love your wives, just as Christ loved the church and gave himself up for her.
Ephesians 5:25

SETTING THE STAGE

According to God's plan, true fulfillment for man comes when he is totally under the lordship of Jesus Christ. This takes expression through his work, what he does during his leisure time, how he serves his country, etc. But, the ultimate "workshop" for fulfilling God's design for man appears to be in marriage. When, in the beginning, God gave man work to do, He also said that it was not good for man to be alone. So God made a female, a companion for Adam, who would not only share his joys and sorrows, but would allow for the continuation of the human race. When this companion was formed from Adam's side, God introduced her to Adam and Adam responded: *"This is now bone of my bones and flesh of my flesh; she shall be called 'woman', for she was taken out of man"* (Genesis 2:23). With these words, God's pronouncement was that they were "one flesh."

Since God's ultimate plan was to form a bride for His Son, Jesus Christ, He would use the earthly relationship of marriage as a means of conforming both men and women to His nature. As husbands and wives become part of the Church (by accepting the atoning work of Jesus' shed blood upon the cross), they become members of the Bride of Christ — the relationship of which will be consummated at the Marriage Supper of the Lamb (Revelation 19:7). To accomplish this goal, God has decreed, in Ephesians 5:25, that husbands are to love their wives, just as Christ loved the Church.

Though Adam was the first earthly man (and had to learn to fulfill his role as husband without any previous models), in this lesson we'll, consider Boaz and his relationship with his wife, Ruth. We'll also see how Boaz foreshadows Christ, and Ruth foreshadows the Church. We will also look at the responsibilities of a faithful and loving husband as seen through Boaz, as well as other scriptural husbands.

INTRODUCING BOAZ

(Based on the book of Ruth, chapters 1-4)

Boaz stands out as a very noble and godly husband who was used by God to provide a continuation of the seed of Eve that would eventually be fulfilled in the birth of Jesus Christ and, ultimately, in the defeat of Satan.

We read in the genealogies of both Matthew and Luke, that Boaz was the son of Salmon. Matthew adds that his mother was Rahab, the harlot of Joshua 2:1-3 & 6:17.

The book of Ruth begins with the story of Naomi and Elimelech, a couple which left famine-stricken Judah to live in the country of Moab. There, their two sons married Moabite women, one of which was Ruth. In time, Elimelech and his two sons died, leaving all three women widows. When Naomi decided to return to Judah, she told her daughters-in-law to go back to their families. Orpha did, but Ruth chose to remain with Naomi. They arrived in Naomi's homeland as two destitute women completely dependent upon the mercy of their kinsmen. One of these kinsman was Boaz, who allowed Ruth to glean in his fields. Naomi wanted to find a place in the family for Ruth and she knew Boaz had shown Ruth favor, so Naomi instructed Ruth to lie at Boaz's feet while he slept. Ruth did as Naomi instructed.

Since Boaz was not the closest male relative according to Levirite law (See Deuteronomy 25; 5-10; Leviticus 25:25-28.), he informed the man who was, so that he could carry out his responsibility. When the other man declined, Boaz followed the procedure to purchase Naomi's land and acquire Ruth as his wife. Thus, he became her "kinsman-redeemer," one who purchased her — a fitting picture of Jesus and the Church.

Boaz's name is significant; it means "in him is strength." (It also graces the north pillar of Solomon's temple. 1 Kings 7:21) Boaz was true to his name, since he was strong in grace, integrity, and purpose. He was also courteous, solicitous, affectionate, devoted, generous, honorable, upright, and hospitable, as well as full of goodness, truth, and honor. Boaz is a fitting example of some of the character qualities of a faithful and loving husband, even as he took on the responsibilities as given by God.

From the union of Boaz and Ruth, Obed was born. Obed was father of Jesse, and grandfather of David...all in the lineage of Jesus Christ.

LESSONS FROM BOAZ
God-given Responsibilities of Husbands

The Hebrew word translated "husband" is the word *ba'al*, which means "master" or "owner." Dictionaries define "husband" as one who is a "master" over his household.

There are two ways to be a master. The first is God's way, using wisdom from above; the second is Satan's way, using earthly wisdom. (See James 3:13-18.) The latter way originates from pride, the desire to be important, to control everything, to lord it over others. To be a master God's way is to be a servant, to be responsible for the welfare of others. The master's status doesn't come from forcing himself on others; he earns his position through service. Jesus was the divine model for this kind of master. He came to serve, not to be served.

As a man takes a wife and, thus, becomes a husband, he assumes new responsibilities. Genesis 2:24 tells us that a man is to leave his father and mother and cleave to his wife. This involves not only physically leaving, but also psychologically leaving childish ways of being carefree and self-centered.

Boaz had the maturity needed by a husband. The phrase *you have not run after the younger men* (Ruth 3:10) indicates that he was older than Ruth. But age isn't the only sign of maturity. Boaz was established in his work (Ruth 2:3-9). He respected Ruth when he could have taken advantage of her sexually (Ruth 3:7-18). He knew and obeyed the laws of the land. Other men in the community respected him (Ruth 4:1-10). Regarding the decisions he made, he sought and received the blessing of the city elders (Ruth 4:11-12).

Do you consider yourself mature as a husband? If so, how did you become so? If not, what can you do to become so?

_____

_____

According to Scripture, what are some of the responsibilities God gives husbands?

_____

_____

He will love his wife.

Husbands, love your wives, just as Christ loved the church and gave himself up for her.... Ephesians 5:25

When we agree, as part of the wedding ceremony, to "love and to cherish" our wives, we may be caught up in the idealism and romanticism of the occasion. How difficult it is to love, let alone cherish when we experience the pressures and frustrations of life in the days and years following!

The Greek language has several words for love. Each word has a very specific meaning. The word translated "love" in Ephesians 5:25, is *agapáo*, God's sacrificial love. *Agapáo* is more than the erotic feeling evoked by physical beauty, it's an act of the will. The word used here is from the same root word that describes God's act of mercy toward us when we didn't deserve it (John 3:16 and Romans 5:8). Loving our wives necessitates more than responding to the flesh; it may mean denying our flesh. The counterfeit love of the world is a type of love that seeks its own pleasure, fulfilling its own desires and needs first. The Bible calls this lust.

List some of the ways you express *agapáo* to your wife:

_____

_____

_____

_____

He will be faithful to his wife until death parts them.

For this reason a man will leave his father and mother and be united to his wife, and the two will become one flesh. So they are no longer two, but one. Therefore what God has joined together, let man not separate. (Matthew 19:5-6)

By law a married woman is bound to her husband as long as he is alive. (Romans 7:2a)

Faithfulness is based on commitment, not feelings. To experience this fully, we must go the way of the cross…laying down our rights as we serve our wives. Proverbs 5:18-23 admonishes men:

May your fountain be blessed, and may you rejoice in the wife of your youth. A loving doe, a graceful deer...may her breasts satisfy you always, may you ever be captivated by her love. Why be captivated, my son, by an adulteress? Why embrace the bosom of another man's wife? For a man's ways are in full view of the Lord, and he examines all his paths. The evil deeds of a wicked man ensnare him; the cords of his sin hold him fast. He will die for lack of discipline, led astray by his own great folly.

What causes unfaithfulness? Why do we so often want what we don't have? How do we justify thinking that we would desire a relationship with another woman?

Put a check by those areas of the flesh, which might lead you to be unfaithful:

____ Lust	____ Physical sight	____ Sexual gratification
____ Pleasure	____ Flattery	____ Feeling needed

How does obedience to the following scriptures help us be faithful to our wives?

- *I made a covenant with my eyes not to look lustfully at a girl.* (Job 31:1)

- *You have heard that it was said, "Do not commit adultery." But I tell you that anyone who looks at a woman lustfully has already committed adultery with her in his heart.* (Matthew 5:27-28)

- *Each one of you also must love his wife as he loves himself.* (Ephesians 5:33)

- *Wisdom will save you from the ways of wicked men...It will save you also from the adulteress, from the wayward wife with her seductive words, who has left the partner of her youth and ignored the covenant she made before God....thus you will walk in the ways of good men and keep to the paths of the righteous.* (Proverbs 2:12, 16-17, 20)

- *Husbands, in the same way be considerate as you live with your wives, and treat them with respect as the weaker partner and as heirs with you of the gracious gift of life, so that nothing will hinder your prayers.* (1 Peter 3:7)

He will assume his role as his wife's spiritual head and covering.

I want you to realize that the head of every man is Christ, and the head of the woman is man, and the head of Christ is God. (1 Corinthians 11:3)

When, in Genesis 3:16b, God told Eve that her desire would be for her husband and that he would rule over her, He was giving her a "covering" from further attack by Satan. As the wife submits to her husband, and her husband submits to Christ, they are protected by God's "divine order." Along with this "benefit" come consequences. When a woman, because of her God-given desire (See Genesis 3:16b.), allows her husband to be her spiritual head, she puts herself in a vulnerable position. If she is abused in any way, she will not respect her husband. If she is affirmed and cared for properly, their relationship will be a good one. As her "head," the husband will pray for his wife, share the Word of God with her, and encourage her in her own walk with the Lord. If she is an unbeliever, she will be sanctified (made holy) through him. (See 1 Corinthians 7:14.)

Though there are different interpretations on how this is to be carried out, and many perceive it as pertaining to the traditional Middle Eastern culture of which Paul was a part, Paul gives a command to women in 1 Corinthians 14:34-35 that: *women should remain silent in the churches…If they want to inquire about something, they should ask their own husband at home….* This implies that her husband should know and be in a position to answer her questions!

As Ruth literally placed herself under the covering of Boaz, he was able to provide her with a new name and standing, even though she was a foreigner.

Do you consider yourself the spiritual head of your family? If not, how can you become so?

He will fulfill his marital duty.

The husband should fulfill his marital duty to his wife, and likewise the wife to her husband. (1 Corinthians 7:3)

In the context of this verse, "marital duty" seems to mean sexual intercourse. For, the surrounding passages also say that each man should have his own wife to keep from immorality, and that the wife's body does not belong just to her, nor does her husband's just to him. Thus, they are not to deprive one another of what belongs in marriage. If they agree to abstain from sexual relationship for a period of time, they need to come together again, lest Satan tempt them. According to Hebrews 13:4, *marriage should be honored by all, and the marriage bed kept pure, for God will judge the adulterer and all the sexually immoral.*

Due to the number of broken marriages, sexual abuse, pornography, etc., it's obvious we are increasingly frustrated in this area of marriage. But be assured, God has set limits for this special part of the marriage relationship, and violating them brings consequences both now and for eternity.

Are you faithful in your "marital duty" to your wife? If not, what can you do?

He will provide for her.

If anyone does not provide for his relatives, and especially for his immediate family, he has denied the faith and is worse than an unbeliever. (1 Timothy 5:8)

Providing for one's wife and family does not only mean meeting physical needs (like food, a place to live, transportation, etc.), it means a husband must also provide understanding, acceptance, etc.

The following are some needs often expressed by wives. Are you aware of these in your wife? If so, how do you make sure these needs are met?

Recognition as an individual with her own talents, abilities, personality, etc.

Fatigue and stress due to daily routine

Isolation, boredom…especially if tied down with young children

Acceptance by in-laws

Sexual and health concerns

Problems with children

Biblical Husbands

Husbands in Scripture had the same problems and needs as men today. Search the following list for those husbands with whom you identify, then read the scriptural passage noted and see what consequence resulted from their actions.

A husband who:

blamed his wife for his own sin	Adam	Genesis 3:1-12, 17-19
saw his wife saved because of his obedience	Noah	Genesis 6:22-7:7
lost his wife because they were both disobedient	Lot	Genesis 19:15-26
didn't protect his wife	Abraham	Genesis 20:1-18
prayed for his wife	Isaac	Genesis 25:19-21
conferred with his wives	Jacob	Genesis 31:4-16
spent time separated from his wife because of his work	Moses	Exodus 18:1-8
did not share intimately with his wife	Samson	Judges 14:1-20
sympathized with his wife	Elkanah	1 Samuel 1:1-8
was opposite in personality and character to his wife	Nabal	1 Samuel 25:1-17, 36-38
was ridiculed by his wife	David	2 Samuel 6:20-23
let his wife dominate him	Ahab	1 Kings 21:1-25
acted on information from his wife	Namaan	2 Kings 5:1-14
tried to use his wife for his own pleasure	Ahasuerus	Esther 1:10-22
had to listen to his wife's angry outburst when he was "down" himself	Job	Job 2:7-10
loved his wife despite her unfaithfulness	Hosea	Hosea 1:2-11; 3:1-3
was unable to communicate with his wife	Zechariah	Luke 1:11-25
protected his wife	Joseph	Matthew 2:13-23
stood by his wife in time of grief	Jairus	Mark 5:21-24, 35-43
lived with his wife unlawfully	Herod	Matthew 14:1-5
did not listen to his wife's advice	Pilate	Matthew 27:13-26
purposed with his wife to lie to others	Ananias	Acts 5:1-11
realized he must respect his wife if he wanted his prayers answered	Peter 1 Peter 3:1-7	Mark 1:29-31;
worked together well with his wife	Aquila	1 Corinthians 16:19; Romans 16:3-5a; Acts 18:18-28; 2 Timothy 4:19

God as Husband / Jesus Christ as Bridegroom

When God made a covenant with Abraham to call out a people of His own, He meant this to be an everlasting relationship. *I will establish my covenant as an everlasting covenant between me and you and your descendants after you for the generations to come, to be your God and the God of your descendants after you* (Genesis 17:7). In this covenant-relationship with His chosen people, God would see Himself as their husband! Jeremiah 3:14-15 reminds us of this as we hear God calling His people back from a time of spiritual adultery. He says, *"Return, faithless people,"* declares the Lord, *"for I am your husband."* (KJV says: *"I am married unto you"*) *I will choose you…one from a town and two from a clan…and bring you to Zion. Then I will give you shepherds after my own heart, who will lead you with knowledge and understanding."*

If we understand this covenant relationship God has with His people, the Jews, we can see how, throughout the whole of Scripture, God is dealing with His "wife"…wooing her back from spiritual adultery, bringing her through the refiner's fire, and anticipating being united with her again (as described in Daniel 12:1-3, when Israel accepts Jesus as her Messiah (Romans 11:25-31). Meanwhile, the Gentiles who have become the Church will be grafted into God's family. (Read the whole chapter of Romans 11 to better understand the relationship God has with both Israel and the Church.)

Jesus, on the other hand, is the Bridegroom of the Church…all those, both Jew and Gentile, who have accepted the work of His atoning blood upon the cross. Ephesians 5:25-32 says it this way: *Husbands, love your wives, just as Christ loved the church and gave himself up for her to make her holy…after all, no one ever hated his own body, but he feeds and cares for it, just as Christ does the church…for we are members of his body. For this reason a man will leave his father and mother and be united to his wife, and the two will become one flesh. This is a profound mystery…but I am talking about Christ and the Church.* The description of this union at the Marriage Supper of the Lamb is found in Revelation 19:6-9.

It's interesting to note that the whole book of Ruth can be seen as an analogy of the relationship of the Jews, the Church, and Jesus Christ. Naomi, as Israel, was dealt with by the Lord. After sojourning in a foreign land, she was restored and became part of the lineage of the Messiah. She should have been the one to marry Boaz, but because she could no longer bear children, she had to allow Ruth to take her place. And so Ruth, a Gentile, the Church, became the bride of Boaz, her kinsman-redeemer.

Ruth had accepted Naomi's God as she left her own family for a new relationship. When Boaz found Ruth in a field at harvest, he showed her much love and mercy…to the extent he was willing to pay a price to have her as his bride. Because of their marriage, she was allowed to inherit all that was his. Out of their union came Obed, father of Jesse, who was father of David…of the lineage of Jesus Christ.

SUMMARY

In our study of Boaz, an example of a godly husband, we have looked at some of the responsibilities Scripture gives husbands…to love their wives, to be faithful to them all their lives, to be their covering and spiritual head, to protect them, and to fulfill their marital duty with them. In the process, we looked at other Biblical couples and learned lessons from their examples. We have also discovered that not only is God the "husband" of Israel, but Jesus is coming as the Bridegroom for the Church, all Jews and Gentiles who have accepted the work of His shed blood upon the cross. Boaz, as Ruth's kinsman-redeemer, is a type of Christ…our "husband" to be!

Consider This

What God-given responsibilities of husbands do you believe you have accepted?

_____

_____

What can you do to become a better husband to your wife?

_____

_____

What difference does it make in our lives if we (as the church) understand and believe that Jesus is a soon-coming bridegroom?

_____

_____

EXAMPLE

John Bevere, pastor and author of *The Bait of Satan*, says he and his wife, Lisa, hurt each other so much during the first five years of their marriage that it seemed impossible to salvage any loving relationship. Lisa, herself an author, agrees.

John was a Christian and diligently prayed for the wife God wanted him to have. When he found Lisa, he believed all would be idyllic. Instead, Lisa's anger, temper, and her need to control exposed the selfish immaturity that was in him — and the battle raged. It was only because they both knew God had ordained their marriage and did not make divorce an option that healing eventually took place.

One of the insights God gave them is the difference between being "yoked" and assuming the "mantle." Lisa's worry and stress of trying to keep everything under control, including John, put a yoke of bondage upon her, and she became even more frustrated and angry. When she finally gave her burden to the Lord, he removed the yoke and she felt great freedom.

Meanwhile, John, due to his immaturity, would not assume the mantle of spiritual leadership.

In Scripture, Samuel had a mantle fashioned by his mother, Joseph had one of many colors, and Elijah, Isaiah and John the Baptist wore mantles of animal skins. Mantles covered nakedness, concealed faults, carried supplies, and announced positions of authority. John and Lisa testify that when her yoke was broken by her submission to God's divine order, John assumed the mantle of spiritual leadership for their marriage. They are not only much happier, but they have since been used by God to minister nationwide helping husbands and wives find the relationship God has ordained in marriage.

Lesson 10
JONATHAN AND DAVID

Friends...Do I Really Need Them?

A friend loves at all times, and a brother is born for adversity.

Proverbs 17:17

SETTING THE STAGE

There was a man all alone; he had neither son nor brother. This verse, Ecclesiastes 4:8a, evokes a feeling of sadness. The next few verses question this man's purpose for living, concluding that life is miserable and meaningless without someone to share it. So it seems when man feels all alone, because God intends for us to share life with others. Wives are a gift of God to meet this need in a special and intimate way, but the need has other aspects that only a male friend, or friends, can truly meet.

Experts estimate that only ten percent of American men have someone that they can truly call a close friend, in the full Biblical sense. Many men may have acquaintances, buddies with whom they enjoy hunting or comparing the latest footfall scores. But these relationships don't always allow sharing true feelings and deep needs. Then, there are those men who suffer from the delusion that real men don't need other people. Society perpetuates this by undermining the ideal of godly friendship between men by emphasizing individualism, autonomy, privatization, and isolation. In our day, men have an additional fear, for they might be suspected of deviant behavior if they have a close friendship with another man.

In light of the above, it seems good to address the issue of friendship between men and see what the Bible says about it. In this lesson we'll use the example of Jonathan and David to examine true friendship and how God has provided for this rewarding relationship in our lives.

INTRODUCING JONATHAN AND DAVID

(Based on 1 Samuel 18:1-4; 19:1-7; 20:1-42; 23:15-18; and 2 Samuel 1:17-27)

The friendship of Jonathan and David is one of the most ideal pictures of what a true godly friendship is and should be. It would be helpful to read all of 1 Samuel 13-23 and 2 Samuel 1 to get the full scope of the events and factors which affected these men's lives, and how friendship was the bonding of these two of God's princes.

Jonathan was the son of King Saul, Israel's first king, whose reign began with high expectations and ended in defeat. Jonathan didn't share his father's weaknesses and propensity toward envy and disobedience. He was a courageous person who wasn't afraid to go to battle against a great army with only his armor-bearer. Jonathan attempted to be loyal both to his father, the King, and to David, God's appointed successor to the throne. Second Samuel 1:17-27 gives us a glimpse of the strong relationship Jonathan and David had, despite the fact that Jonathan was the rightful heir to the throne and David had been appointed by God to take his place. This should have produced envy in Jonathan, but it didn't. Jonathan finally died in battle with his father.

David, a man after God's own heart, had the capacity to be great, do great exploits, and commit great sin. In this lesson, however, we'll focus on the man who became a friend of Jonathan who, like him, not only was a great warrior but also had great fear of God. It may have been the courage and faith that they saw in each other that drew them together. First Samuel 18:1 tells us *Jonathan became one in spirit with David, and he loved him as himself.* Or, as the KJV says: *the soul of Jonathan was knit with the soul of David, and Jonathan loved him as his own soul.*

It appears that their friendship was initiated by Jonathan. Though King Saul loved David (1 Samuel 16:21), this love could turn to anger. Once, when King Saul told Jonathan that he would kill David, Jonathan was, at first, able to get Saul to change his mind. Then, an evil spirit came over Saul and he renewed his pledge to kill David. Jonathan warned David, and David went into hiding, where Jonathan consoled and encouraged him. They made a covenant with each other and devised a plan whereby Jonathan would protect David from King Saul's wrath.

First Samuel 20:41 states that, after making their covenant, they both wept, but David wept the most. The depth of David's love for Jonathan is also evidenced in 2 Samuel 1:26: *I grieve for you, Jonathan my brother, you were very dear to me. Your love for me was wonderful, more wonderful than that of women.* And it wasn't that David didn't love women; He had many wives!

A question, which will probably be answered only in eternity, is: Would David have been the man and King that he was without the love and encouragement of his friend Jonathan? All we do know is that their friendship meant much to both of them in their lives here on earth.

LESSONS FROM JONATHAN AND DAVID

The Friendship of Jonathan and David

To further understand the friendship Jonathan and David had, and how men can have similar friendships with other men, we must look at some of the characteristics of their relationship. Think also of friendships you may have with other men and answer the appropriate question following each section:

Good friends share mutual concerns.

Though Saul's envy and wrath could have cost David's life, both Jonathan and David were mutually concerned about David's safety. They both worked for his protection. What mutual concerns do you share with a friend?

_____

_____

Good friends accept each other's faults and weaknesses.

Jonathan and David had many good experiences together and both had great qualities, but Jonathan had to accept David's fear of being caught, and David had to accept that Jonathan loved both him and his father.

How do you know your friend accepts you the way you are? How do you accept him for who he is? _____

_____

Good friends trust each other.

David and Jonathan were able to trust each other with their very lives; after all, Jonathan was the son of the current king, a man who wanted to kill David. They had to submit to one another and trust that each one would follow through, or David's death would have been the result.

What does it take to be able to trust a friend? _____

_____

Good friends are loyal to one another.

Jonathan and David were so committed to one another that all the tactics of King Saul could not divide their loyalty. David and Jonathan made a covenant in which Jonathan even gave David his own robe and sword. After Jonathan's death, David kept his word to his friend and took Mephibosheth, Jonathan's lame son, to live with him in the palace for the rest of his life.

How do you express your loyalty to your friend? _____

_____

Good friends encourage one another.

Jonathan probably spent more time encouraging David than David did encouraging Jonathan, just because of the circumstances.

How do you and your friend encourage and comfort each other? _____

_____

Good friends want the best for each other.

Jonathan certainly showed that he wanted the best for David despite the fact that David would have the position Jonathan, himself, could have had. Out of respect for the father/son relationship of Jonathan and King Saul, David did nothing to drive a wedge between them. Second Samuel 1:23 confirms this relationship between father and son: *in life they were loved and gracious, and in death they were not parted.*

How do you show your friend that you want the best for him? And he, for you?

_____

_____

Good friends are accountable to one another.

Jonathan and David not only shared mutual concerns and a faith in God, they submitted to one another in the most practical of ways, even when not able to see each other for long periods of time.

Do you and your friend share deep needs and take one another's counsel? Give an example.

_____

_____

Good Christian friends fear God and value His Word.

We know that David had a heart for God even before he became king. We also know that Saul was afraid of David because he could see that the Lord was with David. In 1 Samuel 20:2-23, we find evidence of Jonathan's trust in the Lord on behalf of David.

Do you and your friend share faith in God and share His Word with each other?

_____

_____

Though not specifically noted in the relationship of Jonathan and David, other necessary attributes of friendship include:

the need to take risks, be vulnerable

the need to communicate warmth

the need to be available, even when it is not convenient

the need to spend time together

the need to be willing to forgive and be forgiven

other ?_____

Friendships

Christianity is relational. It's not only about our relationship with Jesus Christ, it's also about our relationship with others. Consider what Jesus said in Matthew 22:37-39 when He was asked which is the greatest commandment: *"Love the Lord your God with all your heart and with all your soul and with all our mind. This is the first and greatest commandment, And the second is like it: Love your neighbor as yourself."* Our neighbor can be our friend. Scripture gives us advice on making friends. It also warns us against making the wrong kinds of friends.

GODLY FRIENDSHIPS

Some of the proverbs tell us the value of good friends:

- Proverb 17:17a, friends are always faithful: *A friend loves at all times.*
- Proverb 18:24, a friend can be closer than a brother: *A man of many companions may come to ruin, but there is a friend who sticks closer than a brother.*
- Proverb 27:6a a friend can give constructive criticism: *Wounds from a friend can be trusted.*
- Proverb 27:10, a friend can be valuable in time of need: *Do not forsake your friend and the friends of your father, and do not go to your brother's house when disaster strikes you…better a neighbor nearby than a brother far away.*
- Proverb 27:17 (KJV), a friend can give help helpful advice: *As iron sharpens iron, so a man sharpeneth the countenance of his friend.*

Some examples of godly friendships in Scripture include:

Moses, Aaron and Hur

We can note the friendships of at least two men in the life of Moses. His brother Aaron not only spoke for him, but accompanied him for forty years in leading God's people out of Egypt into the Promised Land (Exodus 4:27-30). Hur helped Aaron hold up Moses' arms in a time of battle against the Amalekites. (Exodus 17:8-15)

Abraham and God

It's one thing for us to think of friendships with other men, but imagine God saying that you are His friend! Three times in Scripture Abraham is referred to as a friend of God: (See 2 Chronicles 20:7; Isaiah 41:8; James 2:23.)

Elijah and Elisha

In 1 Kings 19:19-21, we find the "call" of Elisha, who would succeed Elijah as prophet to the northern kingdom of Israel. As Elijah cast his mantle upon Elisha, who was plowing the field, Elisha immediately left his work and home to follow and learn from Elijah. We don't hear much more about Elisha until they set out on Elijah's last journey to the Jordan river where God took him to heaven in a whirlwind. On the journey, the two men traveled together from Gilgal to Bethel to Jericho to Jordan. As they began each stage of their journey, Elisha reaffirmed his loyalty by saying, *"I will not leave you."* (2 Kings 2:2, 4, 6)

Paul and Onesiphorus and Barnabas

In 2 Timothy 1:16 and 4:19 we read of Onesiphorus, an almost unknown person, yet a friend of Paul who was kind and often "refreshed" him. Another friend, Barnabas, whose very name means "son of encouragement," not only was a friend and companion of Paul on his missionary journeys, he also tried to repair the friendship of Paul and John Mark. (Acts 15:36-39)

WARNINGS CONCERNING WRONG FRIENDSHIPS

- Deuteronomy 13:6-8 tells us that friends can entice us to sin.
- Psalm 41:9 reminds us that friends can betray us.
- Proverbs 22:24-25 warn that our souls can be ensnared by friendships with angry men.
- Job 19:14 tells us that friends can be unfaithful.
- Proverbs 4:14 says not to walk in the way of evil men.
- First Corinthians 5:9 tells us not to associate with sexually immoral people.
- Second Thessalonians 3:6 commands us to keep away from our Christian "brothers" who do not live like they should.

Have you ever made the wrong kind of friend? If so, what was the result?

_____

_____

Our Best Friend, Jesus Christ

During the week after His triumphal entry into Jerusalem, and prior to His crucifixion at Calvary, Jesus spent much time talking with the twelve men He had discipled for the three years. He told them not only what was ahead for Him, but also that the Holy Spirit would come to take His place as comforter and teacher. They had traveled with Him in ministry and had come to know Him as Christ, the Son of the Living God. They were not only his disciples, they had become his friends. Yet at the very time He was on the cross and needed them the most, they all abandoned Him! Even worse, Judas betrayed Him. Nothing hurts worse than having one's confidence and trust betrayed by a friend. ("Breaking bread" with a friend confirms a friendship, thus the significance of Psalm 41:9, which is prophecy concerning Jesus and Judas: *Even my close friend, whom I trusted, he who shared my bread, has lifted up his heel against me.*)

Jesus wanted His disciples to know that He loved them and, most especially, that they were His friends. John 15:13-15 says He told them: *"Greater love has no one than this, that he lay down his life for his friends. You are my friends if you do what I command. I no longer call you servants, because a servant does not know his master's business. Instead, I have called you friends, for everything that I learned from my Father I have made known to you."*

Jesus wants the same relationship with us. In John 17, He prays not only for these disciples to whom He declared His friendship, but, *"also for those who will believe in me through their message, that all of them may be one, Father, just as you are in me and I am in you"* (Verses 20-21). Romans 8:17 reminds us that *if we are children, then we are heirs...heirs of God and co-heirs with Christ.* And Hebrews 3:1 calls those who partake of the heavenly calling *holy brothers.* Furthermore, our destiny, as part of Christ's Body, is that we will be His Bride (Ephesians 5:30-32). What closer friendship is more desirable than co-heir, holy brother, Bride of Christ!

SUMMARY

There are many rewards of godly friendship with other men. There are also many reasons to be cautious about making the wrong kinds of friends. We can learn much from the example of Jonathan and David's friendship. They shared mutual concerns, were loyal, respected one another, were accountable, and recognized God in their relationship. Because friendship takes time and commitment, it's difficult to have more than a few close friends at a time, but the relationships can be very rewarding. The best friend of all is Jesus Christ, the One who gave His life for you. Spend time with Him and you will have a friend who will never leave you nor forsake you, will always understand you, and will love you as no other person can.

Consider This

Do you have, or have you ever had, a really close friend? If so, how did you both benefit?

_____

_____

Have you ever been betrayed by a friend? If so, what was the result?

_____

_____

How do you make new friends? Or do you just keep the same ones?

_____

_____

Do you consider Jesus your friend? If so, how do you carry on this friendship?

_____

_____

EXAMPLE

Albrecht (or Albert) Durer was born in Germany, son of a Hungarian goldsmith. As he was growing up, he had to help his father in his trade in order to support their large family, even though he was much more interested in drawing and painting. Finally, he was allowed to leave home and study under a great artist, though he also had to earn his own living. When he met another struggling artist, a man somewhat older than he, they decided to pool their resources by living together. It proved to be difficult for both to work and to study, so they decided to take turns. Thus, the older man washed dishes, scrubbed floors — anything to keep food on the table for Albert and himself while Albert studied. Their agreement was that when Albert could earn a living through art, the older man would quit work and begin his study.

The day finally came when Albert brought enough money home, from the sale of one of his woodcarvings, to pay expenses for an extended time. And so, his friend left his menial jobs and took up the brush. However, all the hard work had so stiffened his hands, enlarged his joints, and twisted his fingers that he could no longer hold a brush with any mastery or skill! Not only was he very disappointed, it made Albert extremely sad as well.

One day, Albert happened upon the old man praying in his bedroom. It gave him the idea of a way to show the world of the old man's sacrifice for him. He would paint a picture of his gnarled, twisted hands at prayer. Those who now see this picture and know this story will see beyond the broken fingernails and enlarged joints — not only praying hands, but a masterpiece of friendship between Albrect Durer and a friend who always dreamed of being an artist.

Lesson 11

SOLOMON AND ZACCHAEUS

What's My Attitude Toward Work...and Money?

Whatever you do, work at it with all your heart, as working for the Lord, not for men, since you know that you will receive an inheritance from the Lord as a reward.

Colossians 3:23-24

SETTING THE STAGE

Work and money. Most of the time they go together like a horse and carriage — one follows the other. They consume much of a man's time and energy. There are times when work isn't necessarily rewarded with money, and money or wealth isn't the direct result of work. But the way man obtains his wealth, and what he does with it, matters a great deal to God.

As man was created in the image of God, he was made to work. God Himself was just completing six days of work when He made man and gave him his job: *The Lord God took the man and put him in the Garden of Eden to work it and take care of it* (Genesis 2:15). This took place before sin came into the world. In the curse that resulted after the fall, nature became uncooperative and working conditions became painful. Solomon, in Ecclesiastes 2:4-11 describes this kind of work...work without partnership with God. He recounts all the projects that he had done, all the wealth that he had gathered, and still his heart found no pleasure and life was meaningless. Without God's perspective, man either becomes lazy and slothful or a workaholic, trying to prove his own worth.

God wants to redeem man's work, to give it a purpose and a place. First Corinthians 10:31 tells us: *So whether you eat or drink or whatever you do, do it all for the glory of God.* After all, He is the one from whom we will, in the end, receive reward for our work.

Our attitude toward money will also change when we see our possessions from the perspective of what God wants in our lives. Instead of trying to amass our own fortunes, we'll see ourselves as stewards of God's provision...whether it be money, land, houses, or other material possessions.

To consider these two issues, our attitude toward our work and our attitude toward our money and material possessions, we'll look at the lives of two men in the Bible. King Solomon was one of the wealthiest men who ever lived. But, as he records in the book of Ecclesiastes, all his great fortune was in vain...nothing "under the sun" had really satisfied him. Zacchaeus, on the other hand, had made his wealth as a despised tax-collector. When he heard Jesus teaching, he was changed, because he saw God's perspective. He found new meaning to his life and work as he assumed a new attitude toward his money and material possessions.

INTRODUCING SOLOMON

(Based on 1 Kings 1:11-35; 2-3, 4:20-34; 6:1; 7:1; 10:14-29; 11)

Solomon was the tenth son of David. His mother was Bathsheba, the woman with whom David had committed adultery, whose husband he had killed, and whose baby (they had conceived) died soon after birth. After David's repentance, 2 Samuel 12:24b-25 says,

Bathsheba *gave birth to a son, and they named him Solomon. The Lord loved him, and because the Lord loved him, he sent word through Nathan the prophet to name him Jedidiah* (which means, "loved by the Lord"). This was God's way of showing that David had been restored to God's divine favor after his repentance. Little is known of Solomon's (Jedidiah's) childhood, but we can assume that Bathsheba took an active role in raising her son. That she wanted him to become David's successor as king is confirmed in 1 Kings 1:11-40. The prophet Nathan, no doubt, also exerted a positive influence on young Solomon.

Solomon's reign began with great promise and expectation. The Lord appeared to him in a dream and told him He would give him whatever he wanted (1 Kings 3:5). Solomon wisely chose to be given *"a discerning heart to govern your people and to distinguish between right and wrong"* (1 Kings 3:9a). The Lord was pleased with Solomon's request and humble spirit, and gave him his request. He inherited David's throne and possessions, but he also amassed much wealth on his own. He was a naturalist, wrote one thousand five songs and three thousand proverbs, carried out great public works projects…including numerous palace structures…and built one of the Seven Wonders of the Ancient World, the great temple. He was also an administrator, an architect, a diplomat, a tradesman, and an equestrian. Nehemiah 13:26b says of Solomon: *Among the many nations there was no king like him. He was loved by his God, and God made him king over all Israel….*

Yet with all his great accomplishments, Solomon became a miserable failure because he ignored the great wisdom given him and sinned against God. Though he had been warned (see Deuteronomy 17:16-17) not to acquire great numbers of horses, to take many wives, or to accumulate large amounts of silver and gold, Solomon did these things…partly as a result of the influence his foreign wives had upon him. Solomon partook of all he desired — wisdom and knowledge, wine and women, wealth and fame, music and songs — and his heart turned away from the Lord. His life was characterized by vanity, and the kingdom became divided when he died after forty years upon the throne.

INTRODUCING ZACCHAEUS
(Based on Luke 19:1-10)

Like Solomon, Zacchaeus had built his little kingdom at the expense of others. Scripture identifies him only as a chief tax collector and as being wealthy. The tax collectors, also known as publicans, were part of a system of taxation that allowed, and even promoted, the collection of taxes beyond what was required. Because the tax collector could keep this excess for himself, bribery and extortion were common. Tax collectors were a hated class of people, representing the worst of the oppressive Roman government. Because Zacchaeus was a Jew who earned his living off fellow Jews this way, not only was he doubly despised, he was considered a sinner and outside the law for working with, and for, Gentiles.

Jesus did something quite shocking by selecting a tax collector, Matthew, to be one of His disciples.

Zacchaeus lived in Jericho. When he heard that Jesus was passing through, he wanted to see Him. Because he was short, he had to climb a tree to see what was happening. But he didn't miss the eye of Jesus. Jesus spotted him up in the tree and called to him, *"Zacchaeus, come down immediately. I must stay at your house today"* (Luke 19:5b). Zacchaeus came down at once and gladly welcomed Jesus to his home, to the dismay of the crowd who could not believe that Jesus would invite Himself to eat dinner with a sinner! Confronted by the teachings and acceptance of Jesus, Zacchaeus had a change of heart. He told Jesus, *"Look, Lord! Here and now I give half of my possessions to the poor, and if I have cheated anybody out of anything, I will pay back four times the amount* (Luke 19:8). With that, Jesus recognized that Zacchaeus had become a son of Abraham, and claimed him as one of the lost He had come to save.

LESSONS FROM SOLOMON AND ZACCHAEUS

Work as Ordained by God

Much of man's sense of worth is centered in his work, what he does to earn a living. In fact, inability to work due to health reasons, accidents, unemployment, etc. usually lowers a man's self esteem so that it affects all other areas of his life — his marriage, his family, his ministry, his ability to reach out to others, his attitude toward money and material possessions. This is because God ordained man to work.

On the last day of creation
Just after He had made man, God said to him: *"Be fruitful and increase in number; fill the earth and subdue it. Rule over the fish of the sea and the birds of the air and over every living creature that moves on the ground."* (Genesis 1:28)

Following the fall of man
God said, *"Cursed is the ground because of you; through painful toil you will eat of it all the days of your life...by the sweat of your brow you will eat your food until you return to the ground...."* (Genesis 3:17b-19a)

As the Ten Commandments were given
Remember the Sabbath day by keeping it holy. Six days you shall labor and do all your work. (Exodus 20:8-9)

When the Psalms were written:
Then man goes out to his work, to his labor until evening. (Psalm 104:23)

In the time of the early church
For even when we were with you, we gave you this rule: "If a man will not work, he shall not eat." (2 Thessalonians 3:10)

On Judgment Day
His work will be shown for what it is, because the Day (of Judgment) will bring it to light. It will be revealed with fire, and the fire will test the quality of each man's work. If what he has built survives, he will receive his reward. If it is burned up, he will suffer loss; he himself will be saved, but only as one escaping through the flames (1 Corinthians 3:13-15). This, of course, is more than just the work we do to earn a living, but the total things we do with the time we have.

God's provision seems to come to us also from the combined work of others. In Deuteronomy 15:4-8, we find that He did not intend there to be *any poor among you.* If one followed His commands, he would be blessed. If there was a poor person, people were to give to him whatever he needed — with open hands. We are reminded in Deuteronomy 8:18 that *it is he who gives you the ability to produce wealth, and so confirms his covenant....* He blesses those who follow His commands, so that they can bless others.

Your Attitude Toward Work

We must see work as more than just making a living…paying bills, taxes, spending for needs and even pleasures. We must have a sense of partnership with God. We must understand the sanctity and value of work and how God can be in everything we do. Then, even our workbenches can be altars of worship to Him.

What do the following scriptures tell you about giving your best physical strength to your work?

Proverbs 26:13-16 _____

Matthew 25:26-27 _____

1 Timothy 5:8 _____

What do the following scriptures say about being whole-hearted about your work?

Romans 12:11 _____

Ephesians 6:5-8 _____

Colossians 3:23 _____

What do the following scriptures say about doing your best in your work?

Genesis 1:31 _____

Ephesians 2:10 _____

Scriptural Solutions to Practical Problems

1. You have difficulty working for a harsh boss. According to 1 Peter 2:18-21 and Titus 2:9-10, you are to _____

2. Your co-workers aren't always "nice people" and you want to set them straight. According to Romans 12:14-21 and Ephesians 4:29, you are to

   _____

3. Taxes take a big chunk out of your paycheck and this irritates you, but you remember Luke 20:22-25, which says

   _____

4. You're sick of your workplace, but haven't been able to find another job. Read 1 Peter 1:3-7. _____

5. You work hard, but there's never enough income to live by your standards. Philippians 4: 12-13, & 19, remind you that _____

   _____

6. You're so tired after a full week's work that you decide to take Sunday to do what you want — watching sports, mowing the lawn, taking a trip, etc. When you seem to be losing God's blessing, read Deuteronomy 8:11-14 and remember

   _____

7. You do your best, but it never seems enough. According to Ephesians 6:7-8, you should

   _____

8. You realize that some people at work aren't Christians. You don't think you should take work time to witness to them, but according to 1 Peter 3:15 and Matthew 5:16 you can _____

   _____

9. You aren't sure that your work is worthwhile. According to Psalm 90:17, you can pray

   _____

   According to Colossians 3:17, you can also _____

10. You never hear your boss' approval; you just assume he's satisfied with your work. According to Matthew 25:21, 23, who is it that you should really want to hear say "Well done, good and faithful servant?" _____

    _____

God's Attitude Toward Money and Possessions

Just as God sees our work as something we do as unto Him, He also sees us as stewards of the money and possessions He provides through our work. In scripture, we are reminded:

All things are God's.
The earth is the Lord's, and everything in it, the world, and all who live in it. (Psalm 24:1)
God gives man the ability to get wealth.
Remember the Lord your God, for it is he who gives you the ability to produce wealth, and so confirms his covenant (Deuteronomy 8:18)
Man is not to put trust in earthly treasures.
Do not store up for yourselves treasures on earth, where moth and rust destroy, and where thieves break in and steal. But store up for yourselves treasures in heaven, where thieves do not break in and steal. For where your treasure is, there your heart will be also. (Matthew 6:19-21)
Man is not to love the world and what it offers.
Do not love the world or anything in the world. If anyone loves the world, the love of the Father is not in him….The world and its desires pass away, but the man who does the will of God lives forever. (1 John 2:15-17)
Man cannot serve both God and money.
No one can serve two masters. Either he will hate the one and love the other, or he will be devoted to the one and despise the other. You cannot serve both God and Money. (Matthew 6:24)

Man is to realize everything in this world is temporal.

For we brought nothing into the world, and we can take nothing out of it....If we have food and clothing, we will be content with that....For the love of money is a root of all kinds of evil....Some people, eager for money, have wandered from the faith. (1 Timothy 6:6-10)

God has promised to meet our needs.

And my God will meet all your needs according to his glorious riches in Christ Jesus. (Philippians 4:19)

Obedience to God will bring prosperity.

If they obey and serve him, they will spend the rest of their days in prosperity and their years in contentment. (Job 36:11)

As man gives, it will be given to him.

Give, and it will be given to you....For with the measure you use, it will be measured to you. (Luke 6:38)

Bible Men and Money/Possessions

Can you match the Biblical man with the appropriate attitude he had about money/possessions:

Abraham	prospered twice as much after he lost everything.
Job	acknowledged God for giving wealth for the temple.
David	gave a tithe as he recognized God as His supply.
Solomon	was willing to sell his soul for some money.
Rich young ruler	found he couldn't take wealth with him when he died.
Man who built barns	found all his great work meaningless without God.
Zacchaeus	was sad because he couldn't part with his possessions.
Judas Iscariot	changed his attitude toward his possessions.
Ananias	lied about his possessions and was stricken dead.

(See: Genesis 14:17-24; Job 42:10; 1 Chronicles 29:9-14; Ecclesiastes 2:1-11; Matthew 19:16-22; Matthew 27:1-5; Luke 12:16-21; Luke 19:8; Acts 5:1-11)

Your Attitude Toward Money/Possession

When we claim ownership to money and possessions, we consider ourselves in charge and God as our servant to help us when we call upon Him. When we see ourselves as stewards, we are ready to do His will. Therefore, giving is important because it reminds us who God is, who we are, and what our relationship should be to those things He has allowed us to manage.

So, why does God ask us to give when He owns everything? Because giving isn't only for our own good, it's His way of allowing us to meet one another's needs. Matthew 25:31-46 reminds us that as we do things for others, we are doing them for God.

Scripture tells us we meet others' needs through our giving. Consider the following:

Plenty in God's storehouse to share with others	Malachi 3:10
Support for pastors and church leaders	1 Timothy 5:17,18
Needs of other Christians met	2 Corinthians 8:8-15
Help for relatives	1 Timothy 5:8
Support for missionaries	Luke 10:1-7
Help for the poor and needy	2 Corinthians 9:7-11; Ephesians 4:28

The ways we give can be understood as different "levels." Read the appropriate scripture for each of the following, and then note a time when you gave on that level. (For instance, you might have tithed last Sunday at church.)

Giving a tithe (Malachi 3:10)

_____

Giving out of obedience (Matthew 25:34-36)

_____

Giving out of your abundance (Luke 12:15-21)

_____

Giving sacrificially (Luke 21:1-4)

_____

SUMMARY

Because we give so much time and attention to work, money, and possessions, it's important for us, as Christians, to see these things from God's perspective...and as He wants us to view them. From Solomon, we saw that without submission to God and His will, all our work can be in vain. From Zacchaeus, we saw that God wants us to be honest in our work and generous with what we have. We are His stewards, not owners of what we have earned. Thus, we need to learn to give, whether it's through tithing, through obedience to God's Word, through the abundance with which He has blessed us, or even, at times, through great cost to us personally. God is the supreme example not only of One who worked to complete His job, but One who sacrificially gave His best.

Consider This

Do you feel your job is fulfilling God's call on your life? Or, do you feel it's just a step to what He wants you to do?

_____

_____

How can you have a better attitude in your present job situation?

_____

_____

Do you manage your finances well? Or, do you need help in learning how to do so?

_____

_____

What is your record on giving to others — whether church, friends, relatives, or the poor?

_____

_____

How can you have a better attitude about giving your money and possessions?

_____

_____

EXAMPLE

With the recent increase in droughts, floods, tornadoes, and other results of unusual weather patterns, some farmers are finding that they have to depend, even more, upon God for a good harvest of crops.

Cam Hancock farms in Alberta, Canada. Hancock bought his father's farm in 1966 and has put in and taken off more than 30 crops since that time. Every spring, the thought of new growth and hope of a good crop draws him into the rhythm of work. His enthusiasm, however, is always tempered by experience, for he also has lost crops due to bad weather and poor prices.

His years of experience have taught him something even more valuable — that it's only because of God's faithfulness that he can have success in his work. He has learned to depend upon God's Word for strength, hope, and freedom from fear. Verses such as Genesis 8:22 confirm that *as long as the earth endures, seedtime and harvest, cold and heat, summer and winter, day and night, will never cease.* Hancock has learned to do as James 5:7 commands and wait patiently for the autumn and spring rains. He has followed the advice of Ecclesiastes 11:6 to *sow your seed in the morning, and at evening let not your hands be idle.*

Hancock says God has honored his dependence upon Him, for in thirty-one of the past thirty-two years, he has been able to pay all his bills. He knows his work is in partnership with God. He realizes that he can only do his part and then wait for God to do His. He knows 1 Corinthians 3:7 to be true: *Neither he who plants nor he who waters is anything, but only God, who makes things grow.*

Lesson 12
THE OLD TESTAMENT PROPHETS
Does God Have a Message for Me to Share?

"You are my witnesses," declares the Lord, "and my servant whom I have chosen, so that you may know and believe me and understand that I am he…I have revealed and saved and proclaimed…I, and not some foreign god among you." "You are my witnesses," declares the Lord, "that I am God."

Isaiah 43:10-12

SETTING THE STAGE

God has spoken to men throughout history, and He has used men and women to speak for Him. We usually call the latter prophets, because they utter divine inspiration. Prophets are used by God to proclaim messages of comfort, messages of warning, and reminders of His righteous acts, both for the present and in giving hope for the future. They give God's perspective, even as they are able to see meaning behind the events. They look past the immediate to the ultimate.

Though we'll look at various ways God gave His messages to men in all kinds of circumstances, we'll primarily consider the message and character of the sixteen prophets whose books have been given to us in the Old Testament. All these prophets were used by God to proclaim a message for their day. Many were given insight into both the first and second comings of Jesus.

As we look at the role of the prophets in the Old Testament, we must realize that even then it was the Holy Spirit who gave them their messages. Peter tells us *prophecy never had its origin in the will of man, but men spoke from God as they were carried along by the Holy Spirit* (2 Peter 1:21). We'll also look at the New Testament to see how the Holy Spirit can give men messages from God today. As a caution, we will consider the traits of a false prophet as well.

We'll also discover how the message of the prophets was fulfilled in the New Testament, even to those things which are still to be revealed, as written down for us in the book of Revelation. To conclude this lesson, we'll ask a most important question: Does God have a message for you to share?

INTRODUCING THE OLD TESTAMENT PROPHETS

(Based on the various books by their names)

Isaiah, son of Amoz, lived in Jerusalem during the time Assyria destroyed the Northern Kingdom of Israel. Isaiah tried to warn Judah of what could happen to them because of their apostasy. In his writings, we find the ultimate triumph of God's plan through the coming Messiah who would bring final victory through His own suffering and death.

Jeremiah, the son of a priest named Hilkiah, was from Anathoth just outside of Jerusalem. Jeremiah was appointed by God to be His spokesman during one of the most trying times in the history of God's chosen people. He began his ministry in King Josiah's thirteenth year

(626 B.C.) and continued with a remnant in Jerusalem in the early years after Judah had been taken into exile by Babylon. During his forty-year ministry, Jeremiah spoke of judgment, but the people, whose desperate nationalism was all they had to cling to, rejected it. Jeremiah was regarded as a traitor, and often faced death. We read of some of his suffering in two books, Jeremiah and Lamentations.

Ezekiel, probably having heard Jeremiah while he was still in Jerusalem, lived and preached among a colony of captive Jews who were forced to dig the Chebar canal (about fifty miles from Babylon). Ezekiel had a style and method of teaching all his own. He used symbols, visions, parables and poems as he painted strange pictures often difficult to understand. He was a contemporary of Daniel, who served in the courts of the kings in nearby Babylon.

Daniel, a young man who dared to keep a clean heart and body while serving in the king's courts during Babylonian captivity, was one whom God chose to convey His message to the Gentile nations of the world. God also gave Daniel the interpretation of some the king's dreams, dreams which have made and will make quite an impact on history.

Hosea, a contemporary of Isaiah in Judah, was sent to northern "Israel" and prophesied before their capture by Assyria. In the imagery of Hosea's own experience, Israel's unfaithfulness to the Lord is depicted in terms of a wife who has turned her back upon a faithful husband in order to follow evil lovers. Hosea was called by God to give the clear message that He loved His people as a husband loves his wife, unworthy though she may be.

Joel, as prophet to Judah before the exile, has been called the prophet of religious revival. Because the land had recently suffered a terrible plague of locusts, Joel called the people to consider the cause of the calamity, as he called them to true repentance. If they would repent, he said, the promise would then be that God would completely restore all that the locusts had eaten. Unique to Joel is the prophecy concerning the outpouring of God's Spirit upon all flesh, the ultimate way to restoration and revival.

Amos prophesied about 760 B.C., a time of political security for Israel. He was a shepherd in the desert twelve miles south of Jerusalem. He evidently supplemented his income by taking care of wild fig trees. Although a native of Judah, Amos prophesied in the Northern Kingdom and aroused such antagonism that he returned to Judah. He had a knowledge of history and of the problems of his day. His message is a cry for justice.

Obadiah, a contemporary of Jeremiah, prophesied concerning the judgment of the Edomites who were allied with the enemies of Jerusalem and participated in the sacking of that city.

Jonah, who lived during the reign of Jeroboam II, aided him in making the Northern Kingdom of Israel very powerful and prosperous. An incident in Jonah's life concerning his disobedience to God, and how he ended up in the belly of a big fish, is a story many people know. Jonah finally obeyed God and went to Nineveh, where he preached and many were saved.

Micah, a contemporary of Isaiah (who was preaching in Jerusalem) and Hosea (who was living his message in Israel), cried for justice. Though his burden was for the Southern Kingdom of Judah, he made it clear that God's judgment would fall on the Northern Kingdom. Conditions were the same as he denounced the social sins of the day.

Nahum, probably a native of Galilee, lived during the time of King Hezekiah and Isaiah. About 150 years after the revival of Nineveh, Nahum warned of God's impending judgment on this city because its repentance had not lasted.

Habakkuk, a contemporary of Jeremiah, asked questions and received answers. His book seems to be a dialogue between himself and God. The world-empire of Assyria had fallen just as Nahum had prophesied. Habakkuk, possibly a Levitical chorister in the temple, knew that Judah would fall as well.

Zephaniah, likely a prince in the royal house of Judah, lived during the reign of King Josiah. Zephaniah depicted God as both loving and severe. He denounced various forms of idolatry, the result being that idol worship was destroyed during Josiah's reign.

Haggai was the first post-Exilic prophet to minister to the remnant who returned to Jerusalem from Babylonian captivity. He was sent by God to awaken the people from their lethargy to undertake the restoration of the temple and city.

Zechariah was a young prophet who had stood alongside aged Haggai as the temple was rebuilt by the remnant who had returned to Jerusalem. He tried to build their hopes that one day the Messiah would come and God's chosen people would rise to power.

Malachi was the last prophet to speak to Israel in her own land. Following a period of revival after their return, the people became cold religiously, and lax morally. Malachi encouraged and rebuked, and he became the bridge between the Old and New Testaments.

LESSONS FROM THE OLD TESTAMENT PROPHETS

How God Speaks to Men

It doesn't take a long look at Scripture to realize that God has spoken to men in a variety of ways. Listed below is one example of each of these ways:

How	To Whom	Scripture reference
By His "presence"	Adam and Eve	Genesis 3:8-13, 16-19
By His voice	Abraham	Genesis 12:1-3
From a burning bush	Moses	Exodus 3:4-21
From a dense cloud	Moses	Exodus 19:9
Through fire, smoke, thunder and lightning	Moses	Exodus 19:16-21
Face to face	Moses	Exodus 33:11
Through His Word	Joshua	Joshua 1:7-8
Through judges	His people	Judges 2:16-18
Through an angel	Manoah's wife	Judges 13:3
Through answered prayer	Hannah	1 Samuel 1:27
Through a voice in the night	Samuel	1 Samuel 3:1-9
Through kings	Solomon	1 Kings 9:1-9

Through a still small voice	Elijah	1 Kings 19:11-13
Through a story	David	2 Samuel 12:1-12
Through symbolism	Ezekiel	Ezekiel 2:1-3:10
Through dreams	Joseph	Matthew 2:13, 19-22
Through prophets	His people	2 Peter 3:1-2
Through His Son, Jesus	The church	Hebrews 1:2
Through the Holy Spirit	Us, His disciples	John 14:26; 16:13

The Old Testament Prophets

In the Old Testament, several men were moved by God to prophesy. They were chosen to speak His word to the people, usually ministering the combined gifts of prophecy and knowledge, and often doing other mighty acts by the power of God. Though we have just seen that God can speak to men in a variety of ways, we also find that God often used men called prophets to speak for Him. We have briefly looked at the sixteen who left us books in our Old Testament.

Here are some others:

Moses
In a dream of Abimelech's, God referred to Moses as a prophet. (Genesis 20:7)

Aaron and Moses
Both were called prophets, though they are known for other roles. (Exodus 7:1; Deuteronomy 34:10)

70 Elders
They prophesied when the Spirit of the Lord came upon them (Numbers 11:16-25). Following this incident, Moses declared: *"I wish that all the Lord's people were prophets and that the Lord would put his Spirit on them!"* (Numbers 11:29b)

Balaam
Peter called him a prophet in 2 Peter 2:15-16. In the story about Balaam (Numbers 22-23), his donkey was also used by God. It spoke!

Samuel
He was the first of the prophets attested by all Israel. (1 Samuel 3:1-20)

Nathan
He was a prophet used by God to confront David about his sin. (2 Samuel 7:4-17)

Elijah
As a prophet during the reign of King Ahab and Queen Jezebel, Elijah often spoke for God. He even issued a challenge to 450 prophets of Baal — and triumphed! (1 Kings 18:16-41)

Elisha
He succeeded Elijah as prophet. (1 Kings 19:19-21)

God uses prophets to bring people back to Him: *Although the Lord sent prophets to the people to bring them back to him, and though they testified against them, they would not listen* (2 Chronicles 24:19).

God uses prophets to warn of impending judgment: *The Lord warned Israel and Judah through all his prophets and seers: "Turn from your evil ways. Observe my commands and decrees, in accordance with the entire Law that I commanded your fathers to obey and that I delivered to you through my servants the prophets."* (2 Kings 17:13)

Qualifications for One Who Speaks for God

Though God uses men from all walks of life, of all ages, and from different places, the prophets do have certain qualifications:

Prophets fear God.

They recognize God for who He is, and they see themselves for who they are. This is evident in Isaiah 6:1-8. Isaiah, after experiencing the presence of God in the temple, cried out. *"Woe is me! I am ruined. For I am a man of unclean lips, and I live among a people of unclean lips, and my eyes have seen the King, the Lord Almighty."*

Prophets are willing to do what God asks.

Hosea married a prostitute and tried to win her back after her unfaithfulness so that God could give His people a picture of His desire to win them back after their spiritual adultery. (Hosea 1-3)

Prophets are willing to suffer if necessary.

Jeremiah is known for the suffering he experienced, which included being put into a vaulted cell in a dungeon. (Jeremiah 37:16)

Prophets are willing to speak for God, even if it's contrary to what others are saying.

In 2 Chronicles 18:1-27 we find the story of the prophet Micaiah, who was put in prison because he didn't tell the King of Israel what he wanted to hear — that he would be victorious — as four hundred other prophets (with lying spirits) had.

Prophets know the consequences of not speaking for God when He wants them to.

Ezekiel 3:18 tells us: *"When I say to a wicked man, 'You will surely die,' and you do not warn him or speak out to dissuade him from his evil ways in order to save his life, that wicked man will die for his sin, and I will hold you accountable for his blood."*

Prophets know their message must truly be from God.

Deuteronomy 18:22 says *if what a prophet proclaims in the name of the Lord does not take place or come true, that is a message the Lord has not spoken. That prophet has spoken presumptuously. Do not be afraid of him.*

Prophets know the necessity of God's Word being spoken.

They know that where there is no vision, the people perish (Proverbs 29:18 KJV); that people will grieve if they don't hear God's Word (Nehemiah 8:1-12); that men will stagger and wander when there is a famine of God's Word (Amos 8:11-12); and that people will feel hopeless when no prophet speaks (Psalm 74:9). In being spokesmen for God, men have been willing to allow Him to put specific words in their mouths (Jeremiah 1:9). They have had to realize these words were God's own words (1 Peter 4:11a), and not be afraid of men (Ezekiel 2:6). Thus, they did as admonished in 2 Timothy 4:2: *Preach the Word; be prepared in season and out of season; correct, rebuke and encourage…with great patience and careful instruction.*

Discerning False Prophets

A false prophet:

Prophesies out of his _____ imagination. (Ezekiel 13:2)

Has seen _____ visions and uttered _____ divinations. (Ezekiel 13:7)

Will _____ many people. (Matthew 24:11)

Can perform great _____ and _____. (Matthew 24:24)

Preaches rebellion against _____. (Deuteronomy 13:5)

Proclaims things that do _____ come true. (Deuteronomy 18:22)

Says things that people _____. (2 Timothy 4:3)

Does not acknowledge that Jesus is _____. (1 John 4:1-3)

Will secretly introduce _____ and _____ God. (2 Peter 2:1)

Appeals to the lustful desires of _____. (2 Peter 2:18)

Their message brings _____ response from God. (1 Kings 18:29)

According to Deuteronomy 18:22 *if what a prophet proclaims in the name of the Lord does not take place or come true, that is a message the Lord has not spoken. That prophet has spoken presumptuously.* And 1 John 4:1 reminds us: *Do not believe every spirit, but test the spirits to whether they are from God, because many false prophets have gone out into the world.*

Prophecy in the New Testament

The New Testament is full of references of how Old Testament prophecy has been fulfilled. This is especially true in the life and ministry of Jesus, from His birth to His resurrection. The book of Revelation, most of it yet to be fulfilled, contains many prophecies given in Old Testament times. In Ephesians 2:19-20, Paul showed that the prophets are part of the foundation of the Church: *You are no longer foreigners and aliens, but fellow citizens with God's people and members of God's household, built on the foundation of the apostles and prophets, with Christ Jesus himself as the chief cornerstone.*

Though John the Baptist is called a prophet ("more than a prophet" by Jesus in Luke 7:26), his ministry preceded that of Jesus Christ. Most New Testament prophecy seems to occur after Pentecost (except what Jesus foretold) and for edification of the church. (See 1 Corinthians 14:4.) Many people believe that Joel's prophecy (in Joel 2:28) about the Spirit being poured out on all people was fulfilled in part on the Day of Pentecost when the Holy Spirit came in power (Acts 2:1-5; 1 Corinthians 12:13), laden with gifts for God's people (1 Corinthians 12:4-11). Thus, the gift of prophecy is available, by the Holy Spirit, not only to those who may be called to the office of prophet, but also to those in the Body who may receive the manifestation of this gift. Write down what Scripture says about this gift of prophecy:

1 Corinthians 12:7-10 _____

1 Corinthians 14:1 _____

1 Corinthians 14:3 _____

1 Corinthians 14:5 _____

1 Corinthians 14:39 _____

Romans 12:6 _____

1 Thessalonians 5:20-21 _____

The safeguard is that all prophecy is to be judged, not just accepted as fact. *Two or three prophets should speak, and the others should weigh carefully what is said* (1 Corinthians 14:29).

Present-Day Conveyors of God's Message

As part of the Church of Jesus Christ, we need to hear the message God has for us today, and then share it with others. Those who believe that the gifts of the Spirit are also for modern-day believers may be moved, by the Spirit, to give prophetic words so that the church can be strengthened, encouraged, and comforted (1 Corinthians 14:3) . To others, prophecy may be scripture that has been quickened by the Holy Sprit and proclaimed to others. Thus, some see Spirit-anointed preaching (Acts 10:42-43), teaching (Matthew 28:19-21a), witnessing (Acts 1:8), and worship (Revelation 19:10) as forms of prophecy, because each of these can declare the message God wants to give.

Perhaps the greatest message we can share is God's plan of salvation, whether on a one to one basis, or as missionaries to many around the world. To be able to speak for God, we must have a personal relationship with Jesus Christ, know His Word, and be available to the leading of the Holy Spirit. Romans 10:8-17 tells us that the word of faith which we are to proclaim is in our mouth and in our heart, and that as it is preached to others, *faith comes from hearing the message, and the message is heard through the word of Christ* (v.17). As parents, we may have spiritual truths to share with our children. As pastors, we may have words of comfort and encouragement for the flock. As God-fearing citizens, we may have a message of exhortation for our community and/or nation. It's our responsibility to proclaim the message; it's up to God to bring about the results He desires.

Many feel an urgency to share because of a burden which does not lift until they do something about it. As a result of their obedience, people are won to Christ or forewarned about events to come. (This will always line up with the Word of God.)

Record a burden you may have for declaring God's message, whether for the present time or for what you foresee happening in the future — so that people can be prepared:

_____

_____

How and with whom can you share this burden so that God's message can be heard?

_____

_____

SUMMARY

As we have looked at the sixteen Old Testament prophets who have books named after them and others who prophesied only a few times, we've seen that they were men who heard God speak and then passed on His message. Most of the time, the messages were for the benefit of their contemporaries, though many also foretold events which were eventually fulfilled in the New Testament times and others which will be fulfilled in the years yet to come.

In the New Testament, we find more emphasis on the gift of prophecy inspired by the Holy Spirit and made available to the Church for edification. Some interpret this as preaching and other means God uses to get His message across to man. Each of us must consider what God may be saying to us and then determine how we can impart this message to those He wants to hear it.

Consider This

Which , if any, of the messages of the Old Testament prophets are applicable to us today?

_____

_____

Do you see anyone today in the role of a prophet of God? If so, who?

_____

_____

How has God spoken to you?

_____

_____

What message of God do you feel burdened to share with others? How can you go about doing this?

_____

_____

EXAMPLE

William grew up in a little village in England. He liked natural science and geography, and read so many books about foreign lands that he was nicknamed Columbus.

At sixteen, he was apprenticed to a shoemaker. But as he worked at the cobbler's bench, he was most aware of a large world map which he had hung on the wall. Every chance he got, he talked to people about things going on in other countries, especially news that explorers brought as they returned home to England. Having already learned Latin, he spent his spare time learning other languages, such as French, Spanish and Dutch.

After some discussions about religion, another apprentice told William that he needed to be born again. A nominal churchgoer, William didn't understand what the friend meant until he went with his friend to his church and heard the gospel message. Following his conversion, William couldn't get enough of the Bible — and he learned Greek and Hebrew to better understand it.

His love of the Word, as well as his love of geography, combined to give him a burden for reaching the world with the gospel of Jesus Christ. So, he helped begin the first missionary society and, within a few years, became a missionary himself.

When William Carey and his family, along with the John Thomas family, sailed for India on June 13, 1793, a new era began for the modern-day church. The missionary movement came into being and spread to many denominations, which subsequently sent out thousands of missionaries all over the world.

Though he didn't baptize their first convert for seven years, William taught, supervised mission work, and translated the entire Bible into the four main languages of India. While also publishing newspapers, schoolbooks, and dictionaries, he set up 120 Christian mission schools, an Indian missionary college, and inspired both England and America to send missionaries out into the world. Called the father and forerunner of the modern missionary movement, William Carey made the Bible available to 300 million people in their own language. God spoke to him, a cobbler's apprentice; he heard the message he was to convey, and he shared the gospel in many and various ways all over the world.

Lesson 13

DANIEL AND MORDECAI

How Can I Be a God-Fearing Citizen in a Secular Society?

Remind the people to be subject to rulers and authorities, to be obedient, to be ready to do whatever is good, to slander no one, to be peaceable and considerate, and to show true humility toward all men.

Titus 3:1

SETTING THE STAGE

This lesson deals with our relationship, as Christians, to the world. It will evoke many questions to which there will be many possible answers. For, as we concern ourselves as to what the Christian's attitude should be toward the world, we must recognize that even Christians are divided on how the Church should relate to society…from quite passively to very actively on social and moral issues.

We live in a world which is becoming more and more degenerate, unholy, filthy, violent, etc. The fabric of society is rapidly unraveling. Yet it's also true that we serve an awesome God to whom nothing is impossible, and that He desires all men to be saved. We know that God is the final judge, that His kingdom will prevail, and that it is to Him we all will be accountable. And we know that we, as His people, are but sojourners here on earth; heaven is our real home.

But what are we to do in the meantime? Do we just look for a way of escape, keeping ourselves immune from the world's madness? Or do we put down roots and attempt to help change things? How does God expect us to remain loyal to Him and yet live in a secular society?

This was the predicament for both Daniel and Mordecai. Though at different times and in different ways, they both served pagan kings, yet honored God. Both are good examples of how God can use men, wherever they are, to accomplish His purposes — for them and for the world.

INTRODUCING DANIEL

(Based on the book of Daniel, especially chapters 1-3, 5-6, 9)

Scholars believe that Daniel, one of the most respected of the Old Testament prophets, was born during the time of Josiah's reformation (621 B.C.) As a young man in his late teens, Daniel was part of the first group to be deported to Babylon by Nebuchadnezzar in 602 B.C. (the third year of the reign of Johoiakim, king of Judah). According to Daniel 1:3, Daniel was of a royal family and was selected, along with some friends, to be indoctrinated into the Babylonian system and culture because of his appearance and aptitude.

After three years of special training, Daniel and his friends were assigned to the King's service as consultants and stewards. Daniel served during the reigns of at least four Kings, even when the Babylonian Empire became part of the Media-Persian Empire. Since Daniel 1:21 states that Daniel remained in the king's service until the first year of the reign King Cyrus, he was probably around eighty years old at the time of his retirement. Even years later, Daniel received further revelations from the Lord concerning events in the future. He was probably aware that the time of the seventy-year exile would soon end and God's people would be returning to Jerusalem to rebuild it and the temple.

Whether or not Daniel was of noble birth, he was certainly of noble character. He is a man worth modeling ourselves after. Even during his initial training period, Daniel proved his desire to live a holy life while respecting those in authority over him. Daniel and his friends excelled in all they did and were rewarded with respect and honor, even though there were times when they had to choose between following the King of heaven and submitting to the earthly king they served. On separate occasions this resulted in Daniel's friends being thrown into a fiery furnace and Daniel being put into a lion's den. Yet their intimacy with God enabled these young men to stand alone against a secular society. They served well in the courts of some of the greatest monarchs of all times, but were also true to God. Significantly, Daniel's name means "God is Judge" or "who in the name of God does justice." He had been well named!

Daniel was not only a man of great courage, he was also a man of great prayer, one of which is recorded in his book. He kept his window open toward God. He not only received much wisdom in how to relate to his government and society then, but he was also given revelation as to what will happen in the end times, as well.

INTRODUCING MORDECAI

(Based on the book of Esther)

Mordecai was a Jew of the tribe of Benjamin. His great grandfather, Kish, had been deported by Nebuchadnezzar (King of Babylon) during the reign of Johoiachim (King of Judah). About 115 years after this took place, Mordecai was living in Susa (Shusan), one of the provincial capitals of the Media-Persian empire. Loyal to King Xerxes (Ahasuerus), he appears to have been some kind of official involved in the Kings' Gate (the period's equivalent of our modern-day courthouse or city hall). One day, while there, he overheard a plot to assassinate the king. He told Queen Esther, who told the king, and the king had the conspirators hanged.

Mordecai had raised his niece Esther, after the death of her parents. However, when Esther became queen (following the deposition of Queen Vashti by King Ahasuerus), Mordecai forbade her to tell the King of her Jewish heritage.

Haman, an Agagite, was made chief minister of King Ahasuerus. When he commanded all the kings staff and courtiers to bow down to him, Mordecai refused. This made Haman furious. Discovering that Mordecai was a Jew, he vowed to have him hung and all Jews killed.

One day, the king asked Haman how he should honor a certain man (meaning Mordecai, because Mordecai had never been rewarded for saving his life). Haman thought the king was referring to him, and suggested that he have a parade for all to acclaim such a hero. Through a series of meals, which Esther had arranged after a time of fasting and prayer, she told the king and Haman that she was a Jew and asked the king to spare her people. She had accepted Mordecai's suggestion that she had been put in her position "for such a time as this."

So, through an unusual chain of events, Haman ended up being hung on the gallows; Mordecai was honored with a parade; and the Jews were spared genocide! (Today, this event is celebrated still at the Feast of Purim.)

LESSONS FROM DANIEL AND MORDECAI
Daniel and Mordecai as Examples

Daniel lived in Babylon during the time of the seventy-year exile of the Jews and Mordecai lived in Media-Persia with a remnant of Jews who did not return to Jerusalem. Both lived in pagan lands because of what the Lord had spoken through Jeremiah many years before: *This what the Lord Almighty, the God of Israel, says to all those I carried into exile from Jerusalem to Babylon. "Build houses and settle down; plant gardens and eat what they produce. Marry and have sons and daughters; find wives for your sons and give your daughters in marriage, so that they too may have sons and daughters. Increase in number there; do not decrease. Also, seek the peace and prosperity of the city to which I have carried you into exile. Pray to the Lord for it, because if it prospers, you too will prosper."* (Jeremiah 29:4-7)

As these men lived most of their lives in a secular society, they remained true to their God. What scriptural principles can we learn from them?

God was their highest authority.

Daniel was thrown into the lion's den because he prayed to God during a thirty day period when the king decreed that no man could do so. (Daniel 6:6-16)

Mordecai worked, with Esther, to save God's people, despite the fact that Haman had convinced the king to kill all the Jews. (Esther 4:1-17)

Like the apostles in Acts 5:29, we can say:

_____

They were conveyers of God's Word and Truth.

Daniel interpreted King Nebuchadnezzar's dream with wisdom he credited to God. (Daniel 2:26-28)

Mordecai exposed Haman's dark plot and asked Esther to tell the king the truth so that the Jews would not be annihilated. (Esther 4:6-17)

In our day, we can be the light of God's truth in our dark world. Matthew 5:16 tells us:

_____

They didn't depend upon man for promotion.

Even though he had been instructed in the way of the Chaldeans in order to become a servant in the king's court, Daniel purposed in his heart not to defile himself by what he ate or drank. Because of this, God gave him favor and allowed him to serve kings for sixty years! (Daniel 1:3-20)

Though Mordecai had exposed a plot to assassinate the king, he didn't expect to be honored. But God brought the idea to do so to the king's mind. (Esther 6:1-3, 11-13; 8:2)

Psalm 75:6 reminds us: _____

_____

They lived within the world's system

From the time of his youth, Daniel lived his whole life as a Jew in Babylonian courts. Mordecai, a Jew in the service of the king, lived his whole life in Media-Persia. Romans 13:1-6 tells us that as citizens of a secular society, we are to:

_____

_____

They were men of prayer

Daniel prayed on many and various occasions despite living in a godless society. In Daniel 9: 4-27, we see him praying for God's people and He reveals their future. Mordecai, mourning before God in sackcloth and ashes, encouraged Esther to call a time of prayer and fasting by the Jews, so that God wouldl spare them. (Esther 4:1-17)

James 4:4-10 warns us against being a friend of the world lest we become an enemy of God. Verses 9-10 tell us to _____

_____

They were willing to stand alone, whatever the cost.

Daniel's friends were thrown into a fiery furnace (Daniel 3:8-30), and Daniel into a lion's den (Daniel 6:1-23) because they refused to worship any other than the true God.

Mordecai faced hanging because of Haman's wrath against him. Yet, he was willing to stand with Esther who said, *"If I perish, I perish"* (Esther 4:16), after receiving his advice. (Esther 4:7-17)

In Matthew 5:11-12, Jesus tells us that we are blessed when

_____

_____

And we are to rejoice because _____

_____

God's Perspective of the World

In order for us to know how we should relate to the world and its system, it's important that we know God's perspective of the world. As the creator and sovereign God, He has the right to be LORD. Psalm 24:1-2 says *the earth is the Lord's, and everything in it, the world, and all who live in it; for he founded it upon the seas and established it upon the waters.* Paul declared to the pagan Athenians that: *The God who made the world and everything in it is the Lord of heaven and earth and does not live in temples built by hands. And he is not served by human hands, as if he needed anything, because he himself gives all men life and breath and everything else.* (Acts 17:24-25)

When God finished creating the heavens and the earth, He said everything was good. And that it was — until after Satan's temptation, when man fell and sin entered the world. Because Adam and Eve had chosen to submit to Satan instead of God, they were put out of the Garden, and God allowed Satan to temporarily become the "god of this world." (See 2 Corinthians 4:4 KJV.) Ephesians 2:2 calls him the *ruler of the kingdom of the air, the spirit who is now at work in those who are disobedient.* In John 14:30, Jesus called him *the prince of this world.* 1 John 5:19 sums it up: *We know that we are children of God, and that the whole world is under the control of the evil one.*

So a battle for men's souls is ever present. God calls out a holy people, those who will believe in what He has done for them in sending Jesus to be the sacrifice for their sins so that He can have the relationship He so desired with man in the beginning. And, Satan, as deceiver of the whole world, blinder of men's eyes, accuser of the brethren, and god of this world, wants to keep people in darkness, and part of his kingdom. When we accept Jesus and the atoning work He did on the cross for us, we are transferred from Satan's kingdom to God's kingdom. As Colossians 1:13 tells us *he has rescued us from the dominion of darkness and brought us into the kingdom of the Son he loves, in whom we have redemption, the forgiveness of sins.* Thus, we have two kinds of citizens on earth: those who belong to God's kingdom and those who belong to Satan's kingdom. It's no wonder that Christians have difficulty living their faith and belief in a world under the control of the devil! It's no wonder that God gives us weapons for spiritual warfare so we can help win others to Christ, and also be protected from the wiles of the devil!

Because the world and all its system is under the domain of Satan (as allowed by God), it will eventually be destroyed: *By the same word* (that gave the order to destroy the earth with a flood in Noah's time) *the present heavens and earth are reserved for fire, being kept for the day of judgment and destruction of ungodly men* (2 Peter 3:7). Verse 10 continues: *But the day of the Lord will come like a thief. The heavens will disappear with a roar; the elements will be destroyed by fire, and the earth and everything in it will be laid bare.* Quite an end to secular society according to Revelation 21:1-2! Eventually, there will be a new heaven and a new earth with Jesus and His Bride united at last. Satan will be thrown into the lake of fire to be tormented day and night forever and ever. (See Revelation 20:10.)

Jesus' Relationship to the Secular World

There was no doubt in Jesus' mind as to who He was and His relationship with the world. Is not John 1:3 true? *Through him all things were made; without him nothing was made that has been made.* In John 13:3, we find that *Jesus knew that the Father had put all things under his power, and that he had come from God and was returning to God.* So, while living in the flesh on earth, Jesus was still aware of who He truly was.

Some incidents in Scripture verify that this was true:

- John 18:36a — When asked by Pilate if He were the King of the Jews, Jesus replied, *"My kingdom is not of this world."*
- John 19:11a — When Pilate told Jesus he had the power to set Him free, Jesus' response was, *"You would have no power over me if it were not given to you from above."*

- John 17:9, 11, 16 — In the prayer for His disciples, Jesus made the distinction of not praying for the world, but for those that had been given to Him. In verse 11, He says, *"I will remain in the world no longer, but they are still in the world…They are not of the world, even as I am not of it."*

Yet Jesus related to the needs of those in the world in practical ways. He fed the hungry (over 5,000 at one time!). He told the people to pay their taxes, even render to Caesar's what was his. He healed the sick. He talked with the scribes and Pharisees about the laws. Even from the cross, He delegated the care of his mother to John.

Paul and Secular Society

Paul, who saw himself as a Roman citizen, taught submission to the government authorities (Romans 13:1-7). He also taught, in 2 Corinthians 6:15-17, that we must keep ourselves from being influenced by the world, separating from it if necessary. He further states, in 1 Corinthians 5:9-13, that it's impossible to be in the world and not associate with those who are immoral, greedy, swindlers, and idolaters. But, he warns us not to associate with any of these people who claim to be a brother (fellow Christian), for in so doing, we might be influenced in the wrong way. Paul's main concern was that we do not compromise our faith.

Our Choice

Isaiah 59:19 (KJV) tells us that *when the enemy shall come in like a flood, the Spirit of the Lord shall lift up a standard against him.* There are different ways to deal with an impending flood, just as there is a choice in how to deal with the flood of wickedness in our world.

The fort concept
Do what you can to barricade your home and family against the rising water. Try to make your own dwelling a safe haven as you isolate yourself.

The commune concept
Band together with others of like mind and form your own group to meet one another's needs.

The dam-building concept
Try to confine the flood to certain areas. Design restrictions to keep it under control (such as putting a guard on the Internet, or legislating curfews).

The stop-it-at-its-source concept
Try to restructure the source of the problem (such as eliminating the market for drugs, or putting adult bookstores out of business).

The fatalistic concept
Ignore flood warnings because you know floods will come and there's nothing you can do about them.

The battle-against-it concept
Not only bo on guard against the rising water, but also do all you can to keep it from doing its damage, both to yourself and to others.

The living-above-it concept

Like Noah in the Ark, live above the flood. So fill your lives with God and His Word that you aren't caught in the evil of the world, but can be a light to all.

Social/Moral Issues and What to Do About Them

After considering the role models of Daniel and Mordecai, and after identifying different ways to deal with rising flood waters, what is your stance on the following social/moral issues?

_____ Becoming involved in government, such as voting, running for office, writing to congressmen, paying taxes, etc. (See Romans 13:1-7; 1 Timothy 2:1-2.)

_____ Taking a stand against abortion (See Ezekiel 16:20-21; Psalm 139:13-16.)

_____ Stopping crime and violence (See Genesis 6:11-13; Psalm 11:5.)

_____ Fighting pornography (See Ephesians 4:18-19; 2 Corinthians 12:21. "Debauchery" = "without restraint")

_____ Dealing with homosexual rights (See Leviticus 18:22; Romans 1:26-27.)

_____ Giving to the poor, and problems associated with the poor, such as welfare programs, the homeless problem, food programs, etc. (See 1 Kings 18:2b-15; Ezekiel 16:49.)

_____ Improving the school system (See Deuteronomy 6:6-9; Proverbs 22:6.)

_____ Hearing slander against Christians, whether through the media, in the workplace, etc. (See Matthew 5:11-12, 44; 1 Peter 3:8-9.)

_____ Other?

SUMMARY

We, as Christians committed to remaining faithful to our God and His Word, will always be in conflict with our secular society, whose "god" is Satan. We are of different kingdoms!

We must constantly be choosing how we will relate to each other, especially on the moral and social issues around us. We know God's kingdom is not of this world, which will eventually be judged and destroyed. Will we choose not to get involved, hoping that the evil and antagonism won't affect us too much, or will we do what we can to be light and salt in our society — so that everyone can have a better life here and help bring others to Christ by our actions?

Daniel and Mordecai can be role models for us. They were Jews who had to live in pagan lands. They had to choose between submitting to those who did not know God and remaining faithful to the one true God. They constantly had to make choices, and so do we.

Consider This

Do you see yourself, as a Christian, living in one kingdom with the world in another?

_____

How does understanding this help you relate to others?

_____

_____

What is your stance in dealing with the "flood" of declining social and moral issues?

_____

_____

How has the study of Daniel and Mordecai changed your view on how to relate to a secular society?

_____

_____

If you are an activist, what changes have you seen because of getting involved?

_____

_____

EXAMPLE

It was a beautiful spring day in 1981 when Pastor Roger Story and his wife, Lin, participated in a welcoming ceremony at the White House. After meeting with the Chaplain of the U.S. Senate, they had just walked over from the Senate building and passed a very well known Senator on his way to his office. Soon, the excitement of the morning faded as Roger began to feel guilty about how he had prayed for this man — not for wisdom as he performed his job, but that he would be replaced. So, in the midst of a wonderful occasion in Washington D.C., Roger was brought to his knees in repentance. When he returned home, he shared this experience with his congregation and they began praying weekly for our national leaders.

Eight years later, Roger and Lin left the pastoral ministry and moved to Washington D.C. to put feet to their many hours of prayer. By faith, Roger spent his time sharing the Gospel of Jesus Christ and praying with anyone God would send his way as he walked the halls of our federal government's office buildings. In so doing, he has come to know, in a real way, the spiritual battle against the darkness, unbelief and taunts of Satan which hover in and over our nation's capital. Out of this was born the National Leadership Ministries, an outreach to the leaders in the political, business and Christian community.

In 1991, Lin founded the National Children's Prayer Network, through which Christian Schools, Sunday Schools and families across the nation make a commitment to pray daily for government leaders. In the spring of each year, the children are invited to Washington D.C. to meet with those for whom they have been praying.

Is God pleased when we pray for our national leaders? He must be; He commands it in His Word! Can one man's vision influence our nation? Roger Story would say so.

Lesson 14
NEBUCHADNEZZAR

Do I Act and React With Pride or Humility?

God opposes the proud, but gives grace to the humble.

James 4:6a

SETTING THE STAGE

In this lesson, we will conside, the pitfall of pride, seeing how it not only makes us an enemy of God, but how it also damages our relationships with people as well. We will deal with such Biblical terms as "exalting ourself," being "haughty" or "arrogant" or "thinking of ourself more highly than we ought."

Pride is an inflated sense of superiority. The proud person feels that he can do without God or others; he puts himself in the position of one who knows best. When we are proud, we deny God the glory and honor due Him, and we are unable to accept His grace. When we relate to others in pride, we reject much of Scripture, which teaches the way of lowliness and humility. Satan is the epitome of pride.

Humility is evidence of a surrendered ego, a denial of our self, a yielding of our "rights." It's a true understanding of our position before an awesome God who loved us enough to send His Son to die for our sins. Jesus is the true example of humility.

In this lesson, we'll be looking at both pride and humility. To do this, we'll consider the story of Nebuchadnezzar, a man who was both proud and humble. We'll see what it took to change him from one to the other. We'll also consider other men in Scripture who had to deal with pride. And we'll look at what it takes for us to act and react with humility, rather that with pride. This isn't an easy lesson, especially for men. Let's pray for God to give us open hearts and the willingness to submit to His Word.

INTRODUCING NEBUCHADNEZZAR

(Based on Daniel 4)

Nebuchadnezzar was the great king of the Babylonian Empire. He was the king who took Judah into captivity and who figures prominently in the books of Jeremiah, Ezekiel, Daniel, the Kings and Chronicles. (It is significant that Sadaam Hussein sees himself as a modern Nebuchadnezzar as he tries to restore the former Babylon — now Iraq. It's also significant that Babylon is a picture of the false world system, the system which, as predicted in Revelation 14:8; 16:19, and 18, will be brought down just before Jesus comes again.)

Though Nebuchadnezzar was great in power and position, he was subject to a greater God. Proverbs 21:1 puts it this way: *The king's heart is in the hand of the Lord; he directs it like a watercourse wherever he pleases.* Nebuchadnezzar learned the hard way that he was no match for God. Once, when Nebuchadnezzar was walking on the roof of his royal palace, he said, *"Is not this the great Babylon I have built as the royal residence, by my mighty power and for the glory of my majesty?"* (Daniel 4:30). As soon as he had spoken, a voice from heaven spoke to him, saying he would be driven away from people and would live with the wild animals, where he would eat grass like cattle — until he acknowledged that God alone was sovereign over kingdoms. So, Nebuchadnezzar was driven away. Not only did he eat grass like cattle, his hair grew like eagle feathers and his nails like claws of a bird.

After seven years of living this way, Nebuchadnezzar raised his eyes toward heaven and acknowledged God for who He is *because everything he does is right and all his ways are just* (Daniel 4:37a). At that same time, his sanity was restored, as were his honor and splendor. His advisers and nobles sought him out and he returned to his throne even greater than before. But the most important lesson that Nebuchadnezzar learned during those seven years is summed up in Daniel 4:37b: *Those who walk in pride, he (God) is able to humble.*

LESSONS FROM NEBUCHADNEZZAR

Pride is the root of all sin, for man's pride causes him to be as God rather than submit to Him. Thus, pride is what separates man from God, and from others. When we think we know what is right or best, we put ourselves above God. We not only lose all respect for His authority and power, we also become ungrateful for all He has done. Our iniquities (doing what seems right in our own eyes) are the result of pride. Isaiah 59:2 tells us: *Your iniquities have separated you from your God; your sins have hidden his face from you, so that he will not hear.* A proud person finds himself in opposition to God and, thus, in the position of being unable to hear from God.

Humility, on the other hand, puts us in a submissive position of accepting God and His Word. Thus, we are able to give God His due respect and accept from Him all that He gives us, good and bad. A humble person is also able to relate to others because he respects them as God's creation with unique gifts and abilities.

Satan as the Epitome of Pride

Isaiah 14:12-17 is often seen as a description of the fall of the "morning star, son of the dawn." Many believe this is a description of Satan's fall from heaven, where he was one of the angels surrounding God's throne. Using passages of scripture such as Ezekiel 28:12-19 and Revelation 12:9-12 to complete the story, we find that Satan was cast down to earth because of five "I wills" mentioned in Isaiah 14:13-14 — five things he was determined to do to make himself God, like the Most High. According to 2 Corinthians 4:4, Satan became the *god of this world* (KJV). He continues to try to usurp God's position and will do so until his end (described in Revelation 20:10), when he will be thrown into the lake of burning sulfur to be tormented day and night for ever and ever.

In the meantime, Satan, as the father of lies (John 8:44), deceiver (Revelation 12:9), blinder of men's eyes (2 Corinthians 4:4), accuser of the brethren (Revelation 12:10), does all he can to get men to act and react in pride to become "like God." This was the very temptation that caused the first man and woman to sin (Genesis 3:5). Jesus didn't succumb to pride when He resisted the temptation to use His divine powers for His own benefit at the time of His temptation by Satan (Matthew 4:1-11). Satan's treachery will culminate in the antichrist, who will also try to take his position as god (Daniel 8:9-12). And pride is at the root.

Other Proud Men in Scripture

Listed below are some other men in Scripture who fell victims to pride's deception. Read the scripture following each name. Then state the consequence which resulted.

Pharaoh (Exodus 5:2; 12:31-32) _____

Korah (Numbers 16:1-50) _____

Rehoboam (1 Kings 12:1-15) _____

Naaman (2 Kings 5:1-19) _____

Uzziah (2 Chronicles 26:1-21) _____

Hezekiah (2 Chronicles 32:24-26) _____

Haman (Esther 5:9; 6:4-14:10) _____

Pilate (John 19:8-16) _____

Theudas (Acts 5:35-39) _____

Simon the Sorcerer (Acts 8:9-24) _____

Herod (Acts 12:19b-23) _____

Pride as a Pitfall

Even though pride is not listed seperately in Galatians 5:19-21 as one of the sins of the flesh, we can see that it's part of each of them. It fuels:

> Idolatry — worshiping the results of our own labor
>
> Hatred — opposing anyone who does not agree with us
>
> Discord — the result of pushing our own ideas and ways
>
> Fits of rage — our reaction when others reject our ideas
>
> Selfish ambition — considering our own desires above others
>
> Dissension — becoming aggressively belligerent
>
> Faction — getting people on our side
>
> Envy — not liking it when others are recognized

The following scriptures also describe the results of pride:

- *Pride only breeds quarrels, but wisdom is found in those who take advice.* (Proverbs 13:10)
- *When his heart became arrogant and hardened with pride, he was deposed from his royal throne and stripped of is glory.* (Daniel 5:20)
- *In his pride the wicked does not seek him; in all his thoughts there is no room for God.* (Psalm 10:4)
- *The terror you inspire and the pride of your heart has deceived you.* (Jeremiah 49:16a)
- *Pride goes before destruction, a haughty spirit before a fall.* (Proverbs 16:18)

How God Deals With Pride

Nothing is outside the rule and influence of God. He is Almighty, all-knowing, omnipresent, King eternal. Only pride makes man think he's a match for God. And God, in His Word, has many admonitions and warnings concerning pride and its consequences. Read the following scriptures, then summarize how God deals with pride:

- *He looks down on all that are haughty; he is king over all that are proud.* (Job 41:34)

- *The arrogant cannot stand in your presence; you hate all who do wrong.* (Psalm 5:5)

- *Though the Lord is on high, he looks upon the lowly, but the proud he knows from afar.* (Psalm 138:6)

- *He mocks proud mockers but gives grace to the humble.* (Proverbs 3:34)

- *The Lord detests all the proud of heart. Be sure of this: They will not go unpunished.* (Proverbs 16:5)

- *The eyes of the arrogant man will be humbled and the pride of men brought low.* (Isaiah 2:11)

- *When the Lord has finished all his work against Mount Zion and Jerusalem, he will say, "I will punish the king of Assyria for the willful pride of this heart and the haughty look in his eyes."* (Isaiah 10:12)

- *On that day you will not be put to shame for all the wrongs you have done to me, because I will remove from this city those who rejoice in their pride.* (Zephaniah 3:11)

- *When I fed them, they were satisfied; when they were satisfied, they became proud; then they forgot me. So I will come upon them like a lion, like a leopard I will lurk by the path. Like a bear robbed of her cubs, I will attack them and rip them open. Like a lion I will devour them; a wild animal will tear them apart.* (Hosea 13:6-8)

- *He has performed mighty deeds with his arm; he has scattered those who are proud in their inmost thoughts.* (Luke 1:51)

- *For everyone who exalts himself will be humbled, and he who humbles himself will be exalted.* (Luke 18:14b)

- *God opposes the proud, but gives grace to the humble.* (James 4:6b; 1 Peter 5:5b)

Summary _____

Dealing With Pride — Brokenness

Matthew 21:44 is an interesting verse: *He who falls on this stone will be broken to pieces, but he on whom it falls will be crushed.* "Stone" in this verse refers to a preceding verse (42) where Jesus alludes to Himself as the stone the builders rejected, the cornerstone. Thus, verse 44 can be interpreted to mean that unless we fall on Jesus, and allow ourselves to be broken, He will grind us to powder. We have a choice: We can humble ourselves, or God will humble us. Brokenness is the only way pride can be dealt with. The result is humility.

So, how do we humble ourselves?

We must recognize our sin. (Luke 18:13-14)

We must recognize our unworthiness. (Luke 15:17-21)

We must recognize God's holiness. (Isaiah 6:1-8)

We must recognize God's righteousness. (Philippians 3:4-7)

Next we are to:

clothe ourselves with humility (Colossians 3:12; 1 Peter 5:5)

live in humility (Ephesians 4:1-2)

avoid false humility Colossians 2:18-23

do nothing out of selfish ambition or vain conceit (Philippians 2:3)

look not only to your own interests, but also to the interests of others (Philippians 2:4)

not think of ourselves more highly than we ought to think (Romans 12:3)

not be proud…or conceited (Romans 12:16)

*Nancy DeMoss outlines the traits of proud people compared to those who are broken. Here is a partial list:

Proud People	Broken People
focus on the failures of others	are overwhelmed with a sense of their own spiritual need
are self-righteous; look down on others	esteem others better than themselves
desire to be served	are motivated to serve others
are self-conscious	are not concerned with self at all
are quick to blame others	accept personal responsibility when wrong
are blind to their true heart condition	walk in the light with others
are defensive when criticized	receive criticism with an open spirit
have a hard time saying "I was wrong, will you please forgive me?"	are quick to admit failure and seek forgiveness when necessary

Let's look at some Bible characters who experienced brokenness and became humble:

Moses

As a young man, Moses took things in his own hands, killed an Egyptian and had to flee to Midian (Exodus 2:11-15). It was a different Moses who, after a long period (Exodus 2:23), God called to lead His people into the promised land. Moses' response was *"Who am I, that I should go to Pharaoh and bring the Israelites out of Egypt?"* (Exodus 3:11). During the forty years of wilderness wandering, Moses often fell on his face before the Lord when the people rebelled. (See Numbers 20:6.) Numbers 12:3 declares that Moses *was a very humble man, more humble than anyone else on the face of the earth.*

David

Taking advantage of his position as king, David committed adultery and murder. After God confronted him, through the prophet Nathan, David became a broken man, confessing his sin before God. (See Psalm 51.) God could then say of David: *"I have found David son of Jesse, a man after my own heart; he will do everything I want him to do"* (Acts 13:22b).

Paul

A proud man in his early days of persecuting Christians, Paul was confronted by God on the road to Damascus (Acts 9:1-19). Though he became a different person as he became a follower of Jesus Christ and an apostle to the Jews, he still was strong in personality, even as he was given great revelations from God. So, he was given a "thorn in the flesh" (2 Corinthians 12:7-10). Paul, himself, said this was, "*to keep me from becoming conceited…That is why, for Christ's sake, I delight in weaknesses, in insults, in hardships, in persecutions, in difficulties. For when I am weak, than I am strong.*"

Peter

An impetuous disciple of Jesus Christ, Peter once said to Jesus, "*Even if all fall away, I will not*" (Mark 14:29). Imagine, then, how he then felt after he later denied Jesus three times to those who accused him of being a follower of Jesus (Mark 14:66-72). A broken man, the restored Peter spoke from experience when he wrote: *Humble yourselves, therefore, under God's mighty hand, that he may lift you up in due tim.* (1 Peter 5:6).

Jesus

The ultimate example of humility and obedience to the Father is found in Jesus. This is best described in Philippians 2:5-8: *Your attitude should be the same as that of Christ Jesus: Who, being in very nature God, did not consider equality with God something to be grasped, but made himself nothing, taking the very nature of a servant, being made in human likeness. And being found in appearance as a man, he humbled himself, and became obedient to death…even death on a cross!* Jesus has, thus, dealt with the pride that is in each of us, when He died for us. We appropriate that fact when we look at Him in His suffering and claim that provision as ours.

SUMMARY

Pride is one of the great pitfalls of man. For, it not only keeps us from coming to God in the first place, it also keeps us from going to Him with our petitions, or thanksgiving for what He has done. Pride also keeps us from relating well to others, including our wives, children, bosses, friends, etc. Until we see God in His rightful place — a heavenly Father who not only is over all, but knows everything and has our best in mind — we'll think of ourselves more highly than we should. We are proud. If we don't humble ourselves, God will see to it that we are broken…and this is not easy. Therefore, we must heed the scriptures that command us to humble ourselves or we will to pay the consequences, as we have seen from Nebuchadnezzar and other Bible characters.

Consider This

Do you consider yourself proud? What makes you think you are …or are not?

_____

_____

How do you react to a proud person?

_____

_____

Can you describe a time when God humbled you?

_____

_____

Have you consciously prayed for God to help you become humble?

_____

_____

Have you ever seen the way of humility pay off in a relationship?

_____

_____

EXAMPLE

Many recognize the name Charles Colson. But not everyone realizes that he was President Nixon's "hatchet man" and was involved in the Watergate scandal of the early 1970's. At age 40, Colson was the confidante of the President of the United States. Today he admits that pride had been at the heart of his life as long as he could remember — from High School graduation when he was awarded a full scholarship to Harvard University, to becoming a Captain in the Marine Corps, to being chief assistant to his Senator from Massachusetts, to forming his own law practice, to becoming Special Counsel to the President. He excelled in everything he did, except keeping his first marriage together.

In the summer after the news of Watergate broke, Colson visited with an old friend on what proved to be an unforgettable night. He was curious in the change he saw in his friend — from a businessman of striving ambition to a family man glowing with peace and joy. Colson's friend told him of his conversion to Christ at a Billy Graham Crusade and of the inspiration he had received from reading C.S. Lewis' book, *Mere Christianity*. He read part of the chapter on pride to Colson, explaining how pride has been the chief cause of misery in every nation and every family since the world began. As his friend spoke, and then prayed for him, Charles Colson's life of pride flashed before him. He was reduced to tears when he returned to his car.

Later, sitting alone by the seashore in Maine, Colson finally told Jesus that he believed in Him, and that he wanted Him to come into his heart as he committed his life to Him. When he returned to Washington to face the Watergate trial, he was a new man. God allowed Colson to suffer the consequences of his actions. Colson was sentenced to prison, where God continued the breaking process of Charles Colson. Following his release from prison, Colson began going into prisons to minister and train Christian leaders. This was the beginning of Prison Fellowship, a ministry very active today in prisons all across the United States.

Lesson 15

JOHN THE BAPTIST AND SAMUEL

Does God Have a Plan for My Life?

Before I was born the Lord called me, from my birth he has made mention of my name.

Isaiah 49:1b

SETTING THE STAGE

Inherent in the belief that God created all persons is the belief that He has special plans for each individual. He has known us from our mother's womb (Psalm 139:15-16). In fact, He formed us there (Isaiah 44:2). He knows us by name (Isaiah 43:1). He has a "call" on the ministry or work He desires, as we can see from the lives of many men in the Bible. He wants us to be conformed to the likeness of His son (Romans 8:29a). He wants no one to perish, rather that everyone comes to repentance (2 Peter 3:9).

For those who have repented of sin and are seeking first the Kingdom of God, there are questions: Does God have a special plan for my life? Is there a special work He wants me to do? Is this predetermined before I was born? What is God's will in other areas of my life...my marriage, my leisure time, my future?

As we search Scripture for answers to these crucial questions, we'll use the examples of two men. Through the life of John the Baptist, we will see how God sometimes allows His plan to be known even before the person's birth. In Samuel, we'll see how man seems to have a part in bringing God's plan to pass.

It's difficult for our finite minds to comprehend a God who knows everything even before it takes place, yet allows us free choice, the opportunity to make our own plans. Even more unfathomable is that God can work everything together for good and according to His purpose, especially when we seem to have made wrong choices. But He can and does.

INTRODUCING JOHN THE BAPTIST

(Based on Luke 1:5-25, 41, 57-80; 3:1-20)

The circumstances of John's call, and the events that led up to his birth, are usually incorporated with the story of the birth and ministry of Jesus. This is as it should be; John was commissioned to prepare the way for Jesus, the Messiah (Luke 1:76-79) .

Zechariah and Elizabeth lived in the hill country of southern Judea. Luke 1:6 describes them as *upright in the sight of God, observing all the Lord's commandments and regulations blamelessly.* They were childless, and they were *well along in years.*

One day, when Zechariah was carrying out his priestly duties in the temple, he was visited by an angel of the Lord who told him that his wife would bear a son whom they were to name John. The angel then described the essence of John's calling: *He will be a joy and delight to you, and many will rejoice because of his birth, for he will be great in the sight of the Lord. He is never to take wine or other fermented drink, and he will be filled with the*

Holy Spirit even from birth. Many of the people of Israel will he bring back to the Lord their God. And he will go on before the Lord, in the spirit and power of Elijah, to turn the hearts of the fathers to their children and the disobedient to the wisdom of the righteous...to make ready a people prepared for the Lord (Luke 1:14-17).

Even in Elizabeth's womb, John responded to the voice of Mary, a relative of Elizabeth's. Mary had recently been told that she would give birth to a son who would be named Jesus, who would *be great and will be called the Son of the Most High. The Lord God will give him the throne of his father David, and he will reign over the house of Jacob forever; his kingdom will never end* (Luke 1:32-33).

At the time of John's birth, Zechariah not only announced that his son's name would be John, he also proclaimed the workings of God and the ministry of his son.

John grew up in the wilderness, separated from the world. He preached the message of repentance for the forgiveness of sins. He baptized many, including Jesus whom he recognized as the *Lamb of God, who takes away the sin of the world* (John 1:29b). Declaring that Jesus must increase while he decreased, John continued to preach and baptize in order to point people to Jesus, the Messiah. Because he accused King Herod of adultery, John was thrown into prison, and later, beheaded.

John's ministry fulfilled the prophecy given to his father before his birth. He helped turn the hearts of fathers to their children and the hearts of the disobedient to the wisdom of the righteous. Jesus confirmed that John was, indeed, the Elijah to come (Matthew 11:14).

INTRODUCING SAMUEL

(Based on 1 Samuel 1-2:11; 3)

The physical travail of Samuel's birth was preceded by the spiritual travail of his mother, Hannah. She, as the wife of Elkanah, was childless. Elkanah loved Hannah very much and provided well for her. But Elkanah's other wife had born him several children, and she often provoked Hannah because she was barren. This devastated Hannah.

In the process of crying out to the Lord for a child, Hannah received assurance from Eli, the priest, that God would answer her prayer. In due time, Samuel was born and Hannah fulfilled her vow to the Lord that if He would give her a son, she would *give him to the Lord for all the days of his life, and no razor will ever be used on his head* (1 Samuel 1:11b). She named this son Samuel, saying, *"Because I asked the Lord for him"* (1 Samuel 1:20b). After Samuel was weaned, Hannah gave him to Eli to train and be used in the service of the Lord.

One time, when Samuel and Eli were sleeping in the temple, Samuel heard the voice of the Lord, calling him into what would be the role of priest and prophet (and successor of Eli). First Samuel 3:19-21 tells us *the Lord was with Samuel as he grew up, and he let none of his words fall to the ground. And all Israel from Dan to Beersheba recognized that Samuel was attested as a prophet of the Lord. The Lord continued to appear at Shiloh, and there he revealed himself to Samuel through his word.* Though Hannah had not been foretold about Samuel's life, she had a strong desire for a child and had travailed in prayer for one. God not only heard Hannah's cry, He had a very special plan for the son He gave to her and Elkanah.

LESSONS FROM JOHN THE BAPTIST AND SAMUEL
Pre-Birth Commissions

John the Baptist was born as a result of God's plan, which He told to Zecharaiah and Elizabeth even before the child's birth. John fulfilled His call. Other men in scripture also had "pre-birth commissions."

Jacob and Esau (Genesis 25:21-23)

It appears that these twin boys were the answer to their father's prayer. However, God did tell their mother, before their birth, that they would represent two nations and that the elder would serve the younger.

Samson (Judges 13:2-24; 14: 16:28-30)

An angel appeared to his parents while his mother was still barren and told them that they would have a son set apart for God from birth. Although Samson's life was characterized by moral defeat, God used him, in the end, to defeat Israel's enemy.

Isaiah (Isaiah 49:1-6)

This man recognized that God had set a call upon his life even before he was born. He said that it was God who formed him in his mother's womb to be His servant. And he became one, as a prophet to Judah before its captivity.

Jeremiah (Jeremiah 1:5-10)

Jeremiah also recognized that God had a plan for him before he was born. He, too, says that God set him apart before he was born. God appointed Jeremiah a prophet to the nations.

Jesus (Matthew 1:18-25; Luke 1:26-45; 2:34)

Many prophecies were given before His birth. They foretold such details as where He would be born, what He would come to do, and how He would die. Every one of these prophecies were fulfilled.

The Foreknowledge of God

Read the following scriptures, and summarize what they say to you about the foreknowledge of God...since *the creation of the world*.

Matthew 25:34	Hebrews 4:13
John 17:24	1 Peter 1:20
Ephesians 1:4-5	Revelation 17:8b

Summary: _____

_____

_____

Man's Part in God's Plan

So far, we can conclude that because God is sovereign and knows everything from the creation of the world, He has a plan for every life and knows what choices man will make as well. However, there are scriptures, which support the fact that God delegates some responsibility to man to bring about His will.

After making man in His image, God said (in Genesis 1:28), *"Be fruitful and increase in number, fill the earth and subdue it. Rule over the fish of the sea and the birds of the air and over every living creature that moves on the ground."* He went on to say that all plants and trees would be for man's use, and He told Adam, after the fall, that he would eat his food by the sweat of his brow.

When God later called out a people for His name, He said, *"And now, O Israel, what does the Lord your God ask of you but to fear the Lord your God, to walk in all his ways, to love him, to serve the Lord your God with all your heart and with all your soul, and to observe the Lord's commands and decrees that I am giving you today for your own good"* (Deuteronomy 10:12).

After Jesus came and died for our sins, man, as a born-again Believer, was given another commission. This is found in Matthew 28:19: *"Therefore go and make disciples of all the nations, baptizing them in the name of the Father and of the son and of the Holy Spirit, and teaching them to obey everything I have commanded you."*

From the above scriptures, we can conclude that God's general plan consists of man doing his part:

> Working in partnership with God
>
> Keeping God's commands
>
> Proclaiming the gospel of Jesus Christ

Just as we have considered pre-birth commissions where God seemed to have revealed the plan He had for an individual before he was born, we also have examples of men who evidently also were to fulfill a special plan of God's, but whose birth and call did not come about without some involvement on the part of man. Samuel was one of these. Others include:

Moses (Exodus 2:1-10; 3:7-12)

This baby should never have been born if his parents wanted him to survive, for all boy babies were being killed. But, God evidently had a plan for Moses, though the Bible doesn't say that anyone knew what it was. It took Moses' mother, sister, brother, Pharoah's daughter, Moses' future father-in-law, and others, to be part of his life, so that, eventually, God would make His call known to Moses.

David

We do not hear of David until he was revealed to and anointed by Samuel to succeed Saul as King (1 Samuel 16:13). However, David knew that God had a plan for his life, for, in Psalm 139:16, he says, *"All the days ordained for me were written in your book before one of them came to be."* It took the workings and influence of many people in David's life before he came to sit upon the throne of Israel as God had, evidently, fore-ordained.

Paul (Acts 22:2-21; 26:1-23)

We have no record of God's plan for Paul's life ever being revealed to anyone before God confronted him, as a young man, on the way to Damascus. In fact, Paul's life would seem to indicate that he was against God and His will for man. Gamaliel, Stephen, the high priest Ananias, and others all had part in bringing Paul to the place where he could be used of God to fulfill the plan He evidently had for him.

So the question arises: What if you, not having been told God's plan for your life, make wrong choices and, thus, do things that might not fit in with what He wills for you?

Romans 8:28-29 is the revelation of God's truth that helps us benefit from being in His will — no matter what we do or what choices we make. *And we know that in all things God works for the good of those who love him, who have been called according to his purpose. For those God foreknew he also predestined to be conformed to the likeness of his Son.* There is a prior foreknowing on God's part, a calling we aren't always aware of. When we accept God's plan of salvation by faith, we're then able to trust Him for the rest of our lives. As we do this, He will not only guide our future, He will also redeem all we may have done in the past, to work things out for good according to His purpose. This "safety net" of God's ultimate goodness and purpose will catch us, if we surrender to His care and submit to His rule. For further insight, take the various phrases of the above verse, and elaborate on what they mean to you:

(The first phrase is done as an example.)

in all things <u>not in some things, or easy things, but even when I've made wrong choices</u>

God works for the good _____

of those who love him _____

who have been called _____

according to his purpose _____

God's Plan for Jesus

Even as a child of twelve, when He told His parents that He must be about His Father's business, Jesus knew the call on His life and the work He was to do. He also knew that this "business" would include His own death upon the cross. (See Matthew 16:21.) John 4:34 says that His food was *to do the will of him who sent me and to finish his work.* John 17:4 indicates that He even knew when that work was finished: *"I have brought you glory on earth by completing the work You gave me to do."* What is almost incomprehensible is that Jesus, as the Son of God from the foundation of the world, still had to hear from God. He told His disciples, in John 8:28b: *"I do nothing on my own but speak just what the Father has taught me."* Jesus knew what He had been called to do, sought the Father while doing it, and realized when His job was finished.

Discovering God's Plan for Our Lives

Many a man muddles through life not really sure why he is here or what he is to do. Life, for him, is one long frustration with a few sound-bytes of happiness thrown in. He doesn't know a loving God wants to guide hi, so that he can have both a fulfilling life here on earth, and eternity in heaven.

We who know and belong to God are precious to Him. This is true for His people, the Jews. Deuteronomy 7:6 tells us, *"The Lord your God has chosen you out of all the peoples on the face of the earth to be his people, his treasured possession."* As sons "grafted in," we Gentiles are reminded in Romans 8:16-17 that *the Spirit himself testifies with our spirit that we are God's children. Now if we are children, then we are heirs...heirs of God and co-heirs with Christ.* And John 15:16 reminds us: *"You did not choose me, but I chose you and appointed you to go and bear fruit."* According to these verses then, God wants to give us good gifts (Matthew 7:11). To do this, He will guide us so that we can know His plan for our lives. Part of this plan is that we share His sacrificial love with those who have not found the true meaning of life.

So, how do we go about discovering God's special plan for our lives?

Trust in God	*I will instruct you and teach you in the way you should go; I will counsel you and watch over you.* (Psalms 32:8)
Commit to God	*Commit thy way unto the Lord; trust also in him; and he shall bring it to pass.* (Psalm 37:5)
Acknowledge Him	*In all thy ways acknowledge him, and he will make your paths straight.* (Proverbs 3:6)
Seek His Kingdom	*But seek first his kingdom and his righteousness, and all these things will be given you as well.* (food, drink, clothing, etc.) (Matthew 6:33)
Keep Heart Right	*Today, if you hear his voice, do not harden your hearts.* (Hebrews 4:7)
Study God's Word	*Your word is a lamp to my feet and a light for my path.* (Psalm 119:105)
Pray	*Call to me and I will answer you and tell you great and unsearchable things you do not know.* (Jeremiah 33:3)
Listen to the Spirit	*But when he, the Spirit of truth, comes, he will guide you into all truth.* (John 16:13)
Receive Counsel	*For lack of guidance a nation falls, but many advisors make victory sure.* (Proverbs 11:14)
Assess Gifts	*We have different gifts, according to the grace given us.* (serving, teaching, encouraging etc.) (Romans 12:6-8)
Consider Circumstances	*Now this is what the Lord Almighty says: "Give careful thought to your ways."* (Haggai 1:5)

Genesis 24:27 (KJV) is a very interesting verse. As Abraham's servant is sent to find a bride for Isaac, he isn't given many specific directions on where to go. He had to take one step at a time, which paid off in the end. And so he says, *"I being in the way, the Lord led me to the house of my master's brethren."* As we seek God's will, by any of the various means listed above, we may receive guidance for only the next step. But, God is faithful. He will continue to guide our steps until He has us where He wants us.

What are some of the ways you have seen God's guidance in regard to:

Your work _____

Your marriage _____

Your family _____

Your leisure time _____

Your finances _____

Your role in the Body of Christ _____

Receiving guidance from the Lord is accepting, by faith, that we have heard from Him through prayer, His Word, others, etc. When this word is confirmed, we also step out in faith to do what we believe He has told us. However, until we are sure that the word is from the Lord, it may be best that we stay where we are…bloom where we are planted. This is the message of 1 Corinthians 7:17-24. Rather than stepping out in the flesh, put the burden on the Lord to get the message through to you. Look at where some Bible men were when God called them:

Moses was tending the flock of his father-in-law on the backside of the desert. (Exodus 3:1-10)
Gideon was threshing wheat by a winepress. (Judges 6:11-14)
King Saul was looking for his father's lost donkeys. (1 Samuel 9:2-17)
David was caring for sheep. (1 Samuel 16:1-13)
Peter and Andrew were fishing. (Matthew 4:18-20)
Matthew was collecting taxes. (Matthew 9:9)
Paul was persecuting Christians. (Acts 9:1-15)

SUMMARY

The more we realize the sovereignty of God, the more awed we should be by the way everything fits into His plan and is under His control. This is evident when we look at men in the Bible who were born in certain times for specific purposes. John the Baptist is a good example of one of these men. We also see that although God doesn't always foretell His plan for man, He still has one, and He allows man to participate in bringing it about. Samuel is an example of one of these men. Most awesome of all is the way God can work all things for good and according to His purpose, even when He allows man to make his own choices, good or bad.

God wants to show us His will in our work, our marriage, our families, etc. He wants us, as His children, to look to Him for guidance and wisdom. To do this, we can pray, study His Word, listen to the Holy Spirit, and assess the gifts He has given us. God not only wants us to trust Him, He wants to bless us.

Consider This

Do you believe you are fulfilling God's plan for your life? If so, how did you discover it?

_____

_____

If you are unsure of what God's will is for you…in any area…what can you do to begin to discover it?

_____

_____

What specific guidance have you received through prayer, Scripture, godly counsel, that has made a difference in your life?

_____

_____

EXAMPLE

As Dwight L. Moody closed the Sunday evening service in Farwell Hall, Chicago, on October 8, 1871, fire alarms sounded across the city to announce what became Chicago's worst fire in history: 250 dead, 150,000 homeless, 17,450 buildings destroyed, and $192 million in property damage. Gone were Moody's home, church, mission Sunday School, and Farwell Hall (the country's first YMCA). With a heavy heart, Moody tried to raise financial aid as he began to minister to the great need around him. He was depressed to think not only of rebuilding everything, but also of continuing the endless string of committee meetings, fund-raisers, conventions, and pastoral duties in his church of over 3,000 members. He so longed for a true sense of God's supernatural power and purpose. So he cried out to God to fill him with the Holy Spirit…to give him new direction and a new heart for Him.

In time, he found himself in New York City pacing the streets one miserable night. Suddenly, he felt overwhelmed by the presence of God. He hurried to the closest home of a friend and asked if he could have a room. There, alone with God, he felt his pride of achievement, his old ambition, and many works of the flesh swept away by a holy fire. When he left that room, he knew God had also filled him with the Holy Spirit! Now, at last, he had the water of life springing up inside him!

He went back to preaching, and hundreds were converted. But God had other plans as well. It wasn't long until Moody was traveling…first, to England as an evangelist. It is estimated that, before he died, he had traveled one million miles and preached to 100 million people (all before the days of air travel!). In addition to his remarkable work with Sunday Schools and the YMCA, he founded the Moody Bible Institute, which has since prepared thousands of men and women for evangelistic work around the world. As the fire had leveled much of Chicago, the fire of the Holy Spirit had reduced Moody's former achievements to an ash heap. But when he cried out to God for new direction, God gave Dwight L. Moody His power and His plan for the rest of his life.

Lesson 16
THE TWELVE DISCIPLES

How Do I Determine My Priorities?

But seek first his kingdom and his righteousness, and all these things will be given to you as well.

Mathew 6:33

SETTING THE STAGE

Dave must decide which is the most important thing to do on Saturday morning — work in the yard or go with his children to the town parade. Scott must decide whether to take an urgent work project home to complete or spend a long-anticipated evening with his wife. John must decide whether to go with a friend to a ball game or work on a much over-due project at the home of his elderly parents. Travis must decide whether to go on a mission trip with his youth group this summer or work to earn money for the rest of the school year. Jason must decide whether or not to continue dating Julie now that he's discovered she doesn't share his goals and ambitions. Juan must decide whether to send money to poor relatives in Mexico or keep what he has to support his own growing family. Chris must decide whether or not he and his family will continue in the same church now that the music has become so uncomfortably loud. Big decisions. Small decisions. We all make choices every day that reflect our priorities. But do our priorities line up with God's Word and His principles?

In this lesson, we'll look at the twelve disciples of Jesus Christ, and the choices they had to make. We know all of them chose to leave their former work and follow Him at great cost. But what about the choices they had to continue to make after that time? What were the consequences of their choices? Can their examples help us determine our priorities in life?

INTRODUCING THE TWELVE DISCIPLES

(Based on Matthew 10:2; Mark 3:16-19; Luke 6:13-14)

What would make twelve ordinary men leave their jobs and, perhaps, families, to follow Jesus as their Lord and Master? What would make them, men from all walks of life, bind together with one agenda, one purpose? What would make them be willing to give their lives for the One who died for them? What guided them to choose as they did?

We know, according to Luke 6:12-16, that Jesus spent the night in prayer before calling the twelve. So, God must have prepared their hearts. And it does seem that they chose quickly to respond. However, there were other instances following their initial commitment that also demanded choices. How did they determine their priorities then...and what were some of the consequences?

Peter and Andrew (Mark 1:14-18; Luke 5:1-11; John 1:35-42)

While walking beside the Sea of Galilee, Jesus called Peter and Andrew to leave their fishing nets and, *"Come, follow me."* Scripture says that they left their nets *at once* and followed Him (Mark 1:17-18). Andrew had probably been a follower of John the Baptist, who declared that Jesus was the Lamb of God (John 1:40-42). No doubt he had told Peter what John had said. So, having had their hearts prepared for the coming Messiah; seeing Jesus miraculously fill their empty nets with fish (Luke 5:5-7); and then having His promise that they would become *fishers of men* (Luke 5:10), they were ready to respond, making His call top priority.

At other times however, bold, impetuous Peter didn't respond as he should. When he denied Jesus three times (Matthew 26:69-75), he let fear of his own reputation take priority over his commitment to Jesus.

Andrew introduced his brother Peter to Jesus. It didn't seem to matter to Andrew that, with Peter's natural leadership ability, his own role would not be so significant. But Andrew remained faithful to the end. Both he and Peter died by crucifixion.

James and John (Mark 1:16-20)

John and his younger brother James were also well-to-do fishermen on the Sea of Galilee. They responded to Jesus' call soon after Peter and Andrew did. They were mending their nets on shore and immediately left their father (Zebedee) and followed their new Master. Jesus once called them Sons of Thunder (Mark 3:17), possibly because of their impetuous zeal. He curbed their spirit of retaliation (Luke 9:51-56) when they wanted to call fire down from heaven to destroy Samaritans who refused to welcome Jesus.

According to Acts 12:1-2, James, as a leader in the early church, was put to death by Herod. John lived to be an old man, was exiled on the isle of Patmos and there received the Revelation of Jesus Christ, which has become the last book of our Bible.

Philip and Nathanael (John 1:43-51; 6:5-6)

Though not brothers, these two disciples were called at about the same time. Philip was from the same town as Peter and Andrew. As soon as Jesus asked Philip to follow Him, Philip went to tell Nathanael about Christ. When the hungry multitude gathered at the Sea of Galilee, Jesus tested Philip by asking him how much food it would take to feed the crowd. Philip made a mental calculation, and concluded the project was impossible. It was Andrew who suggested the little boy's lunch, choosing to believe in the supernatural power of His Lord. The historian Eusebius says the Philip was a "great light in Asia" and was buried a martyr in Hierapolis.

Soon after Jesus had asked Philip to follow Him, Philip told Nathanael that he had found the one Moses and the prophets had written about. Jesus praised Nathanael's integrity on their initial encounter. Although we do not hear further of Nathanael, it's possible that he was also called Bartholomew, since Bartholomew is not a proper name, but a way of identifying a person as the son of Tolmai. (The Gospel of John, in 1:43-51, is the only Gospel to mention Nathanael's call. Matthew 10:2; Mark 3:16-19; and Luke 6:13-14 all list Bartholomew with Philip.) Legend has it that Bartholomew was martyred in Armenia.

Matthew (Matthew 9:9-12)

Jesus called a despised tax collector, Matthew (also known as Levi), as one of His disciples. After accepting Jesus' call, Matthew invited Him to dinner at his house…much to the disapproval of the Pharisees. Church historians say that Matthew was martyred in Ethiopia, where he had gone as a Christian missionary.

Thomas (Luke 24:36-49; John 20:24-29)

Also called Didymus, this disciple was the man about whom the phrase "Doubting Thomas" originated…because he could not believe Jesus had risen from the dead until he touched the wounds on His body. When Jesus allowed Thomas to put his hand to His side, Thomas cried out, *"My Lord and my God!"* (John 20:28). At first, Thomas chose to express his unbelief. But after realizing who Jesus really was, he chose to declare Him as Lord and God. According to tradition, Thomas later took the Gospel to Persia and India.

Judas Iscariot (Luke 6:16; John 13:18-30)

Judas is even identified as a traitor when he is listed in Luke 6 as one of Jesus' disciples. The fact is, his priority was thirty pieces of silver, not following Jesus. His subsequent remorse for betraying Jesus led to his suicide.

Simon, the Zealot (Luke 6:15; Acts 1:13)

The sect of Zealots is believed to have been organized by a fierce patriot known as Judas the Galilean who, when Judea was made a Roman province, publicly urged the people to resist Roman rule and refuse to pay taxes. It may well be that Simon the Zealot was one of the followers of Jesus who believed that Jesus might be a political deliverer who would overthrow the hated rule of Rome. One has to wonder what he thought about Jesus' teaching (Matthew 22:21) which says, *"Give to Caesar what is Caesar's."* The Coptic Church of Egypt affirms that Simon went to Egypt, Africa, and Britain, and died in Persia.

Judas Thaddeus also known as Jude (John 14:22-23)

Possibly the son of James, grandson of Zebedee, nephew of John. The only incident in Scripture concerning Jude in the ministry of Jesus occurs in John 14:22-23 when he asked Jesus how He would manifest Himself to the disciples and not to the world. Jesus said that he that keeps the commandments will be loved of the Father and the Father would come and make His home with him. Judas was martyred in Persia.

James, Son of Alphaeus (Mark 3:14-18)

Perhaps a cousin of Jesus and brother of Matthew, he was known as James "the less" or "younger" to differentiate between him and the other James. We know nothing more from scripture about him and there is confusion among historians as to what happened to him.

Jesus…Who Had All Priorities in Order

Everything Jesus did was submitted to doing His Father's will (John 6:38). Even as a young child, He knew He must be about His Father's business (Luke 2:49 KJV). He was baptized with His Father's approval (Matthew 3:17). He had victory over Satan during a time of temptation by choosing to quote God's Word back to Satan (Matthew 4:4, 7, 10-11). When He started preaching in the synagogues, Jesus read from Isaiah (Luke 4:18-19): *"The Spirit of the Lord is on me, because he has anointed me to preach good news to the poor. He has sent me to proclaim freedom for the prisoners and recovery of sight for the blind, to release the oppressed, to proclaim the year of the Lord's favor."* Everything Jesus did in His ministry was a fulfillment of this statement, and He knew when He had completed it (John 17:4b). Nothing kept Him from doing His work, even when people tried to kill him (Luke

4:28-29). Luke 9:51 records that Jesus resolutely set out for Jerusalem, knowing full well that he faced a cruel death upon a cross. The struggle between doing what the Father desired and His own "human" desire to avoid the cross, came to climax in the Garden of Gethsemene where He settled the issue by declaring, *My Father, if it is possible, may this cup be taken from me. Yet not as I will, but as you will*" (Matthew 26:39b). Jesus' top priority was to do His Father's will His whole life through.

LESSONS FROM THE TWELVE DISCIPLES

Godly Guidelines Which Can Help Determine Priorities

As the twelve disciples heard Jesus teach and watched Him minister to people during the three years they spent in close contact with Him, they learned what the Father wanted of them. As they committed themselves to Him, they sought to do His will despite their human frailties. They, like us, had to choose whether or not to submit to the Word of God. So, what are some of the scriptural principles that can be our plumblines, as we determine our priorities?

We cannot serve two masters.

No one can serve two masters. Either he will hate the one and love the other, or he will be devoted to the one and despise the other. You cannot serve God and Money. (Matthew 6:24)

Do not love the world or anything in the world. If anyone loves the world, the love of the Father is not in him…The world and its desires pass away, but the man who does the will of God lives forever. (1 John 2:15-17)

Joshua declared that he and his house would serve the Lord (Joshua 24:15b). Can you recall a time when you (and perhaps your family) chose to serve God instead of submitting to the enticement of the world?

We are to respond with love, not hate.

Greater love has no one than this, that he lay down his life for his friends. (John 15:13)

Do not repay evil with evil or insult with insult, but with blessing, because to this you were called so that you may inherit a blessing. (1 Peter 3:9)

In the Sermon on the Mount, we are told to love our enemies and pray for those who persecute us (Matthew 5:44). Is your priority to bless (or love) someone who has hurt you, or to pay them back?

We should consider eternity, not just time.

Now listen, you who say, "Today or tomorrow we will go to this or that city, spend a year there, carry on business and make money." Why, you do not even know what will happen tomorrow. What is your life? You are a mist that appears for a little while and then vanishes. Instead, you ought to say, "If it is the Lord's will, we will live and do this or that." (James 4:13-15)

Do not store up for yourselves treasures on earth, where moth and rust destroy, and where thieves break in and steal. But store up for yourselves treasures in heaven, where moth and rust do not destroy and where thieves do not break in and steal. (Matthew 6:19-20)

Solomon reminds us in Ecclesiastes 2:17-25 that life without God is meaningless. Can you recall a time when you chose to do something that would be more lasting in God's eyes than something that would satisfy you for the moment?

We reap what we sow.

Do not be deceived; God cannot be mocked. A man reaps what he sows. The one who sows to please his sinful nature, from that nature will reap destruction; the one who sows to please the Spirit, from the Spirit will reap eternal life. (Galatians 6:7-8)

Endure hardship with us like a good soldier of Christ Jesus. No one serving as a soldier gets involved in civilian affairs...he wants to please his commanding officer. Similarly, if anyone competes as an athlete, he does not receive the victor's crown unless he competes according to the rules. (2 Timothy 2:3-5)

Have your priorities ever caused you to reap the consequences for actions you should not have taken?

We must understand our triune nature.

May God himself, the God of peace, sanctify you through and through. May your whole spirit, soul and body be kept blameless at the coming of our Lord Jesus Christ. (1 Thessalonians 5:23)

For physical training is of some value, but godliness has value for all things, holding the promise for both the present life and the life to come. (1 Timothy 4:8)

The mind (part of the soul) of sinful man is death, but the mind controlled by the Spirit is life and peace; the sinful mind is hostile to God. It does not submit to God's law, nor can it do so. Those controlled by the sinful nature cannot please God. (Romans 8:6-8)

Because you are sons, God sent the Spirit of his Son into our hearts, the Spirit who calls out, "Abba, Father." So you are not longer a slave, but a son; and since you are a son, God has made you also an heir." (Galatians 4:6-7)

Because man is body, soul, and spirit, we can act and react physically, emotionally, and spiritually.

Can you recall a time when your decision made a difference because you saw your body as a *temple of the Holy Spirit* (1 Corinthians 6:19)? Can you recall a time when you *put off your old self...to be made new in the attitude of your mind* (Ephesians 4:22b-23)? Can you recall a time when you were *led of the Spirit* (Galatians 5:18)?

What difference does it make when we choose according to our body...our mind...or by the Spirit?

We must know the difference between works of the flesh and living by the Spirit.

So I say, live by the Spirit, and you will not gratify the desires of the sinful nature. For the sinful nature desires what is contrary to the Spirit, and the Spirit what is contrary to the sinful nature" (Galatians 5:16-17).

Since we live by the Spirit, let us keep in step with the Spirit. (Galatians 5:25)

Galatians 5:19-21 describes the works of the flesh. Galatians 5:22-23 describes the fruit of the Spirit. Can you recall a time when you chose to act or react according to the flesh instead of the Spirit? What difference did it make?

We must be focused or we will be doubleminded

But when he asks, he must believe and not doubt, because he who doubts is like a wave of the sea, blown and tossed by the wind. That man should not think he will receive anything from the Lord; he is a double-minded man, unstable in all he does. (James 1:6-7)

Love the Lord your God with all your heart and with all your soul and with all your mind. (Matthew 22:37)

When Paul wrote to the Philippians *"but one thing I do,"* he was stating his focus: that, he was forgetting what was behind in order to press on toward the goal to which God had called him (Philippians 3:13). Are you focused on long-term goals, or are you easily persuaded to change priorities because of momentary circumstances?

We must decide whether we want rewards or punishment.

Without faith it is impossible to please God, because anyone who comes to him must believe that he exists and that he rewards those who earnestly seek him. (Hebrews 11:6)

So then each of us will give account of himself to God. (Romans 14:12)

But the cowardly, the unbelieving, the vile, the murderers, the sexually immoral, those who practice magic arts, the idolaters and all liars... their place will be in the fiery lake of burning sulfur. This is the second death. (Revelation 21:8)

Does the fact that God has a place prepared for both the righteous and the wicked affect the choices you make as priorities?

SUMMARY

We make many choices every day. We simply can't do everything. So we need some guidelines, some over-all principles which help us determine what gets our primary attention. If we have made a commitment to follow the Lord Jesus Christ, we'll want to submit to His Word. As we do, we'll find that there are Biblical principles which will help us make choices pleasing to God.

The twelve disciples made a major decision when they left their past and followed Jesus. With that decision, however, came other choices concerning how they would respond to new circumstances and new teachings. For the disciples, and for us, the top priority should be total commitment God, the Lord Jesus Christ, the Holy Spirit, and the Word of God...all of which agree. When that allegiance is in place, all other priorities will be more easily determined.

Consider This

Have you made following God and His Word your top priority? If so, how has this affected your life since you made that decision?

_____

_____

How do you presently determine your priorities?

_____

_____

After your allegiance to God, in what order do you place your wife, your children, your job, leisure time activities, projects, the Church?

_____

_____

Which describes you? (a) I take on so many things that nothing gets done well. In fact, some things never do get done. (b) I say "no" to some things I am asked to do because I don't have time…then I feel guilty. (c) I have a hard time staying focused. I am easily persuaded to change my mind, even after I have made a decision about what is top priority.

EXAMPLE

Tom Landry had two careers in football. But what happened between them completely changed his attitude about his work, his money and his possessions — and thus changed his priorities.

Born in 1924, Landry grew up in Mission, Texas. The small-town environment, his family, and his church influenced the basic values he learned as a boy. But it was sports that shaped and reinforced those values. Long before he was in any kind of organized sports, he practiced his leadership skills drafting friends and calling the plays in hundreds of football games. When he began playing organized sports, each step up the ladder was exciting…High School championships, University of Texas bowl games, professional football, assistant coach, world championship, acclaim as an NFL coach. Yet, each time he reached the next level of achievement, he asked himself, "What now? Is this all there is?" At age thirty-three he had done everything he wanted to do in football. His "first" career, with football first and God second, came to an end. Because there was no next level, he found himself at a spiritual crossroads, without purpose in life. He tried some business ventures, using the degree in industrial engineering he had earned in 1952. But, because he had given so much time to footfall in the intervening years, he wasn't ready to provide an adequate living for the family through business. During this time, a friend invited him to a men's prayer breakfast which met every Wednesday morning in one of the downtown hotels. At first, he refused. He had gone to church all his life, but studying the Bible had never interested him. When he finally did go, it proved to be the turning point in his life. At this gathering, the scriptures they were studying suddenly came alive to him. In Matthew 6:25-34, he saw that he was to seek God's kingdom first, then things would be added. A spectator to Christianity all his life, he now wanted to become a participant.

Growing into his born-again experience over a period of several months in 1959, Landry found a sense of direction. Before long, he was named head coach of the Dallas Rangers (Cowboys). He began this job by appointing several Christian players to lead voluntary chapel programs and by inviting guest speakers to open Sunday games with short church services. He encouraged weekly husband/wife Bible studies. Tom Landry the coach, who put his faith in God for direction, was a very different man than the Tom Landry who had earlier climbed the ladder of success playing football. His life took on new meaning as his priorities changed with new scriptural guidelines. God became first, and football became a means by which he could serve the Lord.

Lesson 17
PETER

Can I Be Healed of Past Failures and Wounds?

And the God of all grace, who called you to his eternal glory in Christ, after you have suffered a little while, will himself restore you and make you strong, firm and steadfast.

1 Peter 5:10

SETTING THE STAGE

We all like to be complimented and recognized for doing a good job. We want to be successful and come to the end of our lives knowing that we *have fought the good fight... finished the race... kept the faith* (II Timothy 4:7). We want to hear Jesus say, *"Well done, good and faithful servant"* (Matthew 25:21a).

But what if we've stumbled and fallen along life's road? What if we've failed to do what we know is right, or have made foolish mistakes? What if we've experienced such hurts and wounds from others that we find it difficult to function as we should? Is there healing and forgiveness and restoration? Is our God a God of second chances...maybe even of third and fourth?

We've all failed to measure up to the standards set by God. We haven't lived holy lives of sexual purity, we haven't always related as good fathers to our children, we haven't been the husbands our wives deserve, we haven't attained the goals we set for ourselves, nor have we responded to failures of others as we should. Sermons, motivational talks and books inspire us to deeper commitment or give us a list of more things to do. So even trying to live the Christian life can make us feel guilty, because we know we've failed in the past and, therefore, may feel hopeless about changing in the future.

The Bible is full of stories of men who failed in one way or another. But it's also a book about restoration...of these men, of the nation Israel, and ourselves. God has not only set high standards, He has also provided a way for these standards to be met. That's what the Gospel is all about. Jesus came not only to save us for the future, He came to heal us of our past and to be the means of that healing.

In this lesson, we'll look at Peter...his failures, his wounds, his restoration. Perhaps in the process, we can not only see God's grace at work, but we can also have the faith to be healed of past failures and wounds.

INTRODUCING PETER
(Based on Matthew 4:18-22 and all scriptures listed below.)

The Gospel story tells us more about Peter, also called Simon, than any other disciple. He appears to be the leader and spokesman of the twelve. The first half of the book of Acts tell of his ministry as an apostle. As Peter and his brother Andrew were fishing on the Sea of Galilee, Jesus called them to follow Him and become fishers of men.

Some of the events in Peter's life as a disciple include:

- accompanying Jesus to Jairus' house, where a girl was raised from the dead (Mark 5:35-42)
- walking on the water during a night at sea (Matthew 14:22-32)
- confessing that Jesus is the Son of the Living God (Matthew 16:13-20)
- witnessing the transfiguration of Jesus upon a mountain (Mark 9:2-12)
- being told by Jesus, following the "Last Supper," that he would deny Him (Mark 14:12-31)
- falling asleep in the Garden of Gethsemene while Jesus prayed (Mark 14:32-42)
- disowning Jesus three times (Mark 14:66-72)
- absenting himself from the crucifixion of Jesus (Matthew 26:56b)
- being one of the first to enter the empty tomb following Jesus' resurrection (John 20:1-7)
- seeing Jesus several times in His glorified body following His resurrection (John 20:19-21:14)
- eating breakfast on the beach with Jesus following a miraculous catch of fish (John 21:1-14)
- experiencing restoration by Jesus Himself (John 21:15-21)

Briefly, some events in his ministry as an apostle (following Pentecost) include:

- preaching a sermon as 3,000 souls were saved (Acts 2:14-41)
- healing a crippled man in the name of Jesus and power of the Holy Spirit (Acts 3:1-10)
- appearing before authorities to declare that he would obey God before man (Acts 4:8-20)
- confronting Ananias about lying to God (Acts 5:1-11)
- ministering with Phillip and John in Samaria (Acts 8:9-25)
- raising Dorcas from the dead in Joppa (Acts 9:36-43)
- praying for Cornelius and family as the first Gentile converts (Acts 10:30-48)
- experiencing miraculous deliverance from prison as the church prayed for him (Acts 12:6-19)
- debating at the Council in Jerusalem that Gentiles did not have to be circumcised to be saved (Acts 15:5-21)
- traveling to other parts of Asia Minor to establish and organize churches (1 Corinthians 1:10-12; 1 Peter 1:1-2)
- writing two epistles, 1 & II Peter (and perhaps also being the inspiration for Mark's gospel)

Historians believe that Peter went to Italy where he converted Romans to Christianity. Eusebius says that he was among those put to death during Nero's persecution of Christians. Peter himself asked to be crucified upside down because he didn't want to replicate the death of his Lord and Savior, Jesus Christ…the One for whom he was willing to give his life.

LESSONS FROM PETER

The Anatomy of Failure

Why do we fail to do what we should? Paul writes in Romans 7:18b-19, *"I have the desire to do what is good, but I cannot carry it out. For what I do is not the good I want to do; no, the evil I do not want to do…this I keep on doing.* He goes on to describe how he constantly has a struggle within between the delight he has in God's law and the evil that is right there with him.

Even after becoming Christians, this is the battle we all experience between our sinful nature and Christ living in us. The non-believer, who lives by the flesh, has even more opportunity for failure and being wounded, because he doesn't have God's Word cleansing him, Christ living in him, or the Holy Spirit empowering him.

We have several examples of Peter's failures while he was a disciple of Jesus Christ. Some of them are listed below. Read the scriptures describing each instance, then write what you think made Peter respond as he did:

Sinking into the water (Matthew 14:28-31) _____

Cutting off Malchus' ear (John 18:10-11) _____

Boasting of himself (Matthew 26:33) _____

Disowning Jesus (Matthew 26:58, 69-74) _____

Sleeping in the Garden (Matthew 26:40) _____

Deserting Jesus (Matthew 26:56b) _____

Think of a time recently when you failed to act or react as you should. What made you respond as you did? _____

_____

Bridges of Restoration

Some bridges, if crossed, enable us to move from failure to restoration. This is evident in the life of Peter.

True repentance

Peter was truly sorry for what he had done following his disowning of Jesus. Matthew 26:75b says *he went outside and wept bitterly.* Godly sorrow is not the same as remorse. First Corinthians 7:10 tells us *Godly sorrow brings repentance that leads to salvation and leaves no regret, but worldly sorrow* (remorse) *brings death.*

Death to self

Peter had to die to himself, his ability, and his sinful nature. Not only are we told, in Romans 6:11 to *"count yourselves dead to sin but alive to God in Christ Jesus,"* but we are to see ourselves as Paul: *"crucified with Christ and I no longer live, but Christ lives in me."* (Galatians 2:20)

Seeing Jesus for who He is

On Easter dawn, the women who had gone early to the tomb and found it empty, were told by angel to *go, tell his disciples and Peter* (Mark 16:7). God was making sure that Peter saw that Jesus had risen as He said He would. It would be a new day with new hope for Peter.

Returning to where we first met Jesus

Peter had been fishing at the Sea of Galilee when Jesus first summoned him to follow Him. It was there, on the Sea of Galilee, that Jesus manifested His miracle-working power to Peter and the disciples following His resurrection. (John 21:1-14)

Forgiveness

Though there is no specific mention, in Scripture, of Peter asking Jesus for forgiveness, Jesus did bestow upon Peter and the other disciples His peace, and the Holy Spirit, as He told them about the need for forgiveness (John 20:19-23). Jesus went on to talk also about the need to believe…which all of them did, except Thomas who needed more proof (John 20:19-29). Jesus did confront Peter about his love for Him (John 21:15-19). Three times He asked Peter if he loved Him, and three times Peter responded that he did. (Some say that Jesus asked three times to counter the three times Peter denied Him.)

Learning from mistakes

Restoration is complete when we evidence that we have truly learned from our mistakes or failures. After Jesus confronted Peter with the questions about his love for Him, He told Peter some of his future…that he would go where he would not want to go. Then He said to Peter, *"Follow me"* (John 21:19b). For one who had already responded to Jesus' call to follow Him, this was a new invitation, a new chance, a new beginning. And from the acts which followed, we know that Peter did follow Jesus anew. (See also 1 Peter 1:6-7; 4:12-13a; 5:10.)

Other Bible Men Who Failed and Were Restored

The Man	His Failure	How Restored
David (II Samuel 12:1-13)	Committed adultery and murder	Repented and was given another son
Moses (Exodus 2:11-15; 3:1-10)	Tried to save Hebrews in his own strength	Accepted God's call after 40 yrs. in the desert
Jonah (Book of Jonah)	Rejected God's command to preach to Nineveh	Obeyed God after 3 days in fish's belly
Elijah (1 Kings 19:1-12)	Ran away when intimidated by Jezebel	Listened to God's still small voice
All disciples (Matthew 26:56b; John 20:21-23)	Allowed fear and unbelief	Forgiven and filled with Holy Spirit
The prodigal son (Luke 15:11-24)	Lived a godless life	Repented and returned to father

Judas — Some say Judas was predestined to betray Jesus to carry out God's plan (Matthew 26:23, 25; Psalm 109:8). Others say Judas chose to be remorseful instead of repentant for betraying Jesus and suffered the consequences of sin. (Matthew 27:3-5; II Peter 2:20-21) Whichever is true, the result was the same…Judas committed suicide.

From God's standpoint, He is always willing to forgive. John 10:28 says, *"I give them eternal life, and they shall never perish; no one can snatch them out of my hand."* But because man has free will, there seems to be a point when forgiveness is no longer possible.

Hebrew 10:26-27 says *if we deliberately keep on sinning after we have received the knowledge of the truth, no sacrifice for sins is left, but only a fearful expectation of judgment and of raging fire that will consume the enemies of God.* Restoration demands true repentance and sincere desire for the Lord to bring it about. (See Proverbs 29:1.)

Restoration of Those Who Have Been Wounded

So far, we have looked primarily at the failures and wounds that result because of what we have, or have not, done. Now let's look at how we fail because of our reaction to the failures and wounds inflicted upon us by others. Is restoration possible for these as well?

When a person is wounded, his wound gets all of his attention. He becomes blind to other's needs and feelings, even to truth itself. A wounded person is often angry, untrusting of others, super-sensitive, and vulnerable to more wounds.

Perhaps Peter failed at times because of having been offended. As a bold man himself, he might have been disappointed because Jesus seemingly failed the disciples by not being the Messiah they had in mind...One who would stand up for Himself, bring down His enemies, and not allow Himself to be crucified. Failure to have our expectations met often leads to us being wounded.

We all are wounded or offended at some time or another. But many men are afflicted with severe wounds that have festered since childhood. These may come from such things as the divorce of parents, being abandoned by a mother or father, being sexually and/or physically abused, living with drugs and/or alcohol addiction, or attending schools where violence has been perpetrated. Because these past wounds have not healed, these men continue to live dysfunctional lives. As Proverbs 18:14b puts it: *A crushed spirit who can bear?*

Sin begets sin. Our response to the sin of others becomes our sin. Much of this cycle begins in childhood, and unless it's broken, Exodus 34:6-7 comes true: *The LORD, the LORD, the compassionate and gracious God, slow to anger, abounding in love and faithfulness, maintaining love to thousands, and forgiving wickedness, rebellion and sin. Yet he does not leave the guilty unpunished; he punishes the children and their children for the sin of the fathers to the third and fourth generation.*

Our sins do affect our children. King David is one example of this. His sexual sin also resulted in lying and murder. Those sins, though forgiven him, continued in the lives of his sons. But it wasn't God's intent that the children use this as an excuse for their sinning. Ezekiel 18:2 quotes a proverb: *The fathers eat sour grapes, and the children's teeth are set on edge.* Verses 3 and 4 disclaim this: *As surely as I live, declares the Sovereign Lord, you will no longer quote this proverb in Israel. For every living soul belongs to me, the father as well as the son...both alike belong to me. The soul who sins is the one who will die.* God will judge us according to our own sins, no matter who or what caused us to sin. And, we sin when we do not forgive or when we react the wrong way after having been wounded by others.

All sin, and much wounding, begins in childhood, when we are most vulnerable. Jesus realized this. He said, in Matthew 18:6: *"But if anyone causes one of these little ones who believe in me to sin, it would be better for him to have a large millstone hung around his neck and to be drowned in the depths of the sea."* God has great consequences in store for those who cause children to sin. (See verses 7-9.)

Since each person is responsible for his or her own sin, those who have been sinned against are also responsible for how they react (to their wounds and being offended). To consider the healing process of emotional wounds, we should think about the way physical wounds heal. First we must recognize that we even have a wound and what caused it, so we know what kind of medication it may need. Then, the wound must be cleansed, so that it won't become infected. After the proper medicine is applied, it often takes quite a while for the wound to heal from the inside out. All we see is a scab on top as we wait for the complete healing to take place. Finally, the day comes when the scab drops off and the outer layer of skin heals. When the process is complete, we may have a scar to remind us of that wound, but we have no more infection or pain. So, how are emotional wounds — even offenses from childhood — healed?

Recognize that you have a wound that needs healing.

Perhaps you need to look at the situation through the eyes of the one who offended you and determine why it happened. What sin of this person is being passed on to you?

Examine your own response.

Look at the hate, guilt, unforgiveness, blame, shame or other feelings which you harbor from this wound (even the guilt you may have accepted, such as the blame for your parents' divorce). Recognize the fact that your reaction to an offense may also be a sin.

See that the wound is cleansed.

Repent of your sin and ask God to forgive you. Forgiveness is a major ingredient in healing. In fact, healing actually cannot begin until forgiveness takes place. Jeremiah 8:21 speaks of God being crushed when His people are crushed and mentions a balm often used in healing. (Or as the song goes: "There is a balm in Gilead that makes the wounded whole…and heals the sin-sick soul.") Because of the blood Jesus shed for us, we can claim the reality of 1 John 1:9: *If we confess our sins, he is faithful and just and will forgive us our sins and purify us form all unrighteousness.*

Watch to see that infection (bitterness) does not take root.

Just as in the healing of a physical wound, complete restoration may take place over a long period of time. Thus, it's easy to think no healing is taking place, and to rehearse the hurt over and over until bitterness (the infection) takes root. Hebrews 12:15 tells us to *see to it that no one misses the grace of God and that no bitter root grows up to cause trouble and defile many.* For not only does the wounded one continue to hurt, many others (spouses, children, family, friends, co-workers) suffer as well. After asking forgiveness from God and those who perpetrated your wounds (if possible and if wise), make it a daily habit to confess the truth of God's Word instead of reviewing your hurts. This replaces infection with healing. Some good scriptures for this include:

I am a child of God (John 1:12) and He will complete a good work in me. (Philippians 1:6)

I am part of the true vine, a channel of Christ's life. (John 15:1, 5)

God can work all things for my good. (Romans 8:28)

I am a new creation in Christ…the old has passed away. (II Corinthians 5:17)

Check out the wound with a physician.

If a physical wound is deep, or long-lasting, we sometimes need an expert to ensure that proper healing is taking place. The same is true with emotional wounds. If we have long-term, deep hurts, we may need counsel by someone qualified to help us, such as a pastor, counselor, or support group. Just the act of being accountable to someone else often hastens the healing process. (See James 5:16.)

As we are healed, God may use our past — those wounds and offenses — to give us understanding in ministering to others. Just as an ex-drug addict can help present drug addicts; an ex-homosexual can minister to those still in this bondage; an ex-alcoholic can empathize with a present alcoholic; so a person whose emotional wound has been healed can often better help someone else who now needs healing from past offenses. As Jesus told Peter, after telling him that He had prayed that his faith would not fail (when being "sifted" by Satan): *When you have turned back, strengthen your brothers* (Luke 22:32b).

God's restoration often includes a ministry for the person who has been healed. And, in helping others, that person is strengthened himself.

SUMMARY

Every person has failed and made mistakes, and has been been wounded or offended — in different ways and in varying degrees. In lookng through the Old Testament, it's difficult to find an example of anyone who was fully restored. Sins were forgiven through the sacrifices offered. But it was not a time of God's grace. However, once Jesus paid the ultimate sacrifice for our sins, He gave us immediate access to God's throne room, where Jesus Himself is ever interceding for us. Our responsibility is to repent of sin and confess it to Him; the promise is that He will not only forgive us, but will also cleanse us from all sin. We can be new creatures in Him. To maintain the healing, we must forgive ourselves, as well as those who have offended us. Peter is an example of a man who was not only fully restored, but was also used mightily by God to minister truth and healing to others.

Consider This

Do you still feel the guilt of past failures or mistakes that you have made? Or have you experienced both God's forgiveness and the forgiveness of others involved?

_____

_____

What does it take to bring you to repentance?

_____

_____

What wounds or offenses do you still live with from your past?

_____

_____

How can you get free and be healed?

_____

_____

EXAMPLE

Stephen Arterburn knows first hand that God is a God of grace and second chances. He found out the hard way. Though raised in a Christian home, he decided to follow the gods offered by the world — power, pleasure, and possessions. He had to hit the bottom before he could admit that he was ignoring God and trying to control his own destiny.

Though he dreamed of becoming a great musician, he climbed to the top of the ladder in the business world. Through hard work and good breaks, by age thirty-two he became the chairman of a quarter-billion dollar company. Yet, the power he had obtained only brought a feeling of emptiness, not fulfillment.

In following the path of pleasure, he was enticed by anything that fed his empty ego. He liked to make people laugh and be the center of attention, the life of the party. He also became promiscuous and ended up getting a girl pregnant. Not wanting to give up his dreams, he pressured the girl into getting an abortion, a decision that later cost him much pain spiritually, emotionally, and physically.

His desire to acquire possessions caused him to go deeply in debt. He discovered that the cycle of materialism always ends in some form of addiction. What he thought would free him, only enslaved him. When a fire nearly destroyed his home, he was faced with his true priorities.

The turning point in his life came when, after attending a Christian seminar, he truly repented of his sins and determined to seek forgiveness from those he had offended. His whole life changed as he became hungry for God's Word and accountable to other Christians. He still had struggles and strayed from the narrow path at times, but the healing restoration had begun with his acceptance of God's grace.

Today he's happily married and is blessed with a little girl whom the Lord provided through adoption … from an unwed couple who chose not to have an abortion. He is founder of New Life Clinics, which has more than one hundred counseling centers. He has written over twenty books. Most recently, his organization birthed the "Women of Faith" conferences which more than 300,000 women across the United States attended in 1997. Stephen has come to believe that the point of greatest sorrow can become the point of greatest joy, through God's grace and His process of restoration. He is, indeed, the God of second chances.

Lesson 18
STEPHEN AND TIMOTHY

What Is My Function In the Body of Christ?

We will in all things grow up into him who is the Head, that is, Christ. From him the whole body, joined and held together by every supporting ligament, grows and builds itself up in love, as each part does its work.

Ephesians 4:15-16

SETTING THE STAGE

It's awesome, thrilling, supernatural… that we can become children of God through our belief in the atoning work of the blood of His Son, Jesus Christ! John 1:12-13 puts it this way: *To all who received him (*Jesus*), to those who believed in his name, he gave the right to become children of God…children born not of natural descent, nor of human decision or a husband's will, but born of God.* What is just as awesome, thrilling, and supernatural is that, as we are born again to become God's children, we become the Body of His Son, the Lord Jesus Christ! Ephesians 5:23, 30, 32 says it this way: *For the husband is the head of the wife, as Christ is the head of the church, his body, of which he is the Savior…for we are members of his body….This is a profound mystery—but I am talking about Christ and the church.*

Therefore, as true Believers in Jesus Christ, we are part of His Body, whether we want to be or not. And, as part of His Body, we must learn to function together, whether we want to or not! Jesus is coming again for His *radiant church (Bride), without stain or wrinkle or any other blemish, but holy and blameless* (Ephesians 5:27b). We know the need for the various organs/members of our human body to function together. We would think a Bride a mess if her fingers didn't coordinate their function with her hand, or if her tongue wanted to act independently of her mouth.

Jesus prayed, in John 17:21a, that *"all of them may be one, Father, just as you are in me and I am in you."* Thus, to perform as a healthy body…the Body of Jesus Christ…each individual Christian must carry out his particular function. The Father, Son and Holy Spirit each have a role as well.

As we look at Stephen and Timothy, we'll see that the church needs members with different talents and abilities in order to function. We'll also see the importance of each member being submitted to the Head, Jesus Christ. We'll consider what our own function is in the Body of Jesus Christ…that we not only carry out the great commission of Matthew 28:19-20 effectively, but that *when he appears we may be confident and unashamed before him at his coming* (1 John 2:28b).

INTRODUCING STEPHEN

(Based on Acts 6-8:1-3)

Little is known about Stephen's early life. Some believe he may have been among the 3,000 converts who responded to Peter's sermon on the day of Pentecost. Whatever his background, he was recognized in the early church as being full of the Spirit and wisdom, and was selected to be a leader. The apostles had their hands full ministering to all the infant Believers, as well as caring for a multitude of needs…including those of the widows. When complaints were raised, seven men were chosen to carry out the practical matters of the church so the apostles could give their attention to prayer and ministry of the Word.

Stephen was one of these seven deacons. He not only fulfilled his duty well, He was full of God's grace and power, while evidencing great wonders and miraculous power. Certain members of the Synagogue of the Freedmen didn't like this, so they brought false witnesses against him. This set off a riot and Stephen was prosecuted as a criminal.

In his defense before the Sanhedrin, Stephen gave a moving summary of God at work among His people. He insisted that the institution of Jewish life, the law and the temple, were temporary…that God intended them to point beyond to the coming of the Messiah, the One who would fulfill all righteousness for all people. He then called his accusers stiff-necked people, whose fathers had betrayed and murdered the Righteous One who had indeed come. While they gnashed their teeth, Stephen looked up to heaven and saw the glory of God with Jesus standing at His right hand. Enraged, the men dragged him out of the city and stoned him. Falling on his knees, he asked God not to hold this against them! Scripture mentions that as he died, Saul…later to become the Apostle Paul…was there, giving approval to his death.

INTRODUCING TIMOTHY

(Based on Acts 16:1-3; 17:14-15; 18:5; 19:22; 20:4-6; Romans 16:21; 1 Corinthians 4:16-17; 16:10-11; 2 Corinthians 1:1, 19; Philippians 1:1; 2:19-23; Colossians 1:1; 1 Thessalonians 1:1; 3:6; 2 Thessalonians 1:1, 1 & 2 Timothy)

Judging from the large number of scriptures about him, Timothy played a major role in the expanding early church. He was a young man from Lystra, son of Eunice, a Jewess. His grandmother, Lois, was a Believer. His father, a Greek, was probably dead when Paul first visited the home (Acts 16:1). We can surmise some things about Timothy by reading between the lines as he relates to Paul. It's possible that Paul visited Eunice and Lois while visiting Lystra, a town not far from Paul's birthplace of Tarsus. In fact, some say Paul may have recovered from his stoning at Lystra in Timothy's home (2 Timothy 3:10-11). At least he knew that Timothy's mother and grandmother had taught him well (2 Timothy 1:5; 3:15).

As to his function in the early church, we find that Timothy was an ordained minister of the Gospel (1 Timothy 4:14; 2 Timothy 1:6-7). Conscious of Timothy's unique gifts, especially evangelism (Romans 16:21; 2 Timothy 4:5), Paul chose him as a companion and fellow-worker. In fact, Paul had no other companion so like-minded who enjoyed his constant instruction (2 Timothy 2:3; 3:14) . The two epistles Paul addressed to his "son" Timothy are rich in pastoral counsel.

Timothy was charged with difficult tasks. He was given the delicate mission of restoring a backsliding church. He was also a co-sufferer with Paul in the afflictions of the Gospel (2 Timothy 1:8). Tradition says Timothy died as a martyr for his faithfulness as a bishop in the reign of Domitian. While attempting to stop an indecent heathen procession during the Festival of Diana, this God-fearing minister sealed his testimony with his own blood.

LESSONS FROM STEPHEN AND TIMOTHY

What is the Church, the Body of Christ?

The Greek word *ekklesia* means "the church," the "called out ones," and is used to describe a public assembly of citizens in a city. For the Christians, this was a community of Believers who had been called out of an old life and were now a part of a new kingdom with Jesus as the head. This community was characterized by what the Greek called *koinonia*, "fellowship." In Antioch, Believers were first called Christians, "little anointed ones" — a term that was intended to ridicule them as it identified them as followers of Christ. Various analogies in Scripture describe the church:

A human body	1 Corinthians 12:12-31; Ephesians 4:15-16
A building	1 Peter 2:4-8
A community	Acts 4:32-35
Bride of Christ	Ephesians 5:22-32

We describe the church in various ways:

A building, or place for religious ceremony

An organization, including pastor, staff, committees, teachers, etc.

An assembling together for worship and fellowship

A group of people holding the same religious doctrines

How would you describe the church , the body of Christ?

_____

_____

The Church Through the Centuries

The Church is usually considered as being birthed on the Day of Pentecost, fifty days after the Passover and Jesus' crucifixion. When the Holy Spirit fell with manifestations of fire, tongues, and power, people were changed. Acts 2:41 says when Peter began to preach *about three thousand were added to their number that day.* His message was that of repentance and baptism, of being identified with Christ, which gave one entrance to the Church. Believers, full of excitement and growth, *devoted themselves to the apostles' teaching and to the fellowship, to the breaking of bread and to prayer. Everyone was filled with awe, and many wonders and miraculous signs were done by the apostles. All the believers were together and had everything in common....And the Lord added to their number daily those who were being saved.* (Acts 2:42-47)

Before long, the apostles saw the need to travel to other provinces with the Gospel and to establish churches. For the first century, the church proved to be strong and vibrant, even in the face of persecution. By the late second century, the unchallenged leader in church affairs was the local bishop. Those who could trace their line back to the apostles were called "patriarchs" and were given special authority. In the east, there were four patriarchs, each equal with the fifth patriarch, the "pope" ("papa") in Rome.

With the conversion of Constantine in A.D. 312, Christianity not only became legal in Rome, it even became the official religion of Rome. Unfortunately, however, a process of sectarianism and institutionalism began in the church, substituting the form for the power. As the offices of the church had been given more authority, the door to carnal ambition opened wider. When Constantine moved his capital from Rome in A.D. 330 to found Constantinople in the east, a power struggle arose between Rome and the eastern church. Political and ecclesiastical jealousies grew between the church in the east and the church in Rome until finally, in 1054 the Pope and the patriarchs excommunicated each other and the church divided, with the pope governing the western church. The church was influenced by strong Roman belief and organization and gradually became a political force in Europe. Yet despite the fracture over church structure, there was a remnant that kept alive the need for a personal relationship with Jesus, even through the Middle Ages (590-1517).

In the 14th century, two brave souls, John Wycliffe and John Hus, dared to suggest that the church was something other than a visible organization headed by the Pope. They began the stirrings of the Reformation, which were continued by Martin Luther, John Calvin, and others. The four questions raised by these protesters were: How is a person saved? Where does religious authority lie? What is the church? and What is the essence of Christian living? Thus, the Protestant movement came into being in A.D. 1517. This subsequently birthed many denominations which are still alive today.

In 1630, more than 400 emigrants sailed from England to begin a new way of life in the new world. These people were called Puritans because they sought to purify society through their Christian beliefs. In time, "Great Awakenings," revivals, spread across America under the preaching of George Whitefield and Jonathan Edwards.

As social unrest was added to the needs of urban masses, the need for evangelism increased. The missionary movement was born as many denominations sent missionaries both to the cities and foreign fields. The 20th Century brought many new ideologies, and "third world" Christians emerged on the scene in the new age of church history. As liberalism increased in the modern church, a wind of the Holy Spirit began to blow to bring the church back into God's Word and supernatural power. The "Jesus Movement," of the late 1960's and early 1970's, brought the reality of the Holy Spirit and His work into many lives and churches.

As one looks at the Church today, much of it seems lukewarm, powerless and full of compromise. Though the Church may go through the refinement of persecution, many believe we are coming to the end of the Church age, when, at last, she will become the Bride of Jesus Christ as His comes again to earth, this time to rule and to reign.

The Church and Its Function

When Peter confessed that Jesus was the *Christ, the Son of the living God* (Matthew 16:16), Jesus replied (verse 18), *"You are Petras* (a small stone, pebble) *and on this rock* (petra, a mass of rock) *I will build my church.* To be sure, Peter would become one of the "lively stones" he later wrote about in 1 Peter 2:5, but the rock that would be suitable as a foundation of the Church, would be the confession that Jesus is the Son of the living God. (Jesus is the spiritual Rock of 1 Corinthians 10:4.)

With the church built on the rock, Jesus is the foundation stone: 1 Corinthians 3:11 confirms this: *For no one can lay any foundation other than the one already laid, which is Jesus Christ.* He is also the head of the Church, according to Ephesians 5:23: *For the husband is the head of the wife as Christ is the head of the church, his body, of which he is the Savior.*

As head of the Church, and thus responsible for its function, He continues to provide for it. He gave the following offices, or functions as described in Ephesians 4:11; 1 Corinthians 12:27-28; Romans 12:5-8:

Apostle — "Ones that are sent." This usually refers to the original twelve disciples, as well as others in the early Church, such as Paul, who were sent outside of Jerusalem to oversee the Church (Titus 1:5). The mark of apostle was signs, wonders, miracles (2 Corinthians 12:12).

Prophet — One who "speaks forth" for God by the inspiration of the Holy Spirit. Though any Believer may be given the "gift of prophecy," 1 Corinthians 14:29 seems to indicate that certain people are considered prophets.

Evangelist — One who proclaims "good news." The evangelist's primary purpose is to introduce sinners to Jesus Christ.

Pastor — Regarding the role of the pastor (shepherd, bishop, elder), Acts 20:28 says he is to keep watch over the flock. First Peter 5:2-3 says he is to serve as overseer, be an example to others and not be greedy for money. Titus 1:5-9 gives us quite a list. An elder must be blameless, the husband of one wife, have children who are obedient, not be quick-tempered, not be given to drunkenness, not be violent, not be pursuing dishonest gain. They must be hospitable, love what is good, be self-controlled, be upright, be holy, and holding to the message they have been taught, and encourage others.

Teacher — The teacher interprets scripture. This position can often be fulfilled by the pastor. Paul was called both an apostle and a teacher (2 Timothy 1:11).

Added to the above list are those who work miracles, those with gifts of healing, those able to help others, those with gifts of administration, those speaking in different tongues, as well as those who serve, those who encourage others, those who make generous financial contributions, and those who show mercy in specific ways.

All of the above positions were given for the purpose of preparing *God's people for works of service, so that the body of Christ maybe built up until we all reach unity in the faith and in the knowledge of the Son of God and become mature, attaining to the whole measure of the fullness of Christ* (Ephesians 4:12-13).

Through what offices, or in what other ways, do you function in the church?

_____

_____

The Gifts of the Holy Spirit to the Church

Not only does Jesus raise up the various leaders and offices for the church, the Holy Spirit (as sent by the Father in John 14:26) is quietly working in the lives of Believers to *conform (us) to the likeness of his son* (Romans 8:29). Sometimes, the Spirit wants to manifest His special gifts through individuals to benefit the whole body. In 1 Corinthians 12:1-11, Paul speaks of these as spiritual gifts. They include:

Wisdom	can be expressed in many ways, including preaching, teaching, counseling.
Word of knowledge	is, most often, a supernatural revelation needed for specific individuals or situations.
Faith	which comes by hearing the Word, will be made active and appropriate for certain needs.
Miraculous powers	are given as both a sign to unbelievers and special blessings to Believers (such as supernatural healings).
Prophecy	is a forthtelling of the works and character of God to "strengthen, encourage, and comfort." (1 Corinthians 14:3)
Distinguishing between spirits	As our special guide, the Holy Spirit can help us distinguish what is of God, what is of Satan, and what is of the flesh. (1 John 4:1-3)
Tongues and interpretation	Most often used by individuals as a prayer language, tongues can also be manifested in a group where another is able to interpret.

In which, if any, of these gifts have you been used by the Holy Spirit to edify the Church?

_____

_____

Your Function in the Church, the Body of Christ

Below are some of the functions of the Church, the Body of Christ as found in Scripture. Check the ones you now participate in or do.

Worship the Lord with others.

Hebrews 10:25 tells us: *Let us not give up meeting together, as some are in the habit of doing, but let us encourage one another…and all the more as you see the Day approaching.* Only by meeting together for worship, praise, preaching the Word, etc. can we enjoy the fellowship and other benefits of total body experience.

Pray with others.

The effectiveness of agreeing prayer can be seen spiritually in Leviticus 26:8: *Five of you will chase a hundred, and a hundred of you will chase ten thousand, and your enemies will fall by the sword before you.*

Participate with others .

Revelation 1:5b-6 declares that we are part of a kingdom together. *To him who loves us and has freed us from our sins by his blood, and has made us to be a kingdom and priests to serve his God and Father...to him be glory and power for ever and ever! Amen.*

Utilize gifts in the church.

Special abilities and talents can be used in unique ways to bless the rest of the Body and enable the Church to bless others in return. Besides the "offices" as listed in Romans 12, there are other ways listed in verses 9-21 to share gifts. A summary of these include: *Be devoted to one another in brotherly love....Share with God's people who are in need....Practice hospitality....Rejoice with those who rejoice....Mourn with those who mourn....Live in harmony with one another....Be willing to associate with people of low position....Live at peace with everyone.*

Teach others and/or be taught.

According to Ephesians 5:26, one of the ways the church is made holy is by the *washing with water through the Word.* All Christians need to be constantly in the Word, whether by learning from others, or by teaching others. Hebrews 5:11-14 tells us that we need to progress beyond the "milk" of the Word. Verse 14 tells us *solid food is for the mature, who by constant use have trained themselves to distinguish good from evil.*

Share faith with others.

Whether it's done through street or home evangelism, personal witnessing, or other means, we need to share the Gospel with others. Not only is this the "great commission" for disciples of Christ (Matthew 28:19-20), but as Ezekiel 3:18 bluntly puts it: *When I say to a wicked man, "You will surely die," and you do not warn him or speak out to dissuade him from his evil ways in order to save his life, the wicked man will die for his sin, and I will hold you accountable for his blood.*

Be accountable to others.

Not only are we told *"submit yourselves one to another"* (1 Peter 5:5b KJV), we also need each other's help in overcoming sins, in dealing with relationships, and in maturing in the faith.

Serve God and others.

In a sense, whatever we do should be done as serving God. Colossians 3:17 exhorts us: *Whatever you do, whether in word or deed, do it all in the name of the Lord Jesus, giving thanks to God the Father through him.* We are also admonished in Romans 12:11 to *never be lacking in zeal, but keep your spiritual fervor, serving the Lord.* Not only are we to serve the Lord in what we do, but we are also to serve others. Philippians 2:4 reminds us: *Each of you should look not only to your own interests, but also to the interests of others.*

SUMMARY

In considering our function in the Church, we have looked at Stephen and Timothy. Stephen, one of the first deacons of the early Church, confronted the authorities as to the interpretation of the Old Testament in the light of God's plan for the Jews and who Jesus was. For this, he became the first Christian martyr. Our look at Timothy, Paul's young co-worker, gives insight as to how the early Church grew, as well as some of the problems it had.

We've defined the Church as the Body of Jesus Christ…His hands, His feet, His ears, His eyes functioning as He, the Head, wills. This Church has taken many forms down through the centuries and is manifested in a variety of ways even today. Because we are part of Christ's Body…as people who believe in Him and accept redemption by His blood… we each have a function in the Church. Equipped with the gifts of the Holy Spirit, we are able teach, strengthen, and encourage fellow Believers, as well as take the Gospel into all the world.

Consider This

What was your view of the Church prior to this lesson? Has it changed?

_____

_____

Do you presently function in some capacity in the Church? If so, how?

_____

_____

Do you serve the Body of Christ in any way outside of your local congregation/fellowship?

_____

_____

EXAMPLE

Dr. Paul Brand, a world-renowned surgeon, knows the functioning of the human body. He spent many years in India and the United States primarily restoring damaged hands eaten away by leprosy. He can well describe how each organ must perform its particular function if the body is to work properly, as well as how each organ is also dependent upon one another. As a Christian, Brand also gained insight from his work as to the functioning of the spiritual body, for he saw that the human body is composed of more than individual organs. It has a spirit infusing all, or it dies. It is just as necessary for the Spirit to permeate theChurch, or its various members cannot function as they should. And, as the life of the flesh is in the blood, so the shed blood of Jesus Christ gives life to the Church.

Dr. Brand has spent much time studying pain, knowing that it is the lack of pain that allows the leprosy to eat away one's flesh. And so he sees how pain becomes a warning to the body that some part of it needs attention, for when one part of the body suffers, the entire body suffers. But it is the pain God must feel that haunts Dr. Brand. Not only has he read, in Scripture, of how God suffered when His people disobeyed, but he knows God must be suffering today when He sees the persecution and pain His Body is going through. For, as the Head of the Body, Jesus receives the transmitted pain. Dr. Brand concludes that Jesus could have had a perfect body, or no body, when He returned to splendor in heaven, but that He chose to keep the scar on His hand as a reminder of wounded humanity. Meanwhile, we are to function in the Church as He has ordained so the Church can accomplish its purpose here on earth. When Christ comes again, His Body will become His Bride and all pain will be gone.

Lesson 19
PAUL AND CORNELIUS

What Makes for a Fruitful Prayer Life?

And we pray this in order that you may live a life worthy of the Lord and may please him in every way; bearing fruit in every good work, growing in the knowledge of God.

Colossians 1:10

SETTING THE STAGE

If we accept 1 Timothy 2:8 as true: *I want men everywhere to lift up holy hands in prayer,* then all Christian men are expected to spend time in prayer. It's probably also true that Paul didn't mean that men are to use prayer as an emergency ripcord, or panic button, or roadside call box. He, no doubt, meant that men were to *pray continually,* as he admonished in 1 Thessalonians 5:17.

Why, then, is prayer such a difficult thing to do, especially for men? Why do most prayer meetings in churches primarily consist of women? Why don't more men assume the spiritual leadership in their homes, and cover family needs with prayer? Why do relatively few men set aside a committed time each day for personal devotions and prayer? Why don't our prayers seem to bear much fruit?

In this lesson, we'll consider the purpose of prayer and how our prayers can be fruitful…not only in our own lives, but also for those for whom God leads us to pray. The intent of this lesson is to encourage men by giving new reasons to pray, and the inspiration to do so.

Though we have examples of many men throughout Scripture, who prayed for a variety of reasons, we'll primarily consider two men, one a Jew and the other a Gentile. Paul, a Jew who persecuted Christians, became an apostle of the faith after a dramatic encounter with the Lord Jesus Christ. Not only did he become a great man of prayer, he also taught us, through his writings, much about prayer. Cornelius, a Roman centurion, is introduced to us immediately as a man of prayer. As a result of his prayers, the door was opened for him, his family, and, eventually, all Gentiles to become Christians.

INTRODUCING PAUL

(Based on Acts, especially 7:57-60; 8:1-3; 9:1-31; 22:1-21; Philippians 3:5-6; Galatians 1:13-2:1)

With the greater portion of the New Testament attributed to Paul, there is no question that he has had a major impact on the expansion and doctrine of the Church, both then and now.

Paul's credentials are impeccable. He would have received the "man of the year" award from the Sanhedrin. He had had the best training available and was zealous to succeed, even in persecuting Christians. But he came to the end of himself on the road to Damascus, when Jesus confronted him in a most dramatic way. After being prayed for and baptized by Ananias, Paul began to preach the gospel in the synagogues in Damascus. But because of his conversion to Christianity, the Jews conspired to kill him. In Galatians 1:13-24, Paul recounts how he went to Arabia and later returned to Damascus before getting acquainted with Peter in

Jerusalem. Then he went to Syria and Cilicia, all the while spending much time in the scriptures and in prayer. These things took place over about ten years.

As one who had given approval for the stoning of Stephen, Paul was, no doubt, greatly moved by Stephen's prayer when he asked the Lord *not to hold this sin against them* (Acts 7:60). After Paul became a Christian, many were (and still are) moved by his prayers. All of Paul's ministry and writings were laced with prayer; nearly every one of his New Testament letters begins with reference to prayer and ends with a benediction.

If legend is true, Paul's life came to an end when his enemies led him out to the Appian Way in Rome and severed his head from his frail body. He died triumphantly for the Lord he dearly loved. To him life was Christ, and death was gain.

INTRODUCING CORNELIUS

(Based on Acts 10; 11:1-18)

The first mention of Cornelius in Scripture finds him to be a man of prayer, a family man who was God-fearing and devout. He gave generously to those in need, and he prayed to God regularly. What is unusual is that Cornelius was a Roman centurion, a Gentile.

We don't know how he and his family came to know God. We must assume he'd been assigned to Caesarea and, if he was like other Romans, had probably worshipped pagan gods. Perhaps he'd seen the pious purity of Israel's way of life — a stark contrast to what he'd known in Rome. While his devout prayers hadn't obtained his salvation, they had certainly opened the way for God's recognition of him, and for his whole family to eventually accept Christ.

One day, as Cornelius was praying at his regular time, he had a vision. An angel appeared to him and told him to send men to Joppa to bring back a man named Peter. So Cornelius sent two of his servants to Joppa. Meanwhile, Peter was also praying and he, too, had a vision. In his vision, Peter saw a large sheet, containing all kinds of animals, reptiles, and birds being let down to earth. He heard a voice tell him to kill these animals and eat them. Peter, however, considered the animals he had seen "unclean," and said he didn't want to eat them. But the voice told him not to call "unclean" what God had made "clean." Then he was told to meet some men at the door and invite them in. They spent the night there and the next morning he accepted their invitation to go to Cornelius' house (though it was highly unusual for a Jew to visit a Gentile). When they arrived, Cornelius told Peter that he had had a vision and was told to send for him and to hear what he had to say.

Peter then realized why he had been sent. God wanted to show him that He accepts men from every nation who fear Him and want to do what is right. Peter told Cornelius and his family about Jesus as he gave the gospel message. While he was still speaking, the Holy Spirit came on all the people present and Peter heard them speaking in tongues and praising God. So, he baptized them immediately.

The Jewish Christians criticized Peter for doing this, but, after he told them what had happened — and how God had shown him that the Gospel was for Gentiles, too — they accepted what had happened and praised God. Cornelius and his family are remembered as probably the first Gentile converts to Christianity.

LESSONS FROM PAUL AND CORNELIUS

What Is Prayer?

A means of relating to God

Prayer is the means by which we relate everything we do to a sovereign, almighty God. It is the process of acknowledging God as having a right to rule in our lives and to be the source of everything we are and have. He is our life, our hope, and our strength, and we owe Him all thanksgiving, and honor, and praise. Prayer is part of the navigation system by which we stay oriented. We keep our total being locked in to God through His Word and by the link called prayer. (Even Cornelius saw the need of regular times of prayer to relate to God. See Acts 10:2, 30)

A supernatural experience

Some of the most important things in life (for example: love, forgiveness, joy) are not visible to us, but we know they exist. Nor do they emanate from the natural realm. Prayer, because it is a relationship with a "supernatural" God, takes us into a realm beyond the natural. *God is Spirit*, John 4:24 reminds us. Both Peter and Cornelius had supernatural experiences as they prayed.

Look up the following scriptures and note other supernatural experiences that were the result of prayer:

Elijah in 2 Kings 6:8-23 (v.17) _____

Daniel in Daniel 9:20-27 _____

Paul and Silas in Acts 16:25-40 _____

The Church in Acts 12:6-18 (v.12) _____

Paul knew that prayer involved the supernatural, not only in relating to God, but in becoming involved in the battle between good and evil. In 2 Corinthians 10:4 he says *the weapons we fight with are not the weapons of the world.* And in Ephesians 6:12 he tells us *our struggle is not against flesh and blood, but against the rulers, against the authorities, against the dark world and against the spiritual forces of evil in the heavenly realms.* Through prayer we, as God's "army," receive our orders and know how to fight the battle. God is looking for men to stand in the gap: *I looked for a man among them who would build up the wall and stand before me in the gap on behalf of the land so I would not have to destroy it, but I found none.* (Ezekiel 22:30)

Training for the Christian life

Through prayer we:

confess our sins and receive forgiveness and are cleansed from all unrighteousness. (1 John 1:9)

reaffirm our position in Christ. (Ephesians 1:15-23)

take opportunity to give God the thanksgiving He deserves. (1 Thessalonians 5:17-18)

know God and become rooted in Him. (Ephesians 3:14-21)

have opportunity to praise Him for who He is. (Hebrews 13:15)

receive guidance and wisdom. (Colossians 1:9-14)

bring our requests and petitions to Him. (Philippians 4:6-7)

participate in spiritual warfare. (2 Corinthians 10:3-5)

lLearn how to accept the help of the Holy Spirit. (Romans 8:26-7)

interpret tongues. (1 Corinthians 14:13)

lead a peaceful and quiet life. (1 Timothy 2:1,2; James 3:17-18)

receive healing. (James 5:16)

consecrate our food. (1 Timothy 4:4-5)

select and set apart church leaders. (Acts 13:1-3)

open doors to spiritual opportunity. (Luke 2:36-38) (true also for Cornelius)

learn to function together in the Body of Christ. (Acts 1:12-14)

Fruitful Prayers

So we pray, but how do we get results…not just for what we want, but for what God desires? If God is real, then we should expect real answers to our prayers. Let's consider Luke 11 for suggestions on how to pray.

Verse 2	"When you pray." God expects us to pray. It should be as much a part of life as is our breathing.
Verses 2-4	This model prayer outlines the major areas we need to include in our prayers… applying God's kingdom principles to our lives, presenting our needs, obtaining forgiveness, asking that we not be led into temptation.
Verses 5-8	God expects us to press in, travail if necessary, to get our requests answered.
Verses 9-10	We are to ask, seek, knock. Andrew Murray, in his book *With Christ in the School of Prayer* helps us understand the significance of each of these words: When we ask, it is mainly for the gifts that God has for us, the things that meet our needs. When we seek, it is for God Himself, the giver of every good and perfect gift. When we knock, it is for having abiding fellowship with God, that we might dwell with Him forever. This is the intimate fellowship expressed in Revelation 3:20: *"Here I am! I stand at the door and knock. If anyone hears my voice and opens the door, I will come in and eat with him, and he with me."*

We must be specific when we pray.

If we aren't specific, we don't know when they're answered! When the blind man, in Mark 10:46-52, cried out for Jesus to have mercy on him. Jesus asked him, *"What do you want me to do for you?"* (v.51). When the blind man verbalized his need, he demonstrated his faith and was healed. Even though God knows what we have need of before we ask (Matthew 6:8), He wants us to state our needs (Matthew 6:11-13).

How can you be more specific in your prayers?

_____

_____

We must also pray in the name of Jesus.

John 14:13-14 tells us, *"I will do whatever you ask in my name...You may ask me for anything in my name, and I will do it."* Notice the qualification also in John 15:7: *"If you remain in me and my words remain in you, ask whatever you wish, and it will be given you."* And in verse 16: *"You did not choose me, but I chose you and appointed you to go and bear fruit...fruit that will last. Then the Father will give you whatever you ask in my name."* Praying in Jesus' name means praying in the character and nature of Jesus. According to Romans 8:34, Jesus is at the right hand of God interceding for us, so, as we pray in His name, our prayers are passed on to the Father.

Do you pray in the name of Jesus with the understanding of who and where He is?

_____

_____

Our prayers must line up with God's Word.

In John 15:7-8, Jesus says, *"If you remain in me and my words remain in you, ask whatever you wish, and it will be given you. This is to my Father's glory, that you may bear much fruit, showing yourselves to be my disciples."* God, Jesus, the Holy Spirit and the Word all agree. So, if we are praying "in the Spirit" and according to God's Word, then we are in agreement with God. This is why some people like to "pray" scripture, including the special prayers given to us there....the Lord's Prayer, for example.

Do you ever "pray" scripture? If so, how has it built your faith to receive answers to prayer?

_____

_____

Our prayers need the anointing of the Holy Spirit.

Romans 8:26 tells us that when we don't know what we ought to pray for, the Spirit will intercede for us, and *he who searches our hearts knows the mind of the Spirit, because the Spirit intercedes for the saints in accordance with God's will* (verse 27). Praying *in the Spirit on all occasions with all kinds of prayers and requests* is part of the whole armor of God, as found in Ephesians 6:18.

How do you know when you are praying with the anointing of the Holy Spirit?

_____

_____

We must pray according to God's will.

Scripture says, in 1 John 5:14: *This is the confidence we have in approaching God: that if we ask anything according to his will, he hears us.* This means we must have the right motives: *When you ask, you do not receive, because you ask with wrong motives, that you may spend what you get on your pleasures.* (James 4:3). As we seek God's kingdom and His righteousness, all the things we need will be given to us. (See Matthew 6:33.) Sometimes this means denying our own desires, and asking God instead for what we know He wants.

Solomon, in 1 Kings 3:5-15, could have asked God for long life or wealth, or death of his enemies; instead, he asked for a discerning heart to govern the people and the ability to distinguish right and wrong. In return, God blessed him with riches and honor.

What are some of the things you pray for that you now see may not be according to God's will?

_____

_____

We must be in right relationship with God.

Psalm 66:18 says, *If I had cherished sin in my heart, the Lord would not have listened.* Isaiah 59:2 reminds us: *But your iniquities have separated you from your God; your sins have hidden his face form you, so that he will not hear.*

Acts 8:9-24 contains an interesting story about Simon, a sorcerer who believed and was baptized, and even accompanied Philip, seeing all the miracles and signs of God. When Simon saw Peter and John lay hands on people and saw the people receive the Holy Spirit, he wanted the same power Peter and John had. But Peter told him that it wasn't for sale. Peter perceived something else about Simon…that he needed to repent of his bitterness and sin, and therefore, wasn't right with God. So, we learn that before God will be open to hearing and answering our prayers, we must truly repent and accept the blood of Jesus for forgiveness of sins. It is only by His blood that we have access to God (Hebrews 4:14-16; 10:19).

In Luke 18:9-14, we find that of the two men who went up to the temple to pray, God accepted the prayers of the broken and contrite man…not those of the boasting Pharisee. Do you regularly begin your prayers by searching your heart for unconfessed sin?

_____

_____

We must be in right relationship with others.

Jesus taught that if someone has something against you, you are to be reconciled before approaching God (Matthew 5:23-24). From Mark 11:25 we learn that when we pray, we aren't to hold anything against anyone, rather we are to forgive so that God can forgive us.

First Peter 3:7 gives a very specific instruction for husbands: *Husbands…be considerate as you live with your wives, and treat them with respect as the weaker partner and as heirs with you of the gracious gift of life, so that nothing will hinder your prayers.*

How can you better treat your wife, so that your prayers will not be hindered?

_____

_____

We must believe and ask in faith.

But when he asks, he must believe and not doubt, because he who doubts is like a wave of the sea, blown and tossed by the wind. That man should not think he will receive anything from the Lord; he is a double-minded man, unstable in all he does. (James 1:6-8. See also Hebrews 11:6; Mark 11:22-24.)

Do you pray with faith that God is going to answer your prayer? What builds this kind of faith?

_____

_____

Why Praying Is Difficult, Especially for Men

We men like to be self-sufficient. Our feelings of worth are often determined by our accomplishments. So, to ask for help goes against our inner desire to be independent. It's our pride that often keeps us from prayer.

There are other reasons as well:

Like Thomas, we appreciate more tangible things. (John 20:24-29)

Like Gideon, we need proof that God is really in our situation. (Judges 6:36-40)

Like Manoah, we need to know first-hand what God is saying. (Judges 13:8-20)

Like Philip, we don't understand the relationship between God and Jesus. (John 14:8-14)

Like Peter, James, and John, we get too tired and fall asleep. (Matthew 26:36-45)

What have been your reasons for not praying? _____

_____

_____

So, how can we pray with humility?

Like Isaac, we can pray on behalf of our wives. (Genesis 25:21)

Like Moses, we can intercede for others. (Exodus 32:31-34)

Like Joshua, we can ask for help and mercy. (Joshua 7:6-9)

Like David, we can pray for a contrite heart and forgiveness of sin. (Psalm 51:1-17)

Like Solomon, we can acknowledge God's greatness, as we recognize our finiteness. (2 Chronicles 6:12-19)

Like Daniel, we can be faithful in prayer regardless of our circumstances. (Daniel 6:10-17)

Like Cornelius, we can pray regularly. (Acts 10:2, 30)

Like Paul, we can pray for the spiritual growth of other Christians. (Ephesians 3:14-21)

What happens to all our prayers? According to Revelation 5:8 and 8:1-4, they become as incense before God in heaven! They are in His possession to be used by Him for His glory!

SUMMARY

Prayer is, and should be, part of every Christian's life. It's the way we communicate with God, in order to give Him praise and thanksgiving, as well as to confess our sins and share our petitions. We need to know how to pray…in His name, according to His will, with clean hearts, just as we need to pray with faith that our prayers will be answered and fruit may result.

Through the letters he wrote to individuals and to churches in various places, Paul taught us many things about prayer. Cornelius is an example of how prayer opens the door to spiritual opportunity, often beyond our imagination. Prayer is something we learn by doing.

It's not always easy for men to pray, especially on a personal, daily basis, but the rewards are great for those who take the time to have a continuing, intimate relationship with their Heavenly Father.

Consider This

Where and how did you learn to pray?

_____

_____

How would you evaluate your present prayer life?

_____

_____

Do you belong to any men's prayer group? If so, how has this helped your prayer life?

_____

_____

Do you pray regularly with your wife? If not, what hinders you from doing so?

_____

_____

EXAMPLE

When James L. Synder was a boy, his parents took him and his younger brother and sister to church regularly twice a week…on Sunday and to Wednesday night prayer meeting. At the end of each midweek service, the pastor paired up the congregation to pray. Each week he chose a different partner for himself.

One Wednesday night, the pastor chose 15 year-old James. Kneeling beside the Pastor, James coughed a few times, then began to pray by blessing everyone he could think of, including his home state and the United States of America. When he finally said "Amen, " he was both relieved and proud of himself for having made it through. The pastor, however, didn't seem as satisfied and asked James to pray again, saying that this time he wanted him to forget all the blessings and just talk to God as if He were a close friend.

With a whole new attitude, James began to pray a second time. His words were more deliberate as he thought of things he would like to share with someone he knew on an intimate basis. It not only proved to be a rewarding experience, it changed his idea of both God and prayer. And that has lasted through the years as he continues to converse in prayer with his friend, God Almighty.

Lesson 20

JOHN, THE BELOVED DISCIPLE

What Does theFuture Hold...Both Here on Earth and After Death?

"For I know the plans I have for you", declares the Lord, "plans to prosper you and not to harm you, plans to give you a hope and a future."

Jeremiah 29:11

SETTING THE STAGE

Man has always been intrigued about the future, including what happens to him after death. Unfortunately, his attempts to find out what the future holds has led him into New Age beliefs, occult practices, and curiosity about all kinds of "after death" experiences. Our newspapers contain horoscopes, and our billboards advertise psychic readers. Television, Internet and special metaphysical seminars hawk their promises to provide real meaning for this life, and revelation about the future. Countless people dabble in the occult, even to trying to contact the dead; the games, books, seminars, etc. are not only widespread, but also a multi-million dollar business.

God wants us to know the future. In fact, He not only gave us prophets and the written Word, He also gave the Holy Spirit to *"tell you what is yet to come"* (John 16:13b). He has revealed what will be happening at the end of this age, and has said what He has in store for both s and non-believers after they die. Christianity is the only major religion that knows what the future holds with 100% accuracy. We can never completely fathom God, yet we can know the truth of Revelations 15:3b: *Just and true are your ways, King of the Ages.*

Though we will look at some other Biblical authors, we will consider mainly the writings of John, as we see what our future holds...both here and in life after death.

INTRODUCING JOHN, THE BELOVED DISCIPLE

(Based on Mark 1:19-34; John 13:23; 19:26-27; 20:2-5; 21:7, 20, 24; Acts 1:13; 3:1; 8:14-17; Revelation 1:1-5)

Early church tradition attributes the fourth Gospel to John, "the beloved disciple." In fact, John often refers to himself in this way. His name is never mentioned in the book of John. He and his brother James were fishing with their father, Zebedee, when Jesus called them to follow Him. He was one of the disciples with Jesus on the Mount of Transfiguration and in the garden of Gethsemane. He aspired to the seat next to Jesus in the coming kingdom, and was asked whether he, too, could drink of Christ's cup.

At the crucifixion, John was standing near when Jesus said to his mother: *"Dear woman, here is your son,"* and to the disciple, *"Here is your mother."* (John 19:26b-27)

We next see John resurrection morning, when he and Peter ran to the tomb after the women discovered that Jesus was no longer there. In fact, John outran Peter and reached the tomb first to see that it was, indeed, empty. As he stood back to let Peter enter, he also saw and believed.

John, as an apostle in the early Church, is listed among those disciples present on the Day of Pentecost when the Holy Spirit was poured out. He was in the company of Peter when a crippled beggar was healed (Acts 3). Because of the disturbance this caused, both

Peter and John were put in prison. John was also with Peter when some people in Samaria received the Holy Spirit. He also is reported to have encouraged Paul (Galatians 2:9). John probably visited the seven cities in Asia Minor to which he later wrote letters (Revelation 2-3).

The authorship of not only the gospel of John and the three epistles of John, but also the book of Revelation are attributed to him. He lived well into his nineties, so he knew of the destruction of Jerusalem in A.D. 70. He was the last of the apostles to die. He died after being exiled to the island of Patmos, where he received "the revelation of Jesus Christ"…the epic of future end-time events.

In this book, he offers Christians hope, assuring them that in the end Christ will achieve victory over Satan. As we are given warnings and encouragement, we are to rejoice in the awesome power of Christ and to know that God is still in control.

LESSONS FROM JOHN'S WRITINGS

God Wants Us to Know the Future

A brief survey of Scripture will show that God does reveal the future:

- He told Noah that He was going to destroy the wicked and the earth. (Genesis 6:13)
- He told Abraham what He was going to do to Sodom and Gomorrah. (Genesis 18:17)
- He reveals some things to us and our children. (Deuteronomy 29:29)
- Daniel recognized God for revealing deep and hidden things. (Daniel 2:20-22)
- Nebuchadnezzar understood that God had revealed mysteries to Daniel. (Daniel 2:47)
- Amos knew that God doesn't do anything without revealing His plan to His servants and prophets. (Amos 3:7)
- Matthew quotes Jesus as saying that there is nothing concealed that will not be disclosed, or hidden that will not be made known. (Matthew 10:26-27)
- Paul tells us that mystery hidden for long ages past is revealed and made known through the prophetic writings by the command of the eternal God. (Romans 16:25-26)
- Paul also said that the mystery of Christ has been revealed by the Spirit to God's holy apostles and prophets. (Ephesians 3:4-5)
- Jesus related events of the future yet to come, and then told His disciples, *"See, I have told you ahead of time."* (Matthew 24:25)
- Through the Holy Spirit, one of whose roles is *to tell you what is yet to come.* (John 16:13) 1 Timothy 4:1-3 says very specifically that the Spirit has information about the *later times.*

The Demise of Our World System

No matter what environmentalists and other groups would like to say about man being able to make our earth a better place in which to live, Scripture is very specific concerning this world's eventual outcome: *Heaven and earth will pass away.* (Luke 21:33 See also Hebrews 1:10-12.) Many Bible prophecies not only verify this fact, but also give additional details as to what will happen between now and then. In fact, there are four times as many prophecies concerning Jesus' second coming as there are concerning His first coming.

Today, we see some of the end time prophecies being fulfilled as we hear of the following news events: threat of nuclear destruction, wars, changing weather patterns, earthquakes, computer glitches which can affect the world's economic system, plagues, famines, violence, family breakdown, homosexuality, occult practices, persecution of Christians — all of which are on such an increase that life on earth is being changed dramatically.

Which of these events are foretold by Jesus in Matthew 24:1-29 and Luke 21:5-28?

_____

_____

What does Timothy say about the last days? (1 Timothy 4:1-3 and 2 Timothy 3:1-5)

_____

_____

After reminding us that scoffers will also come in the last days to try to make us disbelieve God's Word, Peter tells us that the earth is being kept for a day of judgment (2 Peter 3:3-10). We aren't to know when this will take place; it will come like a thief in the night (1 Thessalonians 5:2-8). God destroyed the earth the first time by a flood because of the wickedness of man. He will destroy the earth a second time by fire for the very same reason.

The Future of Believers and Unbelievers

While s and unbelievers (true Christians and non-Christians) both live in unredeemed society and share a declining earth now, the future for each of these groups is very different. Unlike those who would have us believe that there is nothing beyond this life, or that everyone goes to heaven, the Bible tells us that there is a place called Heaven for those who have accepted Jesus Christ as their Lord and Savior and there is a place called Hell — lake of fire — for those who refuse to accept His invitation.

For the Believer

For God so loved the world that he gave his one and only Son, that whoever believes in him shall not perish but have eternal life. (John 3:16)

I write these things to you who believe in the name of the Son of God so that you may know that you have eternal life. (1 John 5:13. See also verses 11-12.)

For the Unbeliever

Whoever believes in the Son has eternal life, but whoever rejects the Son will not see life, for God's wrath remains on him. (John 3:36)

But the cowardly, the unbelieving…their place will be in the fiery lake of burning sulfur: This is the second death. (Revelation 21:8)

Heaven and Hell

Heaven — The presence of God

Jesus, in John 14:2-3, tells us that He has gone to prepare a place for us, and that He will come again to take us to be with Him. As the Bride of Jesus Christ (Revelation 19:6-8), we will reign with Him forever and ever (Revelation 22:3-5).

Though life after death may go through stages (such as for those who die in Christ before the marriage supper of the Lamb takes place as described in 1 Thessalonians 4:14-15), we will ever be in God's presence. Second Corinthians 5:6-8 reminds us that when we are absent from the body, we are present with the Lord.

Heaven will not include marriage (Matthew 22:30), death (Luke 20:36), flesh and blood (1 Corinthians 15:50), corruption (2 Corinthians 5:1-5), hunger, thirst, heat (Revelation 7:16), tears (Revelation 7:18), sorrow, pain (Revelation 21:4), a curse (Revelation 22:3), night (Revelation 22:5), wicked people (Revelation 22:14), or an end (Matthew 25:46). There will be no need of sun or moon, for God's glory is the light. (Revelation 21:23)

What promises does Scripture give us about heaven, the place where we are ever in the presence of God?

- It will be a place of joy (Luke 15:7,10); rest from labor, (Revelation 14:13), comfort (Luke 16:25) righteousness (2 Peter 3:13), reward (Matthew 5:12), and glory (Romans 8:18).
- It can be described as a glorious city. (Revelation 21)
- It will be shared by saved Israel. (Hebrews 11:10, 16; Romans 11:25-27)
- It will be shared by holy angels. (Daniel 7:8-10; Hebrews 12:22; Revelation 5:11)
- The Father will be there. (Daniel 7:9; Revelation 4:2-3, 8)
- The Son (Lamb) will be there. (Revelation 5:6; 7:17)
- The Holy Spirit will be there. (Revelation 14:13; 22:17)
- Activities will include singing (Isaiah 44:23; Hebrews 2:12; Revelation 5:9; 14:3), serving (Revelation 7:15; 22:3), learning (1 Corinthians 13:9-10).

Hell — The place of separation from God

In this life, though people have belonged to Satan's kingdom, God has still been very much at work in the world and will have the last word, even with Satan. Life after death, for the unbeliever, is complete separation from God. Again, this may be in different "phases" (such as described in Revelation 20:13-14). Eternal life without God will be punishment forever.

What does the Bible say about Hell/lake of fire or eternal life without the presence of God?

- Hell is described as eternal fire (Matthew 25:41), eternal punishment (Matthew 25:46), outer darkness (Matthew 8:12), everlasting destruction (2 Thessalonians 1:9), unquenchable fire (Matthew 3:12), fiery furnace (Matthew 13:41-42), and fire that never goes out (Mark 9:43).
- Hell is prepared for the devil and his angels (Matthew 25:41, Revelation 20:10), the wicked (Revelation 21:8), fallen angels (2 Peter 2:4), the beast and false prophet (Revelation 19:20), worshippers of the beast (Revelation 14:11), and those who reject the gospel (Matthew 10:14-15).
- Punishment is described as bodily (Matthew 5:29-30), of the soul (Matthew 10:28), in varying degrees (Luke 12:47-48)), and unchangeable (Luke 16:22-31, v. 26).
- It will be a place of memory and remorse (Luke 16:19-31), misery and pain (Revelation 14:10-11), frustration and anger (Matthew 13:42; 24:51), and divine wrath (Revelation 14:10).

Our destiny, Heaven or Hell, is determined by what we do in this life…whether or not we accept God's plan of salvation. *The one who sows to please his sinful nature, from that nature will reap destruction; the one who sows to please the Spirit, from the Spirit will reap eternal life* (Galatians 6:8). Death is the means by which we pass from this life to our eternal destination. The fool thinks it doesn't make too much difference what he does about God in this life, or that he can change his destination after death. The wise always have eternity and death in mind, knowing that the sufferings of this present time are temporal and not worth comparing with the glory that is to be revealed (Romans 8:18).

In the Meantime!

For those living in the end times (which many think we are now doing), Scripture does tell of events that will take place. Because the timing is not always clear, there are differences of opinion as to the order. Many, many books have been written on the subject of eschatology ("dealing with last things"), so we will only briefly look at some of the future events and personalities as described in Scripture. Do your own research to come to your own conclusions.

The antichrist and false prophet

In 2 Thessalonians 2:3-4, we are told: *Don't let anyone deceive you in any way, for that day (day of the Lord) will not come until the rebellion occurs and the man of lawlessness is revealed, the man doomed to destruction. He will oppose and will exalt himself over everything that is called God or is worshipped, so that he sets himself up in God's temple, proclaiming himself to be God.* According to Revelation 13:11-12, the antichrist has a helper, a false prophet, who will make the inhabitants of the earth worship him (antichrist or "first" beast).

The tribulation

Matthew 24:4-8 gives some of the "birth pains" that will take place as a time of great tribulation begins all over the earth. There will be wars, famines, earthquakes, and persecution, and the love of many will grow cold. When the antichrist sets himself up to be worshipped, things will get even worse (Matthew 24:15-30) until the sun and moon become darkened and stars fall from the sky. (See also Luke 21:9-26.) According to Daniel 9:25-27, the tribulation period will last a total of seven years. The wicked will get more wicked, and the earth more devastated (2 Timothy 3:13). The Jews, especially, will go through a time of "Jacob's trouble" (Jeremiah 30:7) as God deals one last time with them before He saves those who live through the experience (Romans 11:25-27) and recognize Jesus as their Messiah (Zechariah 12:10).

The millennium or thousand years of peace

At the conclusion of the seven years of tribulation and wrath upon the earth with the antichrist in rule, the greatest battle of all time will take place…the battle of Armageddon. The campaign will rage throughout the land of Israel, beginning in the Valley of Megiddo and will culminate in final fury in the Holy City itself. Jesus Himself will destroy the gathered nations at His Second Coming (2 Thessalonians 2:8; Revelation 19:11-21), as He throws the antichrist and false prophet alive into the lake of fire (Revelation 19:19-21). This will usher in the Millennium, or one thousand years of peace, during which the saints will rule with Christ Jesus from the Holy City (Revelation 20:4-6). During this time Satan will be bound and thrown into a pit to be kept from deceiving people (Revelation 20:2-3) until the thousand years are nearly over. At that time, he will have one last chance to gather nations against Christ. But, fire will come down from Heaven and devour him and he will be thrown into the lake of fire to join the antichrist and false prophet (Revelation 20:7-10).

The nation of Israel

Key in prophecy is the nation of Israel, which was scattered over the face of the earth after its people were taken into captivity and exile during the time of the Kings. Only when

Israel became a nation again, in 1948, did God start bringing Jews back to their homeland from all over the world so that He could deal with them one last time as a nation. It is in the Temple in Jerusalem that the antichrist will try to set himself upon the throne; and the Jews will have to flee their land for a while. When Jesus returns, they will, at last, recognize Him as the Messiah and be saved.

The Bride of Jesus Christ

Many believe the church of Jesus Christ will be spared part or all of the tribulation. This comes mainly from 1 Thessalonians 4:16-17: *For the Lord himself will come down from heaven, with a loud command, with the voice of the archangel and with the trumpet call of God, and the dead in Christ will rise first. After that, we who are still alive and are left will be caught up together with them in the clouds to meet the Lord in the air. And so we will be with the Lord forever.* First Corinthians 15:51-52 gives more details, such as that this will take place in the twinkling of an eye. It is often called the rapture, and many see this as different from the second coming when Jesus will "touch down" on the Mount of Olives, as described in Zechariah 14:4 (instead of us meeting Him in the air). There are those who believe that, though the Church may go through persecution (and much of it has already around the world), God did not appoint His Church to suffer His wrath (1 Thessalonians 5:9). The "marriage supper of the Lamb" will consummate the Church's union with Jesus Christ (Revelation 19:6-9) and she will reign with Christ during the Millennium (Revelation 20:4-6) and then abide with Him as the Holy City, with a new heaven and a new earth. (Revelation 21).

The "Second Coming" of Jesus

According to Revelation 1:7, all the people will mourn when they see Him at last. All will have to bow their knees and confess that Jesus Christ is Lord. (See Philippians 2:10-11.) Unlike His first coming, this one will be spectacular with *"lightning that comes from the east is visible even in the west, so will be the coming of the Son of Man"* (Matthew 24:27). This time, Christ will come riding a white horse, dressed in a robe dipped in blood, and on His robe and on His thigh, will be the words "King of Kings and Lord of Lords" (Revelation 19:11-16).

Resurrections and Judgments

Hebrews 9:27a says *just as man is destined to die once, and after that to face judgment....* We know, from a lengthy explanation in 1 Corinthians 15, that because Christ became the "firstfruits" of resurrection, man will also be resurrected. And, as pictured for us in Daniel 12:2, *multitudes who sleep in the dust of the earth will awake: some to everlasting life, others to shame and everlasting contempt.* After death, man experiences both resurrection and judgment. The judgment for s takes place at the Judgment Seat of Christ, according to Romans 14:10-2 (KJV), where each one will give account of himself to God. This is reiterated in 2 Corinthians 5:10 with additional information: *For we must all appear before the judgment seat of Christ, that each one may receive what is due him for the things done while in the body, whether good or bad.* Many believe this refers to the passage in 1 Corinthians 3:11-15 which tells us that man's works will be judged, whether they have been "gold and silver" or "wood, hay, and straw." There will also be "crowns" given for various reasons. (As described in James 1:12, 1 Corinthians 9:24-27; 1 Thessalonians 2:19-20; 2 Timothy 4:5-8; and 1 Peter 5:2-4.)

The judgment for unbelievers does not take place until after the Millennium, when they will appear before God's great white throne. There, the "books" will be opened. Those whose names are not written in the "book of life" will be thrown into the lake of fire (Revelation 20:11-15).

Judgment for Satan, the antichrist, and the false prophet is also "the lake of fire," where they will be thrown to be *tormented day and night forever and ever* (Revelation 20:7-10).

A new heaven and a new earth

Though there will have to be restoration of the earth for the rule of Jesus and His saints during the thousand years of peace, the new heaven and new earth come into being after the Millennium and the final disposal of Satan. Revelation 21 describes this awesome event…that of the Holy City, the New Jerusalem, coming down from heaven as a bride beautifully adorned for her husband. The chapter goes on to describe this city, with its dimensions and structures. There is no Temple here, because God and Jesus are its Temple. There is no sun or moon, for God's glory is the light and Jesus is the lamp. Nothing impure will ever enter it. The only ones inside are those whose names are written in the Lamb's book of life.

Watch and Pray

In Scripture, we are told several things to do as we await the return of Jesus Christ. Besides watch and pray, Luke 21:34-36 tells us to _____

Matthew 24:42 commands that we keep watch because _____

Second Timothy 4:1-2 tells us to _____

Second Peter 3:3-17 gives several suggestions: _____

_____

Hebrews 10:25 exhorts us to _____

In 1 Thessalonians 3:13, Paul prays that hearts will be strengthened so that _____

_____

SUMMARY

If we really want to know about the future, and life after death, we need to study the scriptures (perhaps with the help of others who have also studied them). Of course, the Holy Spirit is the One who can not only show us insights of prophecies already given, but also tell us of things to come. God not only wants us to know, He wants us to be prepared. Though others in Scripture also had insight, the apostle John gives us much of the "revelation" of the last days. This should be the intense study of every Christian, as many believe that Jesus is coming again very soon.

Consider This

Do you think you are living in the end times? Why, or why not?

_____

_____

What are you doing to be prepared for Jesus' Second Coming, should it be in your lifetime?

_____

_____

Are you afraid of death? Are you ready to die? _____

Are you able to share with others what the scriptures say about the future of man and the earth? Does this give you an urgency to share the gospel?

_____

_____

EXAMPLE

On April 15, 1912, on the Atlantic Ocean about 700 miles east of Halifax, Canada, 2,200 people faced their future in an instant, when the Titanic hit an iceberg and sank to the bottom of the ocean. No passenger or crew member ever have believed such a disaster could happen so quickly, let alone on this magnificent ship's maiden voyage. In the end, 712 of the passengers were rescued, and the rest…millionaires, immigrants, honeymoon couples, musicians, elderly people, young children…drowned or froze to death in the icy waters. Just hours before, each was anticipating his exciting, extravagant voyage to America. Suddenly, all were facing eternity. Some may have been ready. It appears many were not.

It's interesting to note how the different people reacted. Some men were willing to go down with the ship and they helped women and children board lifeboats. Other men dressed as women in order to be helped to safety themselves. Some just couldn't believe what was happening and didn't try to escape. A group of musicians simply provided music to calm the people's nerves while the water invaded the ship. And some, no doubt, spent the time in prayer, crying out to God.

In an article, "Iceberg Dead Ahead," author Bill Cloud points out that according to Proverbs 16:18, pride goes before destruction. All involved with the Titanic were certainly full of pride —from the passengers, to the crew and those who had built it.

According to Greek mythology, the Titans were a group of large beings who tried to overthrow the gods of Mt. Olympus. They were eventually cast down to the lowest region of the underworld. Thus, the name "Titanic" is associated with rebellion and destruction.

Cloud also quotes Luke 17:27 about how revelry preceded the sudden destruction of the earth when God sent a flood. Just as in the days of Noah, some of the pleasure seekers on the Titanic ignored the warnings. Like the story of the tower of Babel (Genesis 11), the story of the Titanic is a grim reminder of what can happen when man becomes enamored with what he can accomplish…so that he forgets to give God the glory and praise due Him.

As we face the future, the question arises: "What would we do if we heard the warning "Iceberg Dead Ahead" and knew that our eternity was beginning right now?

Lesson 21
JESUS OF NAZARETH

What Shall I Do, Then, With Jesus Who Is Called Christ?

Behold the man!
John 19:5b (KJV)

SETTING THE STAGE

There have been thousands of trials, down through the years, which have determined a man's innocence or degree of guilt. Because of modern technology, some of these take place before our very eyes in our own living rooms.

There was a trial that took place nearly 2,000 years ago without benefit of present-day media. This trial's significance and impact on the world has reached far beyond that of any other trial ever held. The defendant was Jesus of Nazareth, a man accused of

> claiming to be "King of the Jews." (Luke 23:3)
> committing blasphemy. (Matthew 26:63-65)
> inciting rebellion. (Luke 23:13-14)
> claiming to be the Son of God. (John 19:7)
> opposing Caesar. (John 19:12)

The prosecutors were the chief priests and Pharisees who had incited a crowd to accuse Jesus, and even got false witnesses to testify against Him. The judges were both Herod and Pilate, Roman rulers in the land of Palestine. Though Pilate was given the responsibility of determining Jesus' fate, he knew that Jesus had been handed over to him because of envy (Matthew 27:18). Even after being warned by his wife, Pilate acquiesced to the demands of the religious leaders and crowd, and turned Jesus over to be crucified.

Pilate, despite his actions, left us a legacy in his declaration: "Behold the Man!" Since that time, each person is confronted with what he sees when he beholds the man, Jesus of Nazareth. And each person must answer the question: *What shall I do, then, with Jesus who is called Christ?* (Matthew 27:22a).

As a means of helping us discover who Jesus is, so we can determine what *we* will do with Him, we will look at the response of some Bible men when they were confronted by Him. We'll begin with (1) those who were given a preview of Jesus before He was made flesh to dwell among us, (2) those who actually saw Jesus in the flesh, or knew someone who did, and (3) those who experienced Jesus after His resurrection.

Those Who Were Given a Preview of Jesus
Before He Was Made Flesh to Dwell Among Us

Adam

He and Eve had listened to the "father of lies" (John 8: 44) and disobeyed God's Word. As part of their "sentencing" they were told that their "seed" (offspring) would, someday, crush the head of the serpent that had misled them (Genesis 3:15.) This was the first Messianic prophesy in Scripture and was fulfilled as recorded in 1 John 3:8b: *The reason the Son of*

God appeared was to destroy the devil's work. (Looking back, we can see that the animal skins covering Adam's sin were a type of the blood covering Jesus would provide by His sacrifice.)

Abraham

In Genesis 14:18-20, we find Abraham giving a tenth of everything he owned to Melchizedek, king of Salem. In Hebrews 7:1-3, we find more description of Melchizedek *like the Son of God, he remains a priest forever.* Hebrews 7:17 declares of Jesus: *You are a priest forever, in the order of Melchizedek.*

Jacob

Jacob attempted to control his own destiny by subterfuge. But a night of wrestling with a "man" changed Jacob, subduing his flesh and giving him a new name (Genesis 32:22-32). Jacob became a "new creature" because of this experience.

Moses

Moses was unable to enter the Promised Land himself, because, when God told him to *"speak to the rock"* (Numbers 20:8-12), he struck it twice instead. Water gushed out to quench the people's thirst, but God was not pleased. First Corinthians 10:4 tells us this *rock was Christ.*

Joshua

(Hebrew for "Jesus") In Joshua 5:13-15, we have a description of an encounter Joshua had with "a man" who claimed to be commander of the Lord's army. As Joshua fell face down on the ground, the man said, *"Take off your sandals, for the place where you are standing is holy."* In Matthew 28:18, we are told that Jesus has all authority in heaven and earth.

Job

In the midst of his loss and suffering, Job declared, *"I know that my Redeemer lives, and that in the end, he will stand upon the earth. And after my skin has been destroyed, yet in my flesh I will see God"* (Job 19:25-26).

Isaiah

It was Isaiah, 800 years before Christ, who "saw" the Messiah as the suffering servant. Though in Isaiah 9:6 he gave prophecy as to how Jesus would be born and what His roles would be — Wonderful counselor, Mighty God, Everlasting Father, and Prince of Peace — he also saw Him as One *like a root out of dry ground…nothing in his appearance that we should desire him…despised and rejected by men…a man of sorrows and familiar with suffering…smitten and afflicted…crushed for our iniquities… righteous servant will justify many* (Isaiah 53).

Daniel

As Shadrach, Meshac, and Abednego, Daniel's friends, were thrown into the fiery furnace by King Nebuchadnezzar, they gave credit to a "fourth man" who appeared in the fire with them and was said to *look like a son of the gods* (Daniel 3:25b). The three Jews came out unharmed…no further mention is made of the fourth man.

Those Who "Saw" Jesus in the Flesh, or Knew Someone Who Had

Matthew

A Jewish tax collector called to be a disciple, Matthew saw Jesus as One who fulfilled messianic expectations and the covenants given to Abraham (Genesis 12:3) and to David (2 Samuel 7:8-13). Thus, his gospel is directed to the Jews concerning the kingdom of heaven, its laws, its participants, and its future.

Mark

This young man probably knew Jesus from the testimony of Peter. Because he was a servant, he was fascinated by Jesus' role of servant. He tells of many of Jesus' miracles as He served those He came to save.

Luke

A Gentile physician, Luke portrays Jesus as the perfect Man. His genealogy goes back to Adam, the first man. Written to the Greeks, his book gives details of Jesus' birth as One who came in the flesh.

John

This disciple saw Jesus as the Son of God, His Word made flesh among us, the One who communicates God's love to us. John speaks of our relationship to God, through Jesus, and of the work of the third person of the trinity…the Holy Spirit.

The Disciples

Though the twelve disciples spent three years with Jesus, they still didn't really understand who He was. Peter, who had confessed that Jesus was the Christ, the Son of the living God, disowned Him. Judas betrayed Him. Even after the resurrection, Thomas wouldn't believe who He was until He saw the nailprints in His hand. Following the resurrection, and empowering of the Holy Spirit, the Disciples not only accepted the reality of Jesus in their own lives, they died proclaiming the "good news" to others.

Pilate

This ruler saw Jesus not as a law-breaker but as an inconvenience, and gave Him over to the crowd to protect his own position.

The women

The women who followed Jesus…Mary, Martha, Mary Magdalene, Salome, and others…felt affirmed and valued by Jesus. They stood beneath the cross while He died, and they were the first to the tomb to find Him risen from the dead.

The soldiers

Most of them mocked Jesus as they pulled out his beard and placed a crown of thorns on His head. After darkness covered the land, an earthquake shook the earth, and the veil in the temple was torn asunder. However one centurion praised God and said, *"Surely this was a righteous man."* (Luke 23:47)

Two thieves crucified with Jesus

As Jesus hung upon the cross between two thieves, one hurled insults at Him. The other one admitted to being punished for his crimes, and knew Jesus had done no wrong. He must have believed in who He was, for he said to Jesus, *"Remember me when you come into your kingdom."* (Luke 23:42)

Two on the road to Emmaus

Two people, walking with Jesus to Emmaus following the resurrection, did not recognize Him at first. It was when they sat to eat and He took the bread and blessed it that *their eyes were opened and they recognized him.* (Luke 24:31)

James

The writer of the book of James is considered, by most scholars, to be a brother of Jesus. He refers to himself as *a servant of God and of the Lord Jesus Christ* (James 1:1). James' idea of who Jesus was had changed, for in John 7:1-5, Jesus' brothers challenged Him to show Himself to the world. But Jesus told them that the right time had not come for Him to do that yet. Verse 5 tells us *even his own brothers did not believe in him.*

Paul

This zealous persecutor of Christians was met by Jesus on the road to Damascus. Blinded by a light from heaven, Paul (then called Saul) fell to the ground and heard a voice ask, *"Why do you persecute me?"* Paul asked who it was and the voice answered, *"I am Jesus, whom you are persecuting"* (Acts 9:3-5). From that time on, Paul's life was changed. He eventually became not only one of the apostles in the early church, but a prolific writer of our New Testament. Though his life in Christ began after the death and resurrection of Jesus, he knew many of those who had actually seen Jesus in the flesh. In his own writings, he presents Jesus in a variety of ways:

- the justifier of our faith and *a sacrifice of atonement* (Romans 3:24-25)
- the man from heaven whose likeness we will bear (1 Corinthians 15:48)
- the One who redeems us from the curse of the law (Galatians 3:13)
- possessing unsearchable riches (Ephesians 3:7-9)
- the One through whom all our needs are supplied (Philippians 4:19)
- *before all things* and *head of the body, his church* and *the beginning and the firstborn from among the dead* (Colossians 1:17-18)
- the mediator between God and men (1 Timothy 2:5)
- the One whose glorious appearance we await (Titus 2:11-15)
- the One who to whom we can be bound as a prisoner (Philemon 1)
- *that great Shepherd of the sheep* (Hebrews 13:20-21)

Yet with all the ways Paul saw Jesus, he yearned to know Him more. And so, he said, in Philippians 3:7-11, *"But whatever was to my profit I now consider loss for the sake of Christ. What is more, I consider everything a loss compared to the surpassing greatness of knowing Christ Jesus my Lord, for whose sake I have lost all things.....I want to know Christ and the power of his resurrection and the fellowship of sharing in his sufferings, becoming like him in his death, and so, somehow, to attain to the resurrection from the dead."*

Those Who Have Experienced Jesus Since His Resurrection

This is the Church through the centuries, including us, for as we receive Christ, abide in His Word, and are filled with the Holy Spirit, we, too, can "behold the man Jesus." We do this by both looking back, and looking ahead. As we look back, we can see Jesus, as His life and mission was predicted, as it came to pass, and as He lives in our hearts today. This has come about through:

Recognizing Christ

No other man in history, except Jesus, requires an answer as to who he is. When Jesus declared, in John 7:37-44, that He was the source of living water, it caused people to wonder who He really was. The prophet? The Christ? An impostor? Jesus not only asked the disciples who others thought He was, He directed the same question to them. It is the question we must answer as well. Our future depends upon it. This question-of-all-questions is found in Matthew 16:15: *"Who do you say I am?"*

Briefly summarize your answer to this question-of-all-questions:

_____

_____

_____

Abiding in God's Word

As God's Word becomes life in us, we begin to see much about Jesus. Not only do the gospels tell us much about the life He lived on earth — from birth to death to His resurrection — they also give us reason to believe that He is the Son of the living God and that He can indwell us, as we accept Him into our hearts.

As we study the New Testament, we see Jesus described in a variety of ways:

Baptizer with the Holy Spirit (Luke 3:16)	The Word made flesh (John 1:14)
Lamb of God (John 1:29)	Savior of the World (John 4:42)
Light of the World (John 8:12)	Our Intercessor (Romans 8:34)

As we begin to see Jesus for who He is, through the New Testament writers, we begin to see Him in the Old Testament as well. We read the many prophesies concerning His first coming and see how they were fulfilled. We read the many more prophecies concerning the Second Coming and realize that they, too, will come to pass. We will also see how men, and events, were types of Jesus and what He would later do. Some of these include:

Seed of woman (Genesis 3:15)	Passover Lamb (Exodus 12)
High Priest (Leviticus 16:14)	Kinsman-Redeemer (Ruth 3:9)
Redeemer (Job 19:25-27)	Good Shepherd (Psalm 23)
Suffering Servant (Isaiah 53)	Sun of Righteousness (Malachi 4:2)

What other analogy in the Old Testament do you see as a "type" of Christ?

_____

_____

_____

Being filled with the Holy Spirit

Ephesians 5:18 says to be *filled with the Spirit.*

In John 16:12-15, Jesus says of the Holy Spirit: *"I have much more to say to you, more than you can now bear. But when he, the spirit of truth comes, he will guide you into all truth. He will not speak on his own; he will speak only what he hears, and he will tell you what is yet to come. He will bring glory to me by taking from what is mine and making it known to you. All that belongs to the Father is mine. That is why I said the spirit will take from what is mine and make it known to you."* The Holy Spirit will also testify of Jesus. (John 15:26)

Do you believe you have been filled with the Holy Spirit? If so, how has this helped to bring glory to Jesus by taking what is His and making it known to you?

_____

_____

As a caution: Satan is always seeking ways to destroy God's Kingdom and His Christ. He does this through deception and counterfeiting what God does. Thus, in 1 John 4:1-3, we are admonished: *This is how you can recognize the Spirit of God: Every spirit that acknowledges that Jesus Christ has come in the flesh is from God, but every spirit that does not acknowledge Jesus is not from God. This is the spirit of the antichrist, which you have heard is coming and even now is already in the world.*

As we look forward, with eyes of faith, we can also see Jesus. John did, through a vision while he was exiled on the isle of Patmos. In Revelation 1:12-18, John says he saw Jesus in all His glory and had no way to describe Him except to use symbolism from Scripture. (See also verses 19-20.) As John fell to the ground, Jesus told him not to be afraid. He affirmed that He was, indeed, the *First and last...the Living One...alive forever and ever...*the one who holds the *keys of death and Hades.*

In the latter part of Revelation, Jesus is:

- The Lamb on Mt. Zion who receives worship (Revelation 14:1-5)
- The Bridegroom of the Church (Revelation 19:6-9)
- The rider on the white horse (Revelation 19:11-15)
- The King of Kings and Lord of Lords (Revelation 19:16)
- The temple in the city (New Jerusalem) (Revelation 21:22,23)
- The One who is coming soon! (Revelation 22:7)

How do you see the Jesus of the future?

_____

_____

May Hebrews 2:9-11 be our testimony of Jesus as well:

But we see Jesus, who was made a little lower than the angels, now crowned with glory and honor because he suffered death, so that by the grace of God he might taste death for everyone. In bringing many sons to glory, it was fitting that God, for whom and through whom everything exists, should make the author of their salvation perfect through suffering. But the one who makes men holy and those who are made holy are of the same family. So Jesus is not ashamed to call them brothers

Men in the Bible who accepted the atoning work of the blood of Jesus Christ are His brothers. Those of us living since that time who also have believed on the Lord Jesus Christ belong to His family and are the church of Jesus Christ. Together, we will — perhaps in the very near future — become the Bride of Jesus Christ, the One with whom we will share eternity.